I0656062

MODERN HUMANITIES RESEARCH ASSOCIATION
CRITICAL TEXTS
VOLUME 60

FRENCH SERIES EDITOR
CLAIRE WHITE

LA BELLE DAME QUI EUST MERCY
AND
LE DIALOGUE D'AMOUREUX ET DE SA DAME

A CRITICAL EDITION AND ENGLISH TRANSLATION
OF TWO ANONYMOUS LATE-MEDIEVAL FRENCH
AMOROUS DEBATE POEMS

MODERN HUMANITIES RESEARCH ASSOCIATION
CRITICAL TEXTS

The MHRA Critical Texts series aims to provide affordable critical editions of lesser-known literary texts that are out of copyright and are not currently in print (or are difficult to obtain). The texts are taken from the following languages: English, French, German, Italian, Portuguese, Russian, and Spanish. Titles are selected by members of the distinguished Editorial Board and edited by leading academics. The aim is to produce scholarly editions rather than teaching texts, but the potential for crossover to undergraduate reading lists is recognized.

Editorial Board
Chair: Dr Claire White (University of Cambridge)
English: Professor Justin D. Edwards (University of Stirling)
French: Dr Claire White (University of Cambridge)
Germanic: Professor Ritchie Robertson (University of Oxford)
Hispanic: Professor Ben Bollig (University of Oxford)
Italian: Professor Jane Everson (Royal Holloway, University of London)
Portuguese: Dr Stephen Parkinson (University of Oxford)
Slavonic: Professor David Gillespie (University of Bath)

texts.mhra.org.uk

La Belle Dame qui eust mercy
and
Le Dialogue d'amoureux
et de sa dame

A Critical Edition and English Translation
of Two Anonymous Late-Medieval French
Amorous Debate Poems

Edited and Translated by Joan Grenier-Winther

Modern Humanities Research Association
Critical Texts 60
2018

Published by

The Modern Humanities Research Association
Salisbury House
Station Road
Cambridge CB1 2LA
United Kingdom

© The Modern Humanities Research Association 2018

Joan Grenier-Winther has asserted her right under the Copyright, Designs and Patents Act 1988 to be identified as the author of this work. Parts of this work may be reproduced as permitted under legal provisions for fair dealing (or fair use) for the purposes of research, private study, criticism, or review, or when a relevant collective licensing agreement is in place. All other reproduction requires the written permission of the copyright holder who may be contacted at rights@mhra.org.uk.

First published 2018

ISBN 978-1-78188-285-6

CONTENTS

ACKNOWLEDGEMENTS

Among the colleagues who have provided me with scholarly and moral support, I am particularly indebted to the late Lionel Friedman, Jesse Hurlbut, Peter Nicholson, and James Laidlaw. My travel and research were supported by generous grants from Washington State University Vancouver, for which I am very grateful. The Interlibrary Loan Office at WSUV, in particular, has continually provided me with invaluable assistance in obtaining research materials.

I am very appreciative of the help I received from the following institutions: the John Work Garrett Library at Johns Hopkins University, Baltimore; the Bibliothèque municipale, Besançon; the Bibliothèque Inguimbertine, Carpentras; the Musée Condé, Chantilly; the Fondation Martin Bodmer, Cologny; the Kongelige Bibliotek, Copenhagen; the British Library, London; the Westminster Abbey Library, London; the Morgan Library, New York; the John Rylands Library, University of Manchester; Art Resource, New York; the Bodleian Library, University of Oxford; the Bibliothèque nationale de France, Paris; the Bibliothèque de l'Arsenal, Paris; the Institut de Recherche et d'Histoire des Textes, Paris; the Musée Jacquemart-André, Paris; the Réunion des musées nationaux, Paris; the Biblioteca Apostolica Vaticana, Rome; the Biblioteca Nazionale e Universitaria, Turin; and the Österreichische Nationalbibliothek, Vienna. In particular, I would like to thank Anne Anderton, Léa Ferrez-Le Guet, Christopher Gardner, Helen Gilio, Yoann Givry, Earle Havens, Catherine Hubbard, Amy Kimball, Anne-Marie Mahe, Liz Kurtulik Mercuri, Marguerite Momesso, John McQuillen, Konstanze Mittendorfer, Samantha Sherbourne, Julianne Simpson, Eva Soos, and Qona Wright, for their kind assistance. In my search for the missing Clumber Library manuscript, I received help from staff at Sotheby's in London; the British Library Repository at Boston Spa; Maggs Bros antiquarian booksellers, London; Eugenio Donadoni at Christie's Auction House; and Raymond Clemens, Diane Ducharme, and June Can at the Beinecke Library at Yale University. I also wish to express my sincere thanks to Gerard Lowe and the staff at MHRA for their expert guidance and patience during the editing and publication process.

To my husband, Douglas Winther, as well as to Mark Winther, Hanne Winther Crawley, and Michael Crawley, who are a constant source of support and encouragement, I offer this book as a sign of my gratitude and affection.

J. G.-W., February 2018

INTRODUCTION

La Belle Dame qui eust mercy [*The Beautiful Lady Who Had Mercy*] and *Le Dialogue d'amoureux et de sa dame* [*The Dialogue between a Lover and his Lady*] are late-medieval French poems of approximately 400 lines each in which a nobleman professes his love and loyalty to a lady in an effort to convince her to accept his suit. The lady in each poem steadfastly refuses the advances of her suitor, expressing doubt about his sincerity, dismissing his suffering from unrequited love, and wishing to avoid falling victim to gossipmongers. *Le Dialogue d'amoureux et de sa dame* ends in the same vein, with the lady never wavering in her rejection of the lover's pleas. *La Belle Dame qui eust mercy*, however, ends with the lady's abrupt change of heart, as she tremulously agrees to his request and joyfully looks forward to their future together.

La Belle Dame qui eust mercy and *Le Dialogue d'amoureux et de sa dame* are important owing to their association with Alain Chartier's *La Belle Dame sans mercy* (written in 1424), as well as with the literary quarrel surrounding this work and the many similar poems that are now grouped into what is called the Belle Dame cycle. The presence of these two poems in numerous late medieval and early Renaissance manuscripts, *incunabula*, and early printed collections further attests to their appeal in the fifteenth and sixteenth centuries.

It is their unusual bipartite structure, however, which distinguishes them from other poems in the Belle Dame cycle, indeed from other lyric works written in the late Middle Ages, and which makes them so intriguing. At the mid-point in each poem, there is a highly unusual shift in the length of the stanzas. Over the period 1890–1908, the Swiss medievalist, Arthur Piaget, made several interesting, but unsubstantiated, claims about *La Belle Dame qui eust mercy*, in particular, and *Le Dialogue d'amoureux et de sa dame*: that Oton de Granson wrote *La Belle Dame qui eust mercy*; that this poem was actually two shorter poems and that the second part was earlier; that *La Belle Dame qui eust mercy* and *Le Dialogue d'amoureux et de sa dame* were related in terms of provenance and dating; that both could have been written as late as the first quarter of the fifteenth century; and that Alain Chartier was familiar with the poems and used them as inspiration for *La Belle Dame sans mercy*. Then, in his 1941 edition of Granson's poetry, Piaget remained absolutely silent on all that he had written earlier about *La Belle Dame qui eust mercy* and *Le Dialogue d'amoureux et de sa dame*. Modern scholarship continues to attribute *La Belle Dame qui eust mercy* to Oton de Granson and to include both poems in discussions of the Belle Dame cycle. Yet nothing more has been said of their unusual stanzaïc structure or of the possibility that they were both composed of two separate poems.

In the following pages, I will review material, stylistic, and thematic evidence that supports many of Piaget's and my own claims about the structure, authorship, dating, and importance of *La Belle Dame qui eust mercy* and *Le Dialogue d'amoureux et de sa dame*. I will also discuss the implications of the poems being composite works in terms of our understanding of the process(es) of poetic creation and of *mise en livre*, as well as the dynamics of courtly love discourse in the late Middle Ages.

§1. Title(s)

La Belle Dame qui eust mercy is found in twenty extant manuscript witnesses and is known by an almost equal number of titles. The title chosen for this edition is an abbreviated version of that used in the primary base manuscript, Paris, Bibliothèque nationale de France (BnF), MS fonds français 1131: *La Belle Dame qui eust mercy de son amant*. In this manuscript, a modern hand has written this title at the start of the poem; it is in the scribal hand in the *explicit*. Since the slightly shortened title is the one used in modern scholarship, it has been adopted here. An alternate title, *La Belle Dame a mercy*, appears in BnF, MSS f. fr. 1642 and 20026, as well as in Copenhagen, Kongelige Bibliotek (KB), Ny. Kgl. S. MS 1768.2. In the two Parisian manuscripts, this title is repeated in the *explicit*; the Danish manuscript ends with *Explicit la belle dame ou a mercy*. In BnF, MS f. fr. 2230, the poem is called *Le Traittie de la belle dame a mercy*. Besançon, Bibliothèque municipale (BBM), MS 554 incorporates the basic title within a longer one referencing Alain Chartier: *Une complainte d'amours que l'on dit autrement La belle dame a mercy faicte par maistre Alain Charretier*. This manuscript ends with the shorter *explicit*, *La complainte d'amours*. A similar title, mentioning Chartier, is found in BnF, MS f. fr. 1727: *Complainte d'amours et response faicte par maistre Alain Charretier secretaire du Roy*. In BnF, MS f. fr. 924 and Rome, Biblioteca Apostolica Vaticana (BAV), MS 4794, the poem is labeled *[L]a belle dame ou a mercy*. The manuscript housed in Yale University's Beinecke Library (YBL), MS 1216, bears the similar title, *La Belle dame ou mercy*.

Two manuscripts, BnF, MS f. fr. 833, and Turin, Biblioteca Nazionale e Universitaria (BNU), MS L.II.12, contain a more descriptive title (also used in Pierre Le Caron's 1489 printed edition): *Comment l'amoureux deprie la dame et est fort repugnant a la belle dame sans mercy selon maistre Alain*. Simpler titles are found in Toulouse, Bibliothèque municipale (TBM), MS 826, which calls the poem *Complainte*, and BnF, MS f. fr. 24440, which labels it *Complainte d'amant a amye*. Paris, Musée

Jacquemart-André (MJA), MS 11 refers to it as *Ung traittie en maniere de prieres en amour*. The word *Balade* appears at the start of the poem in Vienna, Österreichische Nationalbibliothek (ON), MS 2619, probably because the lady and the lover speak to each other in groups of three stanzas, like a series of *balades*. In two manuscripts, Carpentras, Bibliothèque Inguimbertine (BI), MS 390 and Paris, Bibliothèque de l'Arsenal (BA), MS 3523, the rubric *L'Amant* is at the start of the poem, identifying the first speaker. There is no title in BnF, MS Rothschild (BnF-R) I.4.31, but the catalogue description refers to the poem as *La Belle Dame a mercy*. One manuscript witness, London, Westminster Abbey (WA), MS 21, contains only disparate fragments of the poem with no title.

A number of *incunabula* dating from 1478–1495 contain only this one poem. In these stand-alone editions, the poem is called either *La Belle Dame qui eut mercy* or the *Complainte d'amours et response*. Catalogue descriptions of these *incunabula* call it the 'Pseudo-Chartier', with a note that the poem was erroneously attributed to that poet. In addition, the poem is included in many late medieval and early Renaissance printed compilations of works by Alain Chartier and others. Among the titles given to the poem in these collections are *Complainte d'amours et response*, *Complainte d'ung amoureux et la responce de la dame*, and *La Dame qui eut mercy* (see list of variant readings for specific details).

Le Dialogue d'amoureux et de sa dame has come down to us in four manuscripts and a few early printed editions, only one of which presents the title used here: André Du Chesne's 1617 printed edition of the works of Alain Chartier.[1] Since this is the title used to refer to the poem in modern scholarship, it is used here. The other title, *D'un amoureux parlant a sa dame par amour*, appears in three of the four manuscript witnesses to the poem (BnF, MSS f. fr. 1131 and 833, as well as BNU, MS L.II.12), and at least two printed editions. In BA, MS 3523, only Stanzas XIX-XXXVI of the poem are included, with no title given. The two short excerpts of the poem found in the sixteenth century book, *Le Thrésor des joyeuses inventions du paragon des poèsies* (*Thrésor*), use the title *Epistre d'un amant a sa dame* for the three stanzas spoken by the lover and *Rescrit de la dame au dit amant* for the lady's equally long response.

To avoid confusion with Alain Chartier's *La Belle Dame sans mercy*, the title of the poem edited here, *La Belle Dame qui eust mercy*, will always be written in full. *Le Dialogue d'amoureux et de sa dame*, however, will be abbreviated as *Le Dialogue*.

---

[1] Emma Cayley mentioned two other manuscripts, located in Arnhem and Copenhagen, as possibly including *Le Dialogue*, but it has been verified that they do not contain the poem. Cf. *Debate and Dialogue: Alain Chartier in his Cultural Context* (Oxford: Oxford University Press, 2006), p. 153, n. 69.

§2. Overview of the Poems

In the initial exchange between the lover and the lady in *La Belle Dame qui eust mercy*, the lover speaks first, praising the lady for her wisdom and her good reputation in courtly society. In almost the same breath, he apologizes for his own coarseness of speech and his arrogance at aiming his attentions so high. While he has no desire to dishonour her in any way, he states that he must finally reveal that he loves her and that she is the source of his well-being. According to him, if there is blame to be had, it should be laid at the feet of the God of Love. In response, the lady admits that she is flattered, but feels unworthy of this attention. She claims to be naïve in matters of love, but wants to believe that all he says is honourable.

In their second exchange, the lover pledges to serve the lady loyally, but seeks her comfort for the lovesickness that he experiences; she alone controls whether he laughs or cries. If she agrees, he will dedicate himself to serving her and safeguarding her honour. The lady, however, considers this a waste of his words and his efforts, judging it foolish to suffer from such trifles. She is perplexed as to how he came to be so afflicted by love, which she sees as just a fleeting pleasure. She urges him to seek a different lady, one who will be more receptive to his suit. She assures him that she is capable of protecting her own honour.

In their third exchange, the lover claims that the God of Love has ordained that he serve her and no one else. He is enflamed by his love and only she can provide relief; without that, he will die from his sorrows. Like the lady in Alain Chartier's *La Belle Dame sans mercy*, this lady insists that his eyes deceived him if he read anything into a look that she may have given him. She dismisses his threats of death from lovesickness, saying that many are sicker and do not die of their pain. She asserts that no one can be forced to love and that she will only give herself to her future husband and lover.

At this point in the poem, the length of the stanzas changes from eight to thirteen lines. The lover now proclaims that the lady is the source of all honour and joy, and he pledges to live and die in service to her. Appealing to her sense of courtesy, he pleads with her to see his suffering as proof of his sincerity and devotion. While he would welcome death if that is what she demanded, he would prefer to continue serving her, even while enduring pain. The lady responds by reminding him that all ladies need to protect their own reputation. She is adamant that she will not risk hers for him, nor will she be seen as the cause of his death, since she never wished him ill. His suffering saddens her, but she insists that if she had wanted to accept his suit, she would have done so by now. She hopes that the God of Love will grant him a lady more worthy of him.

In their next exchange, the lover accuses the God of Love of failing to come to his aid. He laments his bad luck in love, over which he has no control, and he asks the lady what she would do were she in his situation. In her penultimate speech, the lady decries the amount of time spent on this discussion, questions the lover's sincerity, and reiterates her fear of slander.

In their final exchange, the lover vows that, if the lady continues to reject him, he will put her lack of mercy on display for the world to see by wearing black in springtime, the traditional season of love. If she agrees to his suit, however, they will become as one, joined in love and duty. To this, the lady makes a sudden and unexpected *volte-face*, vanquished, she says, by his sweet words. Unsure of what to expect, she asks him to be honourable, constant, and discreet. She envisions a future in which they will be as one, united as brother and sister, and she looks forward to sharing the same desire, to seeing each other often, and to spending their lives together.

The stages in the debate between the lover and the lady in *Le Dialogue* follow a similar pattern, although the lady never acquiesces to the lover's pleas. The lover begins by saying that he has resisted approaching the lady for a while, but now comes to ask her to hear of the pains that he has suffered without her love. He accuses her, as well as the God of Love, of controlling whether he has pain or comfort from his efforts. Confused, the lady responds by saying that she does not understand why he has chosen her, as she has given him no sign to indicate that she is interested in him. Indeed, she states that she can only be loyal to another, that she is not worthy of her suitor's love, and that others have tried to seek her favour and failed.

The lover next states that he, himself, is unworthy of her love, as she surpasses all ladies in beauty and grace. He claims that the sweet looks from her laughing eyes have ensnared his heart. He is optimistic that, if he serves her well, she will show him mercy, rather than the resistance he has felt thus far. Her response is that if she had wanted to love someone new, she would have done so, but that her heart is already committed to one who fully satisfies her. She advises the lover to seek a prettier and more amenable lady.

In their third exchange, the lover tries to convince the lady of the seriousness of the situation, first saying that she can bring about his destruction with her refusal of his suit, then accusing her of consenting to his death by denying him. He claims that when Love commanded him to court her, he had not been warned of possible rejection. The lady is succinct in her dismissal of the lover's arguments. She denies knowingly or maliciously leading him on in any way and insists that she cannot provide a cure for his lovesickness, since she already has an *amy*. She advises him to accept her refusal gracefully, since she does not want to become fodder for gossipmongers.

At this point, the stanzas change from having ten lines to having thirteen lines. Now, the lover explains that the lady's youth and beauty have brought him to a state of grief and sadness, far from the joy and happiness that he seeks. He maintains that he will die soon if the lady does not provide relief for his suffering. He is assaulted by Desire, but Hope consoles him, saying that Pity is getting ready to grant him what he requires. The lady, however, makes light of his claims, saying that there is nothing she can do; furthermore, she doesn't believe that he is even that sick. If his heart is trembling while he is in bed, it is likely to be laughing at him. She insists that she has never encouraged him. Unlike earlier in the poem, where she claimed to have a satisfying lover and to be worried about falling prey to slander, she now states that others can believe what they like, for she simply has no interest in anyone else. She warns that ladies should be prudent in distributing their favours, and never become '*subjecte ou elle est maistresse*'.

The lover then professes to prefer death over seeking another lady. Incapable of avoiding the assault directed at him by Love, he still holds out hope that his lady will be gracious and return his love. The lady immediately dispels such hope, stating categorically that she did nothing to encourage him and has no plan to accept his suit, regardless of how he or others may perceive her.

In their final exchange, the lover complains that it is not fair that her beauty has made him love her so desperately, suffer for so long, and waste a good deal of his life in a futile pursuit. He calls upon the God of Love to adjudicate this quarrel between his desire and the lady, hoping for even the shortest reprieve in his suffering before he dies of his sorrows. He feels unfairly treated by her, after having served her so well. He makes one final appeal to Love to console his heart, which is now weak and near death. For her part, the lady remains steadfast in her rejection of the lover's claims and pleas. She denies being the cause of his suffering and his wasted time, since she has done him no harm in thought, speech, or deed. In her opinion, if he fell in love with her so cavalierly, it was his own fault. She is free and wants only to protect her reputation. His suffering is exaggerated; no one dies from a lack of comfort in love. Love gives 'only a little bit of pleasant pain' that is fleeting. She ends by advising the lover to seek another lady who will be a hundred times better at 'curing' him.

§3. The Belle Dame Cycle and Poetic Composition

Any discussion of *La Belle Dame qui eust mercy* or *Le Dialogue* must include mention of Alain Chartier's *La Belle Dame sans mercy*. Chartier's poem, written in 1424, was pivotal in its day, as attested by the nearly four dozen fifteenth- and sixteenth-century manuscripts known today to contain it. It was also at the heart of a literary *querelle* that arose in the court of King Charles VII of France in the mid-fifteenth century. In response to Chartier's poem of the merciless lady, a series of letters were written, ostensibly by outraged members of the court, both men and women, complaining of the negative light that Chartier cast upon courtly society and, more particularly, upon courtly ladies. The poet penned an apology (*L'Excusacion aux dames*), but this was followed by another spate of bitter letters accusing Chartier of defaming all women.

La Belle Dame sans mercy exerted considerable literary influence in its day and beyond. Pierre Fabri, author of Le Grand et Vrai Art de pleine rhétorique, published in 1521, extolled Chartier's 'beau langage élégant et substantieux' and the 'doulceur' of both this rhymed and prose work.[2] It was considered to be rivalled only by Le Roman de la rose in terms of its success and the number of sequels and imitations it engendered. Almost four hundred years after its composition, it was partially the inspiration for the ballad of the same name by the English poet, John Keats, written in 1819. It is among the most frequently anthologized and cited late-medieval poems, often for what is seen as the proto-feminist nature of the lady's refusal of an unwanted suitor's request for her love, as well as her denunciation of 'l'hypocrisie des libertins courtois'.[3]

As early as 1876, a link was established between Chartier's La Belle Dame sans mercy and the anonymous La Belle Dame qui eust mercy. In their compilation of fourteenth- and fifteenth-century poetic works, Anatole de Montaiglon and James de Rothschild maintained that these poems, in particular, represented the two main trajectories of a genre of late medieval love literature: 'Tantôt, en effet, l'amant est maltraité de sa mie, et il exhale sa plainte en regrets douloureux, tantôt, au contraire, après un débat plus ou moins long, la dame se laisse fléchir.'[4] A multitude of contemporary works, written to imitate, respond to, and refute La Belle Dame sans mercy, are now considered to belong to this genre, known as the Belle Dame cycle. Some of these poems stage a debate in a quasi-legal trial mise en scène, often with a poet-narrator who overhears the interlocutors and transcribes the arguments for and against the poet and his merciless lady, or ladies and lovers, in general. Other poems present an amorous debate without a narrator, leaving the reader to act as an eavesdropping third agent. In some poems, the cases are referred to a different adjudicator for a new trial. More often, absolute closure is not reached by the end of the works; final judgment, acquittal, and/or punishment is postponed, never articulated, or forgotten because of a distraction. The disputants in these works are left stranded, 'locked in a stalemate with the hope of resolution endlessly deferred'.[5]

In an effort to organize the works in the Belle Dame cycle, Emma Cayley has assigned each of them to one of four groupings based on which character is 'on trial': first, Chartier himself; second, beautiful ladies appearing in sequels to La Belle Dame sans mercy; third, the povre amant; and fourth, beautiful, but

---

[2]   Cf. Alexandre Héron, ed., 3 vols (Rouen: Cagniard, 1889–90), I, p. 11.

[3]   Daniel Poirion, Le Poète et le prince: l'évolution du lyrisme courtois de Guillaume de Machaut à Charles d'Orléans (Paris: Presses Universitaires de France, 1965), p. 260.

[4]   Anatole Montaiglon and James de Rothschild, eds, Recueil de poésies françoises des XVᵉ et XVⁱᵉ siècles, 13 vols (Paris: Jannet; Daffis, 1876), I, p. 194.

[5]   Barbara K. Altmann and Carleton W. Carroll, eds, The Court Reconvenes: Courtly Literature across the Disciplines (Cambridge: Brewer, 2003), p. 28.

merciless, ladies who are locked, with their lovers, in amorous debates which reverse or imitate Chartier's poem (although none of the speakers are made out to be Chartier's characters, per se) *(Debate*, pp. 136–62). Cayley places *La Belle Dame qui eust mercy* and *Le Dialogue* into the fourth group, along with works generally dated after Chartier's poem.

What is most interesting about the poems in this group is the variety of messages they impart. In *Le Desconseillé d'amours*, by Henri Anctil (*c.* 1442), a jaded older man advises younger men that love is but 'temps perdu'. In *Le Loyal Amant refusé,* a merciless lady who has refused her loyal lover dies one year later. In *Le Desloyal d'amours*, the lover's first lady has died; the new object of his affection tells him that he should remain loyal to his first love, and the ladies around her agree. In *La Desserte du disloyal*, a disloyal lover pleads his case, but the lady accuses him of using sweet words only to deceive her. The narrator warns his male readers to be loyal or get their just desserts, like this lover. In *La Sépulture d'Amours*, the lover meets and falls in love with a lady who mocks him. In a dream, he discovers that the God of Love has died, lamented by Hope, Desire, Regret, Comfort, Youth, Loyalty, Virtue, Honour, and Pity. *Le Martyr d'Amours* (*c.* 1464), which is attributed to Franci, depicts the lover abducted by Resistance, Fear, and Refusal, and drowned. His soul goes to the God of Love, who has been told his story by Truth, who calls him a loyal martyr of love and his merciless lady, a 'tres desloyalle amoureuse'. The God of Love sends him back to earth to make his last will and testament. And in *Le Débat de la dame et de l'écuyer* (*c.* 1440–1462), the lady is merciless toward her suitor, then returns to the other ladies, leaving him to die 'le plus tart qu'il pourra'.

Perhaps surprisingly, other poems in this same group contain what could be considered a happy ending. Piaget refers to Achille Caulier's *L'Hôpital d'Amours*, for example, as 'a kind of *Belle Dame qui eut mercy*' ('Imitations,' 34, pp. 560–61). In this poem, the lady is initially resistant to the lover's suit. He then has a dream in which she acquiesces and gives him a kiss. *Danger* (Resistance) sweeps in, however, and the lady returns to being standoffish. Bolstered by Hope, Pity, Remembrance, and Understanding, the lover's appeal to the God of Love pays off; he is able to approach the lady, while *Danger* is sleeping, and receive a second kiss. The lover then awakens, hopeful that his dream will one day become a reality. The sorrowful lover in *Le Traité de réveille qui dort* is eventually comforted by his recalcitrant lady when she sprinkles rose water on his face and speaks sweet words to him. *Le Débat sans conclusion* has two conclusions depending on the version, one hopeful, the other not. In the first one, the lover, who has reached his breaking point from unrequited love, demands that his lady give him death or mercy; she opens her mouth to speak when a hunting party interrupts their discussion, to which they don't return. The optimistic narrator of this version ends the poem saying that he believes that if the lover continues to serve the lady loyally, he will be healed (*guerdonné*). The second version adds a few extra stanzas to show the lover cursing the lady and sending her to the devil for her lack of mercy toward him. This narrator ends the poem by denouncing Love's chicanery and grumbling about women of all stations who believe the sweet words of deceitful suitors and who end up at *l'Hôtel-Dieu* [hospital], *enceinte*.

The level of intertextuality evident in these poems, indeed in all of the poems in the Belle Dame cycle, is exceptional. This was first noted in the early 1970s by Daniel Poirion, who judged the poetic production in late medieval France a prime example of the way that earlier texts are reworked by later ones. Studies by Emma Cayley, Adrian Armstrong, Malcolm Quainton, Jane H. M. Taylor, and others have more recently stressed the social nature of poetic composition in this era.[6] They argue convincingly that the inconclusiveness in many of these late medieval poems was quite intentional and allowed for the formation of an active and organic literary community that was both collaborative and competitive. Cayley states, for example, that 'what we are witnessing is not the recording of an actual dispute between named parties [...], but an intellectual and literary exercise whose continuation is part of an elaborate competition or game between poets and which is fostered by a flourishing climate of cultural and literary debate and exchange in late medieval France' (*Debate*, p. 2). Poets engaging in what she called 'collaborative debating communities' (*Debate*, p. 5) contributed new works, continued existing ones, and added new twists to the basic premise of works like Chartier's *La Belle Dame sans mercy*, all in an effort to compete for prestige in the manner of literary *puys* or contests. Unlike in other literary periods, 'fifteenth-century poets were not looked down upon for borrowing material or ideas from contemporary vernacular texts; they were admired when they succeeded in making subtle and adept manipulations of those recognizable elements to convey a specific argument or critique'.[7] Explicit poetic closure was even to be avoided, according to Cayley, in order to 'encourage the perpetuation of [a] wider debate' on a given topic or theme and/or to engender the continuation of poetic collaboration and competition (*Debate*, p. 129). Poetry from this period, long

---

[6]   Cf. Daniel Poirion, 'Lectures de *La Belle Dame sans mercy*', in *Mélanges de langue et de littérature médiévales offerts à Pierre le Gentil* (Paris: SEDES, 1973), 691–705 (p. 691); Cayley, *Debate*; Jane H. M. Taylor, 'Courtly Gatherings and Poetic Games: "Coterie" Anthologies in the Late Middle Ages in France', in *Book and Text in France 1400–1600: Poetry on the Page*, ed. by Adrian Armstrong and Malcolm Quainton (Aldershot: Ashgate, 2007), 13–30; and Adrian Armstrong, *The Virtuoso Circle: Competition, Collaboration, and Complexity in Late Medieval French Poetry* (Tempe, AZ: Arizona Center for Medieval and Renaissance Studies, 2012).

[7]   Sara Preisig, review of Jane H. M. Taylor, *The Poetry of François Villon*, *Modern Language Notes*, 117.4 (2002), 932–36 (p. 933).

considered formulaic and banal, is now seen to reflect, even communicate with, earlier inspirational works, forming a richly interwoven and consequential body of work.

Drawing on the sociology of Pierre Bourdieu and his concept of 'field' as a relational network, Cayley has framed these medieval debating communities within a field of play where various types of capital operated and various players competed (albeit often in collusion with one another) to gain social and literary dominance. 'Through the increasingly sophisticated manipulation of these intertextual networks,' Cayley writes, 'each successive poet both inscribes himself in an existing space of play (field), and struggles to dominate that field, his poetic capital enhanced in relation to the measure of his skill' (*Debate*, pp. 161–62). If a final judgment or punishment were meted out in any of the interrelated poems, it would disrupt, if not halt, the continuation of this collaboration and/or competition, as well as the opportunity for 'poetic capital' to be gained by anyone else. Such judgment or punishment, therefore, was typically avoided.

The sociology of the *mise en livre* has also come to the forefront of scholarly study in recent years. As Taylor observes, any given poem 'fulfils a function or has a role within an anthology which it does not have outside it, and [...] this coterie circulation of work in manuscript, properly evaluated, articulates artistic preoccupations, and assumptions about the literary process, which reveal much about the socioliterary dynamics of particular texts and about the social history of literature' ('Courtly Gatherings', p. 15). This is certainly true for the imitations, continuations, and reversals of Chartier's *La Belle Dame sans mercy* that were the result of literary collaboration, collusion, and/or competition, as these works were frequently bound together in the same codices with Chartier's poem, providing material proof of this collaborative–competitive dynamic. Cayley confirms this, stating that 'the manuscript collections [...] pivot around the antithetical yet complementary pairings of poets and poems, around the interdependence of *esbatre* and *combatre*, to create spaces of play or *debatre* that confront and collaborate with one another' (*Debate*, p. 187). The frequent proximity in both manuscripts and printed editions of *La Belle Dame qui eust mercy*, in particular, to *La Belle Dame sans mercy*, as well as the letters and *L'Excusacion* written during the *querelle de la Belle Dame*, suggest a deliberate *mise en livre* designed to make the poem ending with a merciful lady serve as a palinode to Chartier's more controversial work about the merciless lady. Although not found in as many of these compilations, *Le Dialogue*, for its part, can also be seen to align with Chartier's *La Belle Dame sans mercy* and other poems of this nature.

§4. Poetic Structure

Late medieval French poems are noted for being carefully crafted works that held to strict rules regarding rhyme schemes and metrical structure. *La Belle Dame qui eust mercy* and *Le Dialogue* are noteworthy in that they adhere to some *formes fixes* rules, but their unusual stanzaïc structure distinguishes them from works written in the same period and suggests that they are both comprised of two separate poems.

La Belle Dame qui eust mercy and *Le Dialogue* each contain thirty-six stanzas. The first eighteen stanzas of *La Belle Dame qui eust mercy* are octosyllabic *huitains* or eight-line stanzas in the *ababbcbc* rhyme scheme so popular among late medieval poets. *Le Dialogue*'s first eighteen stanzas are also octosyllabic, but are *dizains* or ten-line stanzas with the *ababbccdcd* rhyme scheme, again a familiar form in this period. At the nineteenth stanza in both poems, however, there is a rupture in the stanzaïc structure. While both poems continue to have octosyllabic lines, they shift to the extremely rare *treizain* or thirteen-line stanza[8] with four rhymes in an *aabaabbccdccd* pattern. All remaining stanzas are *treizains* in the same pattern. While Daniel Poirion noted that late medieval poets frequently experimented with stanza length, seeking to demonstrate their virtuosity, he documented not a single late medieval poet using the thirteen-line stanza in his overview of poetic structure, nor did he record the use by any poet of a bipartite structure like the one seen here (*Poète*, p. 449).

It was Arthur Piaget, in a short bibliographical notice written in 1894 on one of the manuscripts containing *La Belle Dame qui eust mercy*, who first suggested that this poem was a combination of two poems. (The manuscript he was describing does not contain *Le Dialogue*, so he did not mention it.) Piaget also proposed that the 'second' poem (i.e. Stanzas XIX–XXXVI in *La Belle Dame qui eust mercy*) predated Chartier's *La Belle Dame sans mercy*.[9] While he provided no evidence for his claims, nor reiterated them in any subsequent writing, I contend that material, stylistic, and thematic evidence does exist, and will be presented below, to support the theory that *La Belle Dame qui eust mercy* and *Le Dialogue* are each, in fact, an amalgam of two separate poems.

Looking first at the material evidence, it is noteworthy that in fully one-third

---

[8] A *rondeau* can have thirteen lines (one *tercet* between two *quintains*) which form the whole of the poem (Brandin and Hartog, p. 97), but this is unlike the thirteen-line stanzaïc form seen here. Cf. Louis M. Brandin and Willie Gustave Hartog, *A Book of French Prosody: With Specimens of French Verse from the Twelfth Century to the Present Day* (Glasgow: Blackie, 1904), p. 97.

[9] '[La Belle Dame qui eust mercy] est formée de deux petits poèmes qu'on trouve isolés dans quelques manuscrits; l'un d'eux est probablement antérieur à la *Belle Dame sans mercy* elle-même. Il commence par ces vers: *Jeune, gente, source et riviere, d'amour et de joyeuse chiere* …' Cf. 'Notice sur le ms. 1727 du fond français de la Bibliothèque nationale', *Romania*, 23 (1894), 192–208 (p. 206).

of the extant manuscripts containing *La Belle Dame qui eust mercy*, the first eighteen *huitains* (hereafter referred to as Poem 1) end on one folio, while the thirteen-line stanzas, beginning at Stanza XIX (Poem 2), begin at the top of a fresh folio.[10] This could indicate two separate poems bound together in a single compilation. In one of these manuscripts, BA, MS 3523, an *explicit* — *Et ho* — is written at the bottom of the folio, following the eighteenth stanza, to mark the end of Poem 1. Another *Et ho* is placed at the conclusion of the thirty-sixth stanza or Poem 2. There is little doubt that *Et ho* is used in this manuscript to signal the end of a poem, as it is found nine more times to mark the conclusion of known works. It is reasonable, therefore, to assume that the scribe of this manuscript considered the *huitain* section and the *treizain* section to be two different poems.

In BnF, MS f. fr. 924, Stanza XIX not only starts at the top of a new folio (22^r), but it also has an initial 'J' on the first word 'Jeune', that is larger and more elaborate than preceding initials, as well as ornate flourishes in ink, as might appear at the beginning of a completely new poem.

In another manuscript (BI, MS 390), there is a change in the way rubrics are used to indicate a new speaker at the point of the structural shift. In the first eighteen stanzas, the rubric announcing who is speaking appears at both the beginning and the end of the speech; starting with the nineteenth stanza, the rubric appears only at the start of a speech.

The first *incunabulum* containing *La Belle Dame qui eust mercy*, dating from 1478–1480, provides more material evidence that this poem is an amalgam of two separate works. In this edition, three completely new lines are inserted into Stanza XIX (145bis, 147bis, and 152bis). One can imagine that the editor-publisher was taken aback by the shift that happens at line 145, going from eight- to thirteen-line stanzas. In all probability deciding it was a mistake, he tried to figure out how to maintain the pattern of *huitains* that had been used up to that point. By adding three new lines, he made Stanza XIX into a *seizain* that could be divided into two *huitains*. Lines 151 and 159 are even indented to indicate the familiar eight-line stanzaïc pattern. In subsequent stanzas, he deals with this perplexing situation by breaking each *treizain* into two smaller blocks of six and seven (or occasionally seven and six) lines. Only in the final six stanzas (XXXI–XXXVI) are the *treizains* correctly laid out on the page.

As for *Le Dialogue*, material evidence of composite poems comes again from BA, MS 3523, mentioned above. This manuscript only contains Poem 2 of *Le Dialogue*, and this is bracketed by *Et ho*, indicating a complete work. This is also one of the manuscripts where the poem begins at the top of a new folio. In the modern catalogue description of this manuscript, the entry for the poem explains that it is missing the first part of the poem. Viewed another way,

---

[10]   BnF, f. fr. MSS 924 and 1642; BA, MS 3523; BBM, MS 554; BI, MS 390; and KB, MS 1768.

however, 'Helas! ma dame et ma maistresse' is the *incipit* of a self-contained poem of 234 lines.

Internal tensions in the manuscript witnesses between the first and second parts of *La Belle Dame qui eust mercy* reveal themselves in the variant readings. In Poem 1 in BnF, MS f. fr. 1642, the readings initially show clear affinities with two other Parisian manuscripts, BnF, f. fr. MSS 833 and 24440. At the start of the nineteenth stanza, however, a shift occurs. From this point onward, BnF, MS f. fr. 1642 aligns instead with three other Parisian manuscripts (BnF, f. fr. MSS 924, 2230, and 20026), as well as BI, MS 390 and KB, MS 1768.2. Such a shift suggests that the two separate poems within *La Belle Dame qui eust mercy* had different genealogies, thus different compositional patterns, kinships, and histories.

Stylistically, both poems exhibit differences in versification which argue in favour of separate compositions. Tables 2 and 3 provide details on the rhyme schemes used in the poems, as well as the frequency of rhyme words by gender and quality, but the salient points are highlighted here. First, with regard to *La Belle Dame qui eust mercy*, there is a 5% change in rhyme gender from Poem 1 to Poem 2, with masculine rhymes increasing from 57% to 62% (and feminine rhymes obviously decreasing by the same amount; cf. Table 2). Second, the difference in the use of masculine vs. feminine rhyme words changes by a full 7% (from 58% vs. 42% respectively in Poem 1 to 65% vs. 35% respectively in Poem 2; cf. Table 3). Third, Poem 2 shows a significant (8%) increase in the richer masculine leonine simple, perfect, and pluperfect rhyme words (i.e. not counting simple assonant and consonant rhyme words) over Poem 1 (cf. Table 3). Little difference is found in the use of the richer feminine leonine perfect and pluperfect rhyme words between Poems 1 and 2.

In *Le Dialogue*, the changes in rhyming are even more striking between Poem 1 and Poem 2. First, almost three-quarters of the rhymes in Poem 1 are masculine (74.5%); in Poem 2, masculine rhymes still dominate, but the relationship is more balanced at 56% vs. 44% (cf. Table 2). Second, the same ratio exists in Poem 1 in terms of the rhyme words used (75% to 25%), but the difference is not as great in Poem 2 (60.6% vs. 39.4%), as seen in Table 3. Third, in terms of the richness of the rhyme words used in Poems 1 and 2 in *Le Dialogue*, masculine leonine simple, perfect and pluperfect rhyme words account for 17.4% of the total in Poem 1, but this drops to 9.28% in Poem 2. Richer feminine leonine perfect and pluperfect rhyme words, however, increase from 4.7% of the total in Poem 1 to 8.65% in Poem 2 (cf. Table 3).

A closer examination of the distribution of some of the richer quality rhyme words in Poems 1 and 2 of *La Belle Dame qui eust mercy* provides more stylistic evidence related to versification that points to the presence of two separate poems within a single one. Of the thirty-four masculine leonine perfect and pluperfect rhymes in the whole poem, Poem 1 has only one rhyme between three words (Stanza XVIII, *escouteray* : *aymeray* : *garderay*), with the remaining ten rhymes between just two words (e.g. Stanza II, *humblement* : *grandement*). In contrast, Poem 2 has ten rhymes between two words (e.g. Stanza XXXI, *amitié* : *pitié*), six between three words (e.g. Stanza XXXV, *changier* : *dangier*: *estrangier*), and another seven between four words (e.g. Stanza XXIII, *aymerés* : *laisserés* : *parlerés* : *serés*). While not conclusive, the dissimilarities in versification documented here suggest different authors for these 'poems within a poem' in both *La Belle Dame qui eust mercy* and *Le Dialogue*.

In terms of thematic evidence for composite poems, there is a break in the internal logic of the debates in both *La Belle Dame qui eust mercy* and *Le Dialogue* at the location of the structural shift. The lady's last speech in Poem 1 of *La Belle Dame qui eust mercy* is marked by a clear and adamant refusal of her lover's suit. Reminiscent of Chartier's Belle Dame, she accuses the lover's eyes of having deceived him, as she maintains that she gave him no sign of interest. She dismisses the seriousness of his lovesickness and tells him to seek another ladylove. She ends by saying that she is keeping herself for her future husband, and will never love anyone else. When the lover speaks at the start of Poem 2, though, he seems oblivious to the rejection she has just meted out. Indeed, the first lines of his speech read more like the *incipit* of a fresh appeal for a lady's love, as he extols her beauty, proclaims his devotion, and pledges to serve her even while enduring the suffering caused by her resistance.

The transition between Poems 1 and 2 in *Le Dialogue* is similarly disjointed. In her final speech before the break, the lady categorically refuses her suitor, saying that she is where she wants to be and is with someone who satisfies her. She urges him to accept her refusal graciously, as she fears the harm that slanderers could cause to her reputation. But in the lover's first speech in Poem 2, there is no direct response to anything that the lady has just said. Instead, he complains of his condition (grief and sadness) caused by her beauty (his only source of possible joy and happiness), and pleads with her to provide a cure for his suffering.

Considered together, these factors lead me to concur with Piaget that *La Belle Dame qui eust mercy,* and I would add *Le Dialogue*, are formed of two separate poems. This claim has clear ramifications on the determination of authorship and dating, the discussion of which follows.

§5. Authorship and Dating

Without an authorial manuscript, reference to an author in the poems or elsewhere, or other conclusive evidence, it is difficult to ascribe authorship to a medieval work. Given my contention that both *La Belle Dame qui eust mercy* and *Le Dialogue* are amalgams of separate poems, the task of determining authorship is doubled. Like Arthur Piaget, I believe that Oton de Granson was the author, but I believe that he only wrote the first poems in *La Belle Dame qui eust mercy* and *Le Dialogue*, during the last quarter of the fourteenth century. I do not believe that Granson wrote the second poems in either *La Belle Dame qui eust mercy* or *Le Dialogue*, and these must remain anonymous. My rationale for this partial attribution is detailed below.

In the nineteenth century, Montaiglon and Rothschild remarked that, while *La Belle Dame qui eust mercy* was placed after Chartier's *La Belle Dame sans mercy* in André Du Chesne's 1617 edition of Chartier's works as a kind of 'réponse ou contre-partie', Du Chesne chose to call the poem simply *Complainte d'amour et response* so that his readers would not think that Chartier had written it (p. 192). They noted that almost a century earlier, in his 1529 edition of Chartier's works, Galliot du Pré had done something similar, calling the poem *Comment l'amoureux deprie sa dame*. They stated that 'l'on a voulu attribuer' *La Belle Dame qui eust mercy* to the poet, Jean Marot (1450–1526), which was, in their estimation, as foolish as saying that Chartier wrote it.[11]

In an article written in 1890, in which he introduced the fourteenth-century Savoyard knight, diplomat, and poet, Oton de Granson, and presented a few of Granson's poems,[12] Piaget also dismissed the idea that Jean Marot had written *La Belle Dame qui eust mercy*. The evidence he cited came from Marot *fils*, the Renaissance poet, Clément Marot, who considered such works unworthy of Chartier's name and compared them to other 'lourderies' that were sometimes attributed to his father or himself.[13]

In this same article, and twice more — in his 1901–05 *Romania* series on the 'imitations' of Chartier's *La Belle Dame sans mercy* and in his 1908 edition of *Le Miroir aux dames*[14] — Piaget ascribed authorship of *La Belle Dame qui eust mercy* to Oton de Granson. (Piaget never commented on authorship of *Le Dialogue*.) Advanced over a century ago, this attribution persists, despite the fact that Piaget tacitly rescinded it in his 1941 edition of Granson's complete poetical works, making no mention at all of the poem of the merciful lady.[15] Nevertheless, there is much in Granson's life and *œuvre* to support the assertion that he wrote Poem 1 in *La Belle Dame qui eust mercy* and *Le Dialogue*.

---

[11] The 'someone' was the French scholar and paleographer, Paulin Paris, in his mid-nineteenth-century inventory of French manuscripts. See *Les Manuscrits françois de la Bibliothèque du roi*, 7 vols (Paris: Techener, 1845), VII, p. 252.

[12] 'Oton de Granson et ses poésies', *Romania*, 19 (1890), 237–59, 403–48.

[13] Clément Marot, *Œuvres complètes*, ed. by Pierre Jannet, 4 vols (Paris: Picard, 1868), IV, p. 195; qtd in Piaget, 'Oton de Granson', 404.

[14] 'La Belle Dame sans merci et ses imitations', *Romania*, 30 (1901), 22–48, 317–51; 31 (1902), 315–49; 33 (1904), 179–208; 34 (1905), 375–428, 559–97; and *Le Miroir aux dames: poème inédit du XVe siècle* (Neuchâtel: Attinger Frères, 1908), p. 26.

[15] *Oton de Grandson, sa vie et ses poésies* (Lausanne: Payot, 1941).

Oton III de Granson, lord of Sainte-Croix, Cudrefin, Grandcour, Aubonne, and Coppet (in northwest Vaud, in modern Switzerland; historically, part of the County of Savoy), was born in the mid-1340s and died in a judicial duel in 1397 in Bourg-en-Bresse. Celebrated in his day for his military prowess and diplomatic acumen, in both the French and English courts, Granson was also lauded for his poetic works, by the nobility and by contemporary poets. In 1401, for example, Queen Isabel of France purchased two gold clasps for her copy of Granson's *Le Livre messire Ode* (Piaget, *Oton de Grandson*, pp. 110–11). Along with Geoffrey Chaucer, Granson was an early adopter and developer of the motif of the unhappy lover on Saint Valentine's Day. Chaucer, who no doubt had contact with the Savoyard poet at the English court, adapted three of Granson's *balades* in his 'Complaint of Venus' and ended this complaint by acknowledging the knight-poet as 'Graunson, flour of hem that make in Fraunce'.[16] In his *Débat de réveille matin*, Chartier himself praised Granson and Guillaume de Machaut as the masters of the complaint on desperate love.[17] Martin le Franc, author of *Le Champion des dames* (1441), advised reading the works of Granson in order to fully comprehend the suffering that resulted from unrequited love.[18] And the nineteenth-century French medievalist, Amédée Pagès, noted that Granson was 'un poète de haut vol [...] qui paraît avoir exercé le plus d'influence sur les trois littéraires hispaniques', especially in the development of the figure of the 'caballero de la trista figure' by both Castilian and Catalan poets.[19]

Granson's poetic output was considerable; somewhat surprisingly, the manuscript tradition of his poetry exceeds those of two of the more widely known poets of the era, Jean Froissart and Eustache Deschamps.[20] The corpus of his works — over one hundred *balades* and *rondeaux*, one *virelai*, three *lais*, four longer pieces in rhyming couplets, ten *complaintes*, one *pastourelle*, one *tençon*, and one letter inserted into a longer poem — respects all of the poetic norms of his era. As Jean-François Kosta-Théfaine notes, Granson's poetry fits 'de manière incontestable dans le sillage de celle de ses prédécessurs, mais aussi

---

[16] *The Riverside Chaucer*, ed. Larry D. Benson, 3rd edn (Boston: Houghton Mifflin, 1987), p. 649.

[17] *The Poetical Works of Alain Chartier*, ed. James C. Laidlaw (Cambridge: Cambridge University Press, 1974), p. 314.

[18] *Le Champion des dame*s, ed. by Robert Deschaux, 5 vols (Paris: Champion, 1999), III, lines 14125–28.

[19] Amadée Pagès, *La Poésie française en Catalogne du XIIIᵉ siècle à la fin du XVᵉ siècle* (Toulouse: Privat, 1936), pp. 89–93 and 100; 'Le Thème de la tristesse amoureuse en France et en Espagne du XIVᵉ au XVᵉ siècle', *Romania* 58 (1932), 29–43 (p. 29); Piaget, *Oton de Grandson*, pp. 175–76; and Jaune Massó i Torrents, 'Oto de Granson i les balades de Lluis de Vilarasa', in *Mélanges delinguistique et de littérature offerts à M. Alfred Jeanroy* (Paris: Droz, 1928), pp. 403–10.

[20] Marc René Jung, 'Répertoire des poèmes d'Oton de Grandson', in *Moyen Âge et Renaissance: Hommage au Professeur François Rouy* (Nice: Faculté des Lettres, Arts et Sciences Humaines, 1995), pp. 91–125 (p. 91).

de ses contemporains, qui ont écrit et exploité à profusion le thème d'amours malheureuses, dont le poète est lui-même le sujet'.[21] At the centre of most of his work is the lament of the forlorn and unfortunate lover, perpetually left 'à soupirer après merci' ('Imitations,' 33, p. 204). Indeed, Granson's 2,500-line *Le Livre messire Ode* provides unquestionable proof that love relationships were filled with despair, suffering, and an illusory joy, and were always unattainable because the object of the lover's suit [was] forever resistant.[22] In his own 1941 edition of Granson's works, Piaget called *Le Livre messire Ode* 'un catalogue [des] joies et [des] tourments d'amour' (p. 145).

Piaget's justifications for attributing *La Belle Dame qui eust mercy* to Granson came in his 1904 article in *Romania*. First, he described the poem as having 'un certain air vieillot, vieux jeu' typical of works from the late fourteenth century. Second, he felt that 'langage amoureux' in the poem was as different from that used by fifteenth-century poets, including Chartier, as Chartier's differed from that of his successors. Third, he found the lamentations of the lover in *La Belle Dame qui eust mercy* to echo those of the unfortunate lover so ubiquitous in Granson's poetry. And finally, he maintained that the lack of a single textual reference in *La Belle Dame qui eust mercy* to *La Belle Dame sans mercy* was proof that the former was written prior to the latter, thus by Granson, or at least by someone of his generation ('Imitations,' 33, p. 204).

Piaget also advanced two stylistic arguments for assigning authorship of *La Belle Dame qui eust mercy* to Granson: the presence in this poem and in Granson's works of a certain type of hiatus and of the square *huitain*. The type of hiatus that concerned Piaget was that placed on the feminine final letter 'e' before monosyllabic words beginning with a vowel.[23] This hiatus was commonly found at the cæsura in ten- and twelve-syllable lines (after the fourth and the sixth syllable respectively), to create the desired pause. Its usage was accepted by most late medieval poets, including Jean Froissart, Christine de Pizan, Charles d'Orléans, René d'Anjou, and Granson himself. Its presence in the eight-syllable line was uncommon; if used, it was both mobile (occurring after any syllable) and weak (Brandin and Hartog, p. 24). Piaget cited a line in Granson's *virelai*, *Je vous aime je vous desir* (*Je suis vostrë ou que je soye*, line 3)[24] and suggested that the frequency of this hiatus in Granson's poems and

---

[21]   Jean-François Kosta-Théfaine, 'Du Chant d'amour au chant du désespoir, ou l'écriture d'une poétique de la tristesse dans la lyrique d'Othon de Grandson', *Romanistische Zeitschrift für Literaturgeschichte*, 23 (1999), 297–310 (p. 301).

[22]   Jean-François Kosta-Théfaine, 'De la Continuité à l'innovation: *Le Livre messire Ode* d'Othon de Grandson et *Le Livre du duc des vrais amans* de Christine de Pizan', *Cahiers de recherches médiévales* 11 (2004), 239–51 (p. 246).

[23]   Piaget had already studied the use of this type of hiatus by another fifteenth-century knight-poet in his article '*Le Chemin de vaillance* de Jean de Courcy et l'hiatus de l'*e* final des polysyllabes aux XIVe et XVe siècles', *Romania*, 27 (1898), 582–607.

[24]   Cf. *Oton de Granson: Poems*, ed. and trans. by Peter Nicholson and Joan Grenier-Winther

in *La Belle Dame qui eust mercy* was evidence that Granson authored the poem ('Imitations' 33, p. 205).

In fact, *La Belle Dame qui eust mercy* contains only one example of hiatus in an octosyllabic line (line 72, which coincidentally has the same wording as the line in Granson's *virelai*), but this reading varies by manuscript. BnF, MS f. fr. 1131, for example, reads *Je suis vostre quel que je soye*, thus avoiding the hiatus that Piaget had studied. As for Granson, his poetic *œuvre* runs to approximately 8,500 lines, one fifth of which are octosyllabic. Of these, there are fifteen examples of this hiatus, or less than 1%. So while it can be said that Granson did occasionally use this kind of hiatus, its low frequency in his works and the virtual lack of it in *La Belle Dame qui eust mercy* undermine it as a strong factor in proving authorship.

Piaget also judged that the presence of square *huitains* (stanzas of eight octosyllabic lines) with the interlacing *ababbcbc* rhyme scheme in both Granson's poetry and *La Belle Dame qui eust mercy* was added proof that Granson wrote the poem. Like many of his contemporaries, Granson makes good use of this type of *huitain*; it can be found in the fifteen stanzas of his *Complainte de Saint Valentin* and the thirty-four stanzas of the *Complainte de Saint Valentin Garensson*. Two of his *balades* are written in octosyllabic *huitains* (lines 1195–1218 and 1365–88 in *Le Livre messire Ode*), but these have a different rhyme scheme (*ababbccb*). He also used *ababbcbc* in many of his decasyllabic lines, but not to the exclusion of other rhyme schemes.[25] His familiarity with the square *huitain* supports consideration of him as the author of Poem 1 of *La Belle Dame qui eust mercy*, but not to the exclusion of many other poets who used this popular stanzaïc form.

Material evidence, i.e. inclusion in one or more manuscript compilations, may provide some information relative to authorship, but it is rarely conclusive. Many times, 'the size of a work, as much as its subject, determines the sort of manuscript in which it appears'.[26] Nevertheless, Piaget included material evidence for attribution of *La Belle Dame qui eust mercy* to Granson, based on the frequency with which this poem was bound in the same manuscripts with other works by the Savoyard knight-poet. In London, WA, MS 21, for example, fragments of this poem immediately follow Granson's 'Lai de plour' from *Le Livre messire Ode*, a few *balades*, and a fragment of his *Complainte de Saint*

(Kalamazoo: Medieval Institute Publications, Western Michigan University, 2015), *Virelai* 10, p. 52.

[25] Twenty *balades*, plus the 64-line *Complainte de l'an nouvel*, as well as in the 72-line *complainte* at lines 1534–1605 in *Le Livre messire Ode*. Six of his *balades* in decasyllabic eight-line stanzas exhibit yet another rhyme scheme, *ababbccb*, while one *balade* uses *ababccdd* (with the fifth line having seven, not ten syllables).

[26] James C. Laidlaw, 'The Manuscripts of Alain Chartier', *Modern Language Review*, 61 (1966), 188–98 (p. 193).

Valentin. In BnF, MS f. fr. 1727, *La Belle Dame qui eust mercy* follows Granson's *Le Livre messire Ode*, while in BnF, MS f. fr. 1131, the poem is situated among Granson's *Complainte amoureuse de Saint Valentin*, two complaints, and *La Pastourelle Granson*. (*Le Dialogue* immediately follows *La Pastourelle* in this manuscript.) In total, *La Belle Dame qui eust mercy* appears in eight of the same manuscripts containing works by Granson. While material proximity is not solid evidence of authorship, the frequent pairing of works by Granson and these two poems is worth noting.

Piaget concluded his 1904 *Romania* article on *La Belle Dame qui eust mercy* by saying that the totality of his observations authorized his attribution of the poem to Oton de Granson (pp. 204–05). In the very next article in the series, however, dealing with *Le Dialogue*, he retreated from this attribution, focusing instead on the significance of the two poems relative to *La Belle Dame sans mercy*. He stated that *La Belle Dame qui eust mercy* and *Le Dialogue* were closely related; that the latter was the counter-point to the former; and that the two poems emerged from the same *milieu*, exhibiting 'la même inspiration, le même langage, le même verbiage amoureux' (pp. 207–08). And he proposed that *La Belle Dame qui eust mercy* and *Le Dialogue* were written around the same date, possibly as late as the first quarter of the fifteenth century. Oton de Granson had died in 1397.

Four years later, in his edition of *Le Miroir aux dames*, Piaget again linked *La Belle Dame qui eust mercy* and Granson, saying that the poem was 'faussement attribué à Alain Chartier, puis à Jean Marot, et qui est probablement d'Oton de Grandson'. Then, in 1941, he neither included *La Belle Dame qui eust mercy* in his edition of the complete works of Oton de Granson, nor made any mention of it.

Strange as it may seem to be attributing any part of *La Belle Dame qui eust mercy* and *Le Dialogue*, with their outspoken and confident female voices, to the author of over one hundred poems on unrequited love in which the dominant voice is male, I would assign authorship of Poem 1 in each of *La Belle Dame qui eust mercy* and *Le Dialogue* to Oton de Granson, and for many of the same reasons proposed by Piaget. In my opinion, however, the most convincing evidence that Granson wrote them is their kinship with three specific and somewhat unusual works by this poet: *La Pastourelle Granson* and two *balades* with the identical refrain, *Je n'ay riens fait qu'Amours ne m'ait fait faire*.[27]

Going by the number of its manuscript witnesses (nine of a total twenty-two), *La Pastourelle Granson* was the poet's most popular work. His only love debate poem, it contains nineteen octosyllabic *dizains* with a rhyme scheme of *ababbccdcd*, identical to that found in Poem 1 of *Le Dialogue*. The first twelve lines are spoken by a narrator, who tells that he has come across a group of

---

[27] Cf. Nicholson and Grenier-Winther, *Balades* 49 and 50, pp. 102–05 and *La Pastourelle Granson* 73, pp. 150–61.

young shepherds and shepherdesses relaxing on the bank of a river. Two, in particular, have captured his attention: a lovelorn shepherd and an intelligent and charming shepherdess. The remaining eighteen stanzas contain the debate between these two, in alternating stanzas spoken first by the shepherdess and then by the shepherd, who ends the poem.

Although *La Pastourelle Granson* has a narratorial introduction not found in either *La Belle Dame qui eust mercy* or *Le Dialogue*, Granson's work displays a stronger kinship with these two poems than with *pastourelles* written before or during his time. The earliest *pastourelles* were written in the twelfth century, by troubadours such as Marcabru, Giraut de Bornelh, and Gui d'Ussel. The form was redeveloped and formalized by Granson's contemporaries in the fourteenth century, including Jean Froissart, Eustache Deschamps, and others. The structure of the later *pastourelles* was most often at the intersection of the *balade* and the *chant royal*, with five stanzas of eight-syllable lines with a refrain, reflecting the 'prestige du nombre impair' (Poirion, *Poète*, p. 370). In terms of structure, the extended length of his *Pastourelle* and the equal weight given to the voices of the shepherd and shepherdess, speaking in alternate stanzas, prove that Granson was moving into new territory, one that more closely resembles Poem 1 in both *La Belle Dame qui eust mercy* and *Le Dialogue*.

As for the key figures in the debate, Granson's *Pastourelle* also exhibits subtle differences relative to earlier *pastourelles*, perhaps reflecting his exposure to and knowledge of the dynamics of courtly life in the second half of fourteenth-century France and England. Some early *pastourelles* depict an amorous debate between a stereotypical shepherd and shepherdess. In others, a knight-poet encounters a coy shepherdess with whom he engages in, and loses, a battle of wits. Sexual relations, either consensual or forced, often followed, with the knight then departing. Granson's *Pastourelle* turns on its head any depiction of a naïve country lass or a coy flirt who serves as an 'object of male fantasies of domination' (Nicholson, Grenier-Winther, p. 26). Instead, Granson's shepherdess is immediately (and somewhat surprisingly) labelled as *gentil* or *gente* (depending on the manuscript witness), terms clearly used to mean noble, well-mannered, and well-bred (P1) [this abbreviation will be used for all line references to Granson's *Pastourelle*]. She is described by the narrator as *plaisant et belle* (P11) and *jolie* (P93), again, descriptors often reserved for noblewomen. The shepherd addresses her as *Belle* (P21, 61, 83, 121) and *Cuer gracieux* (P41), familiar endearments usually applied to courtly ladies. And the narrator is heard to call her *la bien sachant pastoure* (P56), emphasizing her wisdom and prudence, both qualities cultivated by and admired in noblewomen. Piaget himself calls her 'très experte dans les choses d'amour … [qui] … continue à éduquer à sa manière son ami le berger' ('Oton de Granson', 405). The shepherd is called a *simple loyal bergier* (P2), but he holds his own in the debate and even makes a pseudo-literary reference when he says that he wishes to read from the *Livre de Joye* (P146) in order to comfort his heart. Clearly, we are not very far from the figures of the courtly lover and lady in *La Belle Dame qui eust mercy* and *Le Dialogue* (and Chartier's *La Belle Dame sans mercy*).

The debate that is overheard by the narrator is also akin to that heard in *La Belle Dame qui eust mercy* and *Le Dialogue*. The despondent shepherd laments the torment that Love makes him suffer. He is racked by jealousy when he sees other men surrounding the shepherdess and he blames Love for not coming to his aid. The shepherdess admonishes him, saying that he should be happy to be in the service of Love and be satisfied with what he receives. Furthermore, no one can control what someone else thinks, nor can one be prevented from laughing or looking. She is young and enjoys the company of others, so he must trust that she will act honourably and, in doing so, will protect her reputation. He fears that others will misinterpret her *regard* and her *contenances* (P127) and will boast about it; she replies that *riens que je face ne dye | A mon propos n'est pas pour eulz* (P133). In any case, it doesn't matter to her for she is *Franche* [...], *loyal, nette, et pure* (P137), and stands in defiance of the slanderers. Needless to say, these words confirm the affinities between the shepherdess and the ladies in *La Belle Dame qui eust mercy* and *Le Dialogue*, regardless of any societal distinctions.

Five other poems by Granson feature the solo voice of a woman. Four of these bear little resemblance to the voices of the ladies in *La Belle Dame qui eust mercy* and *Le Dialogue*: one laments her separation from her lover; one professes her loyalty regardless of the gossip surrounding her; and two complain of the inconstancy of their lovers. The fifth lady appears in the second of a pair of *balades* (decasyllabic *dizains* in *ababbccdcd*, the same structure and rhyme scheme as in Poem I of *Le Dialogue*) with identical refrains, *Je n'ay riens fait qu'Amours ne m'ait fait faire*. These two poems form a mini-debate in which many familiar and new questions of love are discussed. In the first *balade*, the lover speaks of his devotion to his lady; his decision to come forward to demand her love after having remained silent; his pain and sorrow at having been rejected for another; and his blame of the God of Love for having made him fall victim to her *beaulx yeux*. In the second *balade*, the lady scolds him for not being satisfied with the rewards from her love that he has been enjoying for quite some time and for complaining that she now loves another. Such is Love's game, she says; in this, she is not false, she is merely doing what Love has wished of her. In her no-nonsense and pragmatic tone, it is clear that the lady in Granson's *Balade* 50, like the shepherdess in *La Pastourelle Granson*, shares a deep kinship with the ladies in *La Belle Dame qui eust mercy* and *Le Dialogue*.

In my opinion, therefore, the structural and thematic elements present in Oton de Granson's *Pastourelle* and *Balades* 49 and 50 permit attribution of authorship of Poem 1 in *La Belle Dame qui eust mercy* and *Le Dialogue* to the Savoyard knight-poet, with a dating to the last quarter of the fourteenth century, obviously prior to his death in 1397. The material proximity of many of Granson's works to the two poems edited here, while not conclusive, supports this attribution.

My reticence to attribute to Granson the 'second poems' in *La Belle Dame qui eust mercy* and *Le Dialogue*, thus the poems in their entirety, relates primarily to their structure. Granson never once used the *treizain*, nor did he ever disrupt the structure of a poem in the way that is seen here. Knowing of no other contemporary poet who made use of the *treizain*, and lacking any other conclusive evidence, I must refrain from assigning authorship to Poem 2 of *La Belle Dame qui eust mercy* or *Le Dialogue* and they must, for now, remain anonymous.

Cayley's 'collaborative debating communities,' Armstrong's 'virtuoso circles,' and Taylor's 'coterie poetics,' however, provide insights into the compositional process that may help to explain how the 'second poems' in *La Belle Dame qui eust mercy* and *Le Dialogue* came to be. These concepts encourage us to envisage poets responding to earlier works by reworking and/or writing continuations of them in order to create poetic capital. As Armstrong notes, 'the view that poetry is a craft to be mastered emerges implicitly from the dynamics of intertextual response, as poets engage with specific pre-existing texts' (*Virtuoso Circle*, p. xvii). With this in mind, it seems to me that the poems now known as *La Belle Dame qui eust mercy* and *Le Dialogue* can be seen to be the end result of the melding of separate poems during one or more of three specific processes: composition, transcription, and compilation.

At the point of composition, one or two poets wrote continuations of Granson's eighteen-stanza poems in which a lady refuses a lover's suit. One continuation, in *treizains*, was a palinode to the depiction of a merciless lady. The other continuation, also in *treizains*, was a reaffirmation of the lady's right to decide whom she would love. It bears consideration that competition was at play here, i.e. that these continuations were written in the unusual *treizain* structure precisely for the effect that the rupture in stanzaïc structure would have on the reader, drawing attention to the continuation itself. The poets of the continuations could then have employed scribes to append their new works to Granson's original poems, with the separate poems being transcribed as the single poems that have come down to us as *La Belle Dame qui eust mercy* and *Le Dialogue*. Subsequent scribes simply copied the composite poem as one.

Alternatively, at the point of compilation, decisions would have been made to bind separate works such as these together, either based on superficial similarity or to advance a specific agenda or theme.

Piaget maintained that Chartier knew *Le Dialogue* and *La Belle Dame qui eust mercy* (whether in their entirety or in sections is not stated), just as he was familiar with other works by Granson and his contemporaries. Furthermore, he claimed that Chartier reworked and rejuvenated this existing genre when he composed his poem about the merciless lady. Somewhat ironically, therefore, these two poems from the Belle Dame cycle which have always been thought to be imitations of Chartier's work may have been the inspirations for Chartier — and his *La Belle Dame sans mercy*, the imitation. In a final salute to the two lesser known works, Piaget concluded that Chartier had found in *La Belle Dame qui eust mercy* and *Le Dialogue* 'quelques-uns des traits qui ont fait le succès de la *Belle Dame sans merci*' ('Imitations', 33, p. 207).

It is entirely possible, however, that the continuations date from after 1424, and were written in the context of the *querelle* surrounding *La Belle Dame sans mercy*, since numerous poems both for and against the lady were written throughout the century. While poets like Christine de Pizan and others came 'increasingly to manage their own work and to valorize it in single-author codices' (Taylor, 'Courtly Gatherings', p. 15), there is no single extant manuscript of Chartier's complete *œuvre*. Roughly two hundred manuscripts exist containing his poetry and/or prose, one quarter of which includes *La Belle Dame sans mercy*. And there is no evidence that the copying of any of these manuscripts was overseen by the poet; it is more likely that 'almost all the surviving manuscripts were copied after his death' (Laidlaw, 'Manuscripts', p. 43). In the preparation of these compilations, works by authors other than Chartier (Oton de Granson, Baudet Herenc, Achille Caulier, among others) were included, probably due to the pragmatic facets of publication (availability of works, choice of theme or genre, length of text, cost of medium, destination and/or marketability of the compilation, etc.), as well as the social and literary milieu in which they were created and for which they were destined. This would have allowed for the composition, transcription, and compilation of the poems into the forms that have come down to us. There is simply not enough evidence to draw any firm conclusions about the authorship and dating of the *treizains* in *La Belle Dame qui eust mercy* and *Le Dialogue,* but continuation, collaboration, and probable competition undoubtedly factored into their history.

§6. Manuscripts, *Incunabula*, and Early Printed Editions

Twenty manuscripts are known to contain all or fragments of *La Belle Dame qui eust mercy*.[28] Four of these manuscript witnesses are complete: BnF, MSS f. fr. 1131 and 1642; TBM, MS 826; and ON, MS 2619. *Le Dialogue* comes down to us

---

[28] Piaget documented fifteen manuscript witnesses to *La Belle Dame qui eust mercy*, omitting the Carpentras, Copenhagen, Toulouse, Paris-Musée Jacquemart-André, and Yale University-Beinecke Library manuscripts.

in four manuscripts, all incomplete. The best of these is BnF, MS f. fr. 1131, which is missing four lines (compared to the next most complete, which is missing sixteen). For its relative completeness and its legibility, therefore, BnF, MS f. fr. 1131 was chosen as the base for this edition and translation of both poems; it was also the one used by Hult and McRae in their 2003 edition of some of the poems in the Belle Dame cycle. The three other complete manuscripts of *La Belle Dame qui eust mercy* were the first to be consulted for emendations and corrections where the primary base manuscript was manifestly faulty, but all variants were considered. As for *Le Dialogue*, BnF, MS f. fr. 833 and BNU, MS L.II.12 served as secondary sources, since they contain the four lines missing in the base manuscript and, while lacking sixteen and eighteen lines respectively, are otherwise fairly good witnesses to the poem.

The earliest *incunabulum* containing *La Belle Dame qui eust mercy*, published in Vienne (south of Lyon) by Johannnes Solidi (Schilling), dates from 1478–1480. It is a single quire of eight folios containing only this poem and is called *Complainte d'amours et réponse*. Variant readings from this print edition have been included here. Five other publishers working in Lyon also produced *incunabula* devotedly solely to *La Belle Dame qui eust mercy*, including Jean Du Pré (1485), Matthias Huss (1490), Jean de Vingle (1495), Pierre Mareschal and Barnabé Chaussard (1495).

Apart from these self-contained editions, many compilations of works primarily by Alain Chartier include both *La Belle Dame qui eust mercy* and *Le Dialogue*. The first printed edition of French prose and verse works by Chartier was published by Pierre Le Caron on 5 September 1489, about 40 years after the poet's death. Although bearing the title *Les fais maistre Alain Chartier, notaire et secretaire du Roy Charles VIe*, this edition also contained poems now known to be by Michault Taillevent, Oton de Granson, Achille Caulier, and others, as well as several anonymous works, including *La Belle Dame qui eust mercy* and *Le Dialogue*. Le Caron is likely to have based his edition on two manuscripts: BnF, MSS f. fr. 833 and 24440, as these manuscripts contain several unique readings found in Le Caron's text, as well as lines that are missing from other, similar manuscripts.[29] Le Caron's edition sold out quickly, as Chartier was considered to be 'le grand maître de la poésie et de l'éloquence' (Piaget, 'Notice,' p. 192). Another Le Caron edition appeared that same year, reproducing the text of the first, with only minor modifications.

It was Le Caron's 1494 edition, however, which became the base for the half-

---

[29] In his edition of the poetry of Oton de Granson, Arthur Piaget accused Le Caron of being poorly informed as to the relatively limited number of works by Chartier in his edition, of trusting the contents of the manuscripts he used, and of gathering together 'une foule de pièces étrangères à l'auteur de *La Belle Dame sans merci*' (*Oton de Grandson*, p. 124). He also criticized this edition for faulty and missing lines and stanzas, as well as language modernized to Le Caron's time ('Notice', p. 192).

dozen more print editions that were produced over the next four decades. While this edition was, according to Piaget, 'simplement copié et rarement corrigé' from his earlier editions ('Notice,' p. 192), subsequent editors who based their work on it included: Le Caron himself, for the bookseller, Antoine Vérard c. 1494; Michel Le Noir in 1514; La Veuve Feu Jean Trepperel and Jehan Jehannot in 1515; Philippe Le Noir in 1520 and 1523; and Pierre Vidoue for Galliot du Pré in 1529. According to Laidlaw, 'the later fifteenth-century and sixteenth-century collected editions are so similar to [Le Caron's third edition] that they can almost be considered reprints of it' (*Poetical Works*, p. 142). In the preface of his 1529 edition, Galliot Du Pré claimed to have carefully corrected the errors that he found in earlier editions, but Piaget dismissed this claim, saying that Du Pré was only mocking his readers, for (according to Piaget) he had neither reviewed nor corrected the text and was, moreover, guilty of inserting even more mistakes ('Notice', p. 194).

The next print versions of *La Belle Dame qui eust mercy* and *Le Dialogue* appeared in 1617, included in a compilation of works again purported to be by Chartier, published by the noted geographer and historian, André Du Chesne. In the preface to this, his only edition of vernacular literature, Du Chesne stated that, in order to honour the memory of such an excellent author as Chartier, he had decided to rely principally on manuscripts to produce his compilation, rather than on the earlier and, in his opinion, faulty printed editions that he had consulted.[30] He chose BnF, MS f. fr. 1727 as his primary source, but when this manuscript did not contain a particular work by Chartier, Du Chesne borrowed from Galliot Du Pré's 1529 edition. In those cases where he used manuscript readings to correct Du Pré's edition, Du Chesne wrote in the margins *Ajoustés [nouvellement] du Ms.* Laidlaw notes, however, that Du Chesne's editing was inconsistent and that BnF, MS f. fr. 1727 was really 'quite a good manuscript of Chartier's poetical works, [which] could have been used to greater advantage, if only in making good omissions and irregularities'.[31] In the end, Du Chesne published all of the other works appearing in the earlier printed editions, including *La Belle Dame qui eust mercy* and *Le Dialogue*. In fact, of the 809 pages in Du Chesne's edition of Chartier's works, only 425 of them contain pieces that are indisputably by that author. Nevertheless, this 1617 edition was the primary source for Alain Chartier's poetical works until James C. Laidlaw's edition appeared in 1974.

---

[30] 'Mais les lisant & conferant toutes les unes avec les autres [éditions], j'y ai recognu tant de fautes & de corruptions en la diction, aux noms propres, voire aux periodes entieres, que m'estant resolu de renouveller la memoire d'un Autheur si celebre & renommé, je n'ay pas creu pouvoir bien m'en acquitter autrement que par l'aide & secours des Exemplaires escrits à la main.' (Du Chesne, fol. b.i^r).

[31] 'André Du Chesne's Edition of Alain Chartier', *Modern Language Review*, 63 (1968), 569–74 (p. 574).

* * * * *

The manuscripts used in this edition are identified below and in the list of variant readings by an italicized *siglum* borrowed from the system developed by Laidlaw for his Chartier edition (pp. 43–60). Parisian manuscripts containing *La Belle Dame sans mercy* and similar poems were designated by *P*, followed by a small *a, b, c,* and so on (excluding the letter 'i'). Manuscripts located outside of Paris, but containing these poems, were identified by *Q* plus a small letter. The *siglum Qx* was added in McRae's study of the *querelle* to represent WA, MS 21 (which contains no works by Chartier), so that has been used here.

Variant readings from a small selection of *incunabula* and early printed editions in which *La Belle Dame qui eust mercy* and *Le Dialogue* appear are also documented here. Laidlaw chose *X* plus a small letter for the five early printed editons (single works and collections of works) that he used in his Chartier edition, two of which are used here: *Xa* for Le Caron's 1489 edition and *Xd* for Du Chesne's 1617 edition. Other early printed books containing *La Belle Dame qui eust mercy* and *Le Dialogue* were consulted and assigned a *siglum* based on the order in which they are numbered in the *Gesamtkatalog der Wiegendrucke* (*GKW*). Thus, Johannes Solidi's 1478–1480 stand-alone edition of *La Belle Dame qui eust mercy* is identified by *Xe*, while the 1568 *Le Thrésor des joyeuses inventions du paragon des poésies* is labelled *Xn*. A listing of the manuscripts, *incunabula,* and early printed editions used in the preparation of the present edition follows.

La Belle Dame qui eust mercy

Primary Base Manuscript

Pc   Paris, Bibliothèque nationale de France, MS f. fr. 1131, fols 184^r–189^v (mid-15th c.)

Other Manuscript Witnesses, *Incunabula*, and Early Printed Editions

Pa   Paris, Bibliothèque nationale de France, MS f. fr. 833, fols 128^r–134^r (late 15th–early 16th c.)

Pb   Paris, Bibliothèque nationale de France, MS f. fr. 924, fols 19^r–26^v (late 15th c.)

Pd   Paris, Bibliothèque nationale de France, MS f. fr. 1642, fols 285^r–290^r (late 15th – early 16th c.)

Pe   Paris, Bibliothèque nationale de France, MS f. fr. 1727, fols 125^r–130^r (mid-15th c.)

Pf   Paris, Bibliothèque nationale de France, MS f. fr. 2230, fols 160^r–168^r (mid-15th c.)

Pj   Paris, Bibliothèque nationale de France, MS f. fr. 20026, fols 39^v–47^v (mid-15th c.)

Pk   Paris, Bibliothèque nationale de France, MS f. fr. 24440, fols 160^r–165^v (15th c.)

Pl   Paris, Bibliothèque nationale de France, MS Rothschild I.4.31, fols 107^r–114^r (mid-15th c.)

Po   Paris, Bibliothèque de l'Arsenal, MS 3523, pp. 339–50 (15th c.)

Pp   Paris, Musée Jacquemart-André, MS 11, fols 75^r–85^{rbis} (15th c.)

Qa   Besançon, Bibliothèque municipale, MS 554, fols 79^v–87^r (15th c.)

Qb   Carpentras, Bibliothèque Inguimbertine, MS 390, fols 61^r–68^v (15th c.)

Qd   Toulouse, Bibliothèque municipale, MS 826, fols 5^r–63^v (early 15th c.)

Qh   Copenhagen, Kongelige Bibliotek, Ny. Kgl. S., MS 1768.2, fols 16^r–23^r (late 15th c.)

Qn   New Haven, Yale University Beinecke Library, MS 1216, fols 102^r–104^r (*c.* 1490)

Qp   Turin, Biblioteca Nazionale e Universitaria, MS L.II.12, fols 103ra–105vb (mid-16th c.)

Qq   Rome/Vatican, Biblioteca Apostolica Vaticana, MS 4794, fols 25^r–30^v (15th c.)

Qr   Vienna, Österreichische Nationalbibliothek, MS 2619, fols 143rb–146ra (mid-15th c.)

Qx   London, Westminster Abbey Library, MS 21, fols 80^r–80^v (mid-15th c.)

Xa   Paris, Bibliothèque nationale de France, Rés. P. Ye 30–31, *GKW* 6557; fols Ciii^r–Cvi^r, published in Paris by Pierre Le Caron (September 5, 1489)

Xd   Paris, Bibliothèque nationale de France, Imprimé 705, pp. 684–94; published in Paris by André Du Chesne, printed by Samuel Thiboust (1617)

Xe   Paris, Bibliothèque nationale de France, Réserve P. Ye 137, *GKW* 6569; fols Ai^r–Aviii^r, published in Vienne by Johannes Solidi (*c.* 1478–1480)

Le Dialogue d'amoureux et de sa dame

Primary Base Manuscript

Pc   Paris, Bibliothèque nationale de France, MS f. fr. 1131, fols 195^r–201^r (mid-15th c.)

Other Manuscript Witnesses, *Incunabula*, and Early Printed Editions

Pa   Paris, Bibliothèque nationale de France, MS f. fr. 833, fols 181^v–184^v (late 15th – early 16th c.)

Po   Paris, Bibliothèque de l'Arsenal, MS 3523, pp. 351–57 (15th c.)

Qp   Turin, Biblioteca Nazionale e Universitaria, MS L.II.12, fols 150vb–154ra (mid-16th c.)

Xa   Paris, Bibliothèque nationale de France, Rés. P. Ye 30–31, *GKW* 6557; fols Iviii^r–Kiii^r, published in Paris by Pierre Le Caron (5 September 1489)

Xd   Paris, Bibliothèque nationale de France, Imprimé 705, pp. 782–92; published in Paris by André Du Chesne, printed by Samuel Thiboust (1617)

Xn   *Le Thrésor des joyeuses inventions du paragon des poésies*; pp. 39–42, published in Paris by La Veuve Jean Bonfons (1568)

A full description of the base manuscript, BnF, MS f. fr. 1131, is given below, including a list of its contents. A description of the other manuscript witnesses, *incunabula*, and early printed editions consulted in this edition is also provided, with foliation for *La Belle Dame qui eust mercy* and *Le Dialogue*, but without an inventory of the works they contain.

Primary Base Manuscript

Pc — Paris, Bibliothèque nationale de France, MS f. fr. 1131 (Codex Colbert 3329, Regius 7372³); <http://gallica.bnf.fr/ark:/12148/btv1b9058815c.r=la%20 belle%20dame%20qui%20eust%20mercy>; mid-15th c.; title printed on spine, 'Al. Chartier'; yellow parchment binding; 208 parchment folios; 295 × 210 mm; 34–36 lines per folio; justification 210 × 115 mm; some catchwords; a few remaining signatures and rubrics; large, regular and uniform handwriting; modern foliation in Arabic numerals; incomplete decoration, several spaces reserved for miniatures are left blank; several smaller initials marking the start of a stanza are outlined in gold and framed in blue, with red interior, but other large initials are missing; the volume contains:

> fols 1ʳ–50ᵛ *Le Livre des quatre dames* by Alain Chartier
> fols 51ʳ–68ᵛ *Le Debat du gras et du maigre* by Alain Chartier
> fols 69ʳ–71ᵛ *La Complainte amoureuse de Saint Valentin* by Oton de Granson
> fols 73ʳ–80ʳ *Le Breviaire de nobles* by Alain Chartier
> fols 80ʳ–84ʳ *Le Lai de paix* by Alain Chartier
> fols 84ᵛ–87ᵛ *Le Lai de complainte pour les guerres* by Eustache Deschamps
> fols 88ᵛ–90ᵛ *La Complainte contre la mort de la dame* by Alain Chartier
> fols 91ʳ–103ᵛ *La Belle Dame sans mercy* by Alain Chartier
> fols 103ᵛ–104ᵛ *La Complainte envoyee aux dames par les poursuivans de la court*
> fol. 104ᵛ *Lettres closes envoyees a Maistre Alain par les dames*
> fols 104ᵛ–108ᵛ *Response faite par Maistre Alain*
> fols 108ᵛ–116ᵛ *Le Parlement d'amours* by Baudet Herenc
> fols 117ʳ–130ᵛ *Le Jugement de la belle dame sans mercy*
> fols 131ʳ–146ʳ *La Cruelle Femme en amours* by Achilles Caulier
> fols 146ʳ–166ᵛ *L'Ospital d'Amour* by Achilles Caulier
> fols 167ʳ–172ʳ *Le Debat du reveille matin* by Alain Chartier
> fols 173ʳ–183ᵛ *Le Traité de reveille qui dort*

fols 184ʳ–189ᵛ *La Belle Dame qui eust mercy de son amant*

fols 189ᵛ–190ᵛ *Complainte* 'Ma treshonnouree princesse, ma dame ma seule maistresse'

fols 191ʳ–192ʳ *Complainte* by Granson 'Helas se je me complains'

fols 192ᵛ–194ᵛ *La Pastourelle d'Othon de Granson*

fols 195ʳ–201ʳ **D'un Amoureux parlant a sa dame par amour**

fols 201ᵛ–208ᵛ Moral texts

Other Manuscript Witnesses, *Incunabula*, and Early Printed Editions

Pa — Paris, Bibliothèque nationale de France, MS f. fr. 833 (Codex Colbert 2258, Regius 7215 2.2); <http://gallica.bnf.fr/ark:/12148/btv1b90588050.r=833.langEN>; late 15th–early 16th c.; title *Oeuvres d'Al. Chartier*; on fol. 1 *Les faicts maistre Alain Charetier*, with verses by Chartier at the bottom and on the back; contemporary binding made of wood plates covered with stamped brown leather with a criss-cross pattern forming diamond-shaped compartments, each bearing a circle; traces of two clasps; parchment; 195 folios; 330 × 240 mm; 34 long lines; some folios with double columns; justification 235 × 140 mm; irregular quires; no catchwords or signatures; black ink, with a few initials in blue or brown; large initial, five lines high, at start of each group of three stanzas spoken by the lady or the lover in *La Belle Dame qui eust mercy*; two-line high initial at start of *Le Dialogue*; one-line high initials begin all other stanzas; regular hand; right-justified rubrics 'La dame' and 'Lamant / L'amoureux' at start of each speech; modern foliation in Arabic numerals; no decoration; *La Belle Dame qui eust mercy* is found on fols 128ᵛ–134ʳ although its rubric is at the bottom of 128ʳ and reads *Comment l'amoureux deprie la dame Et est fort repugnant a la belle dame sans mercy selon maistre Alain, Le dixieme Livre*; library catalogue gives title as *Complainte d'amour*; *Le Dialogue* appears on fols 181ᵛ–184ᵛ.

Pb — Paris, Bibliothèque nationale de France, MS f. fr. 924 (Codex Colbert 2117, Regius 7274 2.2; <http://gallica.bnf.fr/ark:/12148/btv1b90071477.r=Français+924. langEN>; late 15th c.; *Oeuvres d'Alain Chartier*; binding of wooden plates covered in parchment, back of the skin; paper, except fols 1 and 18, which are parchment; several watermarks (a barred 'P' with a fleuron and cross, a unicorn, a coat of arms, a pot surmounted by a cross, and a balance); 282 folios; 275 × 184 mm; 24 long lines per folio; justification 190 × 100 mm; irregular quires; catchwords in items copied on more than one quire; no signatures; black ink; no titles or *explicits*; regular cursive hand; two numbering systems, an old one in Roman numerals and a modern one in Arabic numerals, always parallel with one another; on fol. 1, lines drawn in red ink set out a frame filled with fine foliage in golden swirls, with little flowers, fruits, and blue and gold acanthus; very careful and delicate decoration; capitals in red; initial at the start of fol. 1, the colour of slate with geometrical lines in gold on a blue background, watermark in white; rubrics 'La dame' and 'Lamant' at start of each speech in *La Belle Dame qui eust mercy*; Stanza XIX starts at top of new folio (22^r) and has an initial 'J' that is larger and more elaborate than preceding initials, as well as ornate flourishes in ink; the manuscript belonged to Jacques Thiboust of Bourges (d. 1555), notary and royal secretary to Henry II; under the rubric *La belle dame ou a mercy*, the poem is found on fols 19^r–26^v; the title in the library catalogue is *La belle dame a mercy*.

Pd — Paris, Bibliothèque nationale de France, MS f. fr. 1642 (formerly 7640); late 15th to early 16th c.; title: *Ouvrage de Mr Allain Chart*; on fol. 1, the title *Les faiz maistre Allain Charretier ou vivant du roy Charles VIIeme son notaire et secretaire*; 18th-c. binding with the arms of this king on the cover; paper; watermarks, five types of Saint Catherine-style endentured wheels, coming possibly from the Auvergne region (Briquet 13.364, 365, 358, 357, 491); 479 folios; 290 × 200 mm; 35 lines per page for the poetry, 40 lines per page for prose, and double columns on fol. 177^v; justification 210 × 112 mm; catchwords at right angles; regular quires; black ink (faded brown); no rubrics; regular writing style; modern foliation in Arabic numerals; alternating blue and red initials, decorated with tiny flowers; corner frames with initials decorated with flowers, fruits, and blue and gold acanthus appear at the start of each work; a capital letter, two lines high, begins each poem; *La Belle Dame qui eust mercy* appears on fols 285^r–290^r.

Pe — Paris, Bibliothèque nationale de France, MS f. fr. 1727 (formerly 7689); mid-15th c.; title printed on spine *Alain Chartier*; binding on marbled leather with a narrow border of little blades of golden leaves; ribbed spine in red with either a lily or interlacing surmounted by a crown in the compartments, each flanked with four corners of a golden fleur-de-lys; paper; watermark of grapes within a border of branches and foliage, 65 × 50 mm (Briquet 13055, dating from 1453); 189 folios; 280 × 200 mm; 35–45 long lines per folio for the poetry, 38–39 for prose; justification 205 × 110 mm (margins reduced by the most recent binding); regular catchwords, some at right angles; one signature on fol. 12; brown/black ink; no rubrics; cursive hand, not always regular, with occasional corrections and words crossed out; modern foliation in Arabic numerals; light decoration limited to a few capitals at the beginning of a text or of a grouping within a text; many of the capitals are missing; the manuscript belonged to the Dupuy brothers and was used by DuChesne in his 1617 edition of the works of Alain Chartier; at the bottom of fol. 124^v is the title *Complainte d'amours et Response faicte par maistre Alain Charretier secretaire du Roy*, while the poem is found on fols 125^r–130^r; in the library catalogue, it is listed as *La belle dame qui eut merci*.

Pf — Paris, Bibliothèque nationale de France, MS f. fr. 2230 (formerly 8009);

mid-15th c. (after 1445); title *Le Lai de paix et d'amitié*; red-brown binding, bearing a crown and a golden fleur-de-lys of Louis XVIII on the outer and inner covers; parchment; 249 folios; 215 × 148 mm; 29 long lines per folio; justification 137 × 77 mm; regular quires with catchwords (a single catchword is missing on fol. 120^v); traces of signatures; black ink; careful handwriting; no particular decoration for the lyric pieces, apart from alternating red and blue capitals (2–3 lines high); the manuscript belonged first to the library of Charles d'Orléans, then to that of his brother, Jean d'Angoulême, as attested by the two coats of arms on the first two pieces in the manuscript; *Le Traitté de la belle dame a mercy* appears on fols 160^r–168^r; the title given in the catalogue is *Le Traité de la belle dame qui eut mercy*.

Pj — Paris, Bibliothèque nationale de France, MS f. fr. 20026 (formerly 2045 fonds St. Germain); <http://gallica.bnf.fr/ark:/12148/btv1b8451111w/f92.image. r=Français2020026.langEN>; mid-15th c. (after 1440); title on the spine in gold letters, *Le Livre des quatre dames*; wood plate binding, covered by dark speckled paper; parchment; 178 folios; 221 × 152 mm; 29–30 long lines per folio; justification 140 × 75 mm; catchwords; traces of signatures; regular quires; no rubrics; black ink; regular hand; modern foliation in Arabic numerals; the folios bearing the beginning of a text are framed by a delicate swirling leaf pattern with small flowers; capital letters at the start of a text have a floral decoration of alternating blue and red with white, on a gold background; rubrics 'La dame' and 'Lamant' at start of each speech in *La Belle Dame qui eust mercy*; groups of three stanzas from I–XVIII contained on each folio; thirteen-line Stanza XIX starts at the bottom of fol. 42^v and the 39 lines in this speech by the lover are grouped into five stanzas of 8, 8, 9, 8, and 6 lines as the scribe tries to maintain the eight-line format; the lady's next speech reverts to the thirteen-line format, which is used until the end of the poem; regular handwriting; the coat of arms of Marie de Clèves, wife of Charles d'Orléans (Orléans and Clèves impaled) appears on fol. 1^r along with her device *Rien ne m'est plus*; on fol. 177^v, a monogram followed by La Tremouille, Ysabeau de Beaumont, the letters H and M interlaced, above which is a coat of arms in blue, black, orange and gold; the poem is found on fols 39^v–47^v and is called simply *La dame a mercy*, while in the library catalogue the word 'Belle' is added.

Pk — Paris, Bibliothèque nationale de France, MS f. fr. 24440; <http://gallica.bnf. fr/ark:/12148/btv1b9007145d.r=24440.langEN>; 15th c.; title typed in gold *Alain Chartier, Oeuvres poetiques*; binding of thick wood plates, with the profile of a man carved into the top plate; parchment; 270 folios; 295 × 125 mm; 30–39 long lines per folio; justification 190 × 122 mm; regular catchwords; some vestiges of signatures; brownish black ink; several rubrics; likely two different hands (fols 1^r–230^v and 231^r–269^r), both neat and regular; foliation in Arabic numerals;

texts were destined to have a preceding minature, but only one exists, 21 lines high, which shows the author seated in an armchair, looking at a manuscript resting on a lectern in the form of a coffer; decorated, flourished, and coloured initials; the rubrics 'Lamie' and 'Lamy' are placed in the left margins, otherwise the stanzas are not easily recognizable by spacing, but rather by a small initial; *La Belle Dame qui eust mercy* is located on fols 160^r–165^v and is labelled *Complainte d'amant a amye*.

Pl — Paris, Bibliothèque nationale de France, MS Rothschild I, 4, 31 (formerly 440); mid-15th c.; title *Oeuvres d'Alain Chartier*; brown vellum binding; parchment; 212 unnumbered folios; 204 × 132 mm; 26 long lines per folio; justification 130 × 81 mm; regular quires with catchwords and some signatures; black ink; no rubrics; luxury edition; irregular hand; red-ruled lines; capitals in blue, red and gold, decorated with vegetation; manuscript belonged to Renée de Daillon; no title given for the poem, found on fols 107^r–114^v, but the catalogue calls it *La belle dame qui a mercy*.

Po — Paris, Bibliothèque de l'Arsenal, MS 3523 (formerly 316 B. F); 15th c.; paper; several watermarks (Briquet 1725, 1547, 1684, 6909, 1739 or 1740, dating from 1445–1480); 818 pages; 290 × 195 mm; 30 long lines; justification 210 × 100 mm; the manuscript is in many different hands; the names of Jehan Maciot, Glaude Maciot and Gilbert Coquille appear on p. 818; the manuscript contains works by Chartier, François Villon, and other anonymous poets; the Belle Dame poem appears on pp. 339–50, but has no title, simply the rubric 'Lamant' at start of poem; at the end of Stanza XVIII, at the bottom of p. 343, is the *explicit* 'Et ho,' which indicates the end of a work throughout the manuscript; this *explicit* is repeated at the end of Stanza XXXVI; the poem is referred to as *Dialogue entre l'amant et la dame* in the library catalogue; as for *Le Dialogue*, only Stanzas XIX–XXXVI from are found here, on pp. 351–57.

Pp — Paris, Musée Jacquemart André, MS 11 (formerly 686); 15th c.; binding in brown leather on cardboard plates with diamond-shaped compartments on cover; vellum; 310 pages; 285 × 150 mm; 37 long lines per page; justification 193 × 76 mm; regular quires; some catchwords and signatures; black ink; some rubrics; neat handwriting; modern pagination in Arabic numerals; no decoration; on pp. 1 and 309 is the signature of Moisan de Brieux; the title that appears with the poem on pp. 75–85bis is *Ung traittié en maniere de prieres en amours*, while the catalogue gives the title as *La belle dame qui eut pitié*.

Qa — Besançon, Bibliothèque municipale, MS 554; 15th c.; provenance Ile de France; contemporary binding in brown stamped (calf) leather on wooden boards; paper; watermark of an ox head (Briquet 15100 or 15103, 104, 109); several worm holes; water stains; 214 folios plus two parchment end-leaves;

208 × 140 mm; 21–30 long lines; justification 135 × 109 mm; collation 1–9^{12}, 10^{10}, 11–18^{12}; catchwords (vertical) and signatures; brown ink; some rubrics; neat handwriting; modern foliation in Arabic numerals; no decoration; possible scribal signature on fol. 214^{v}, 'Ja.de bosco'; manuscript belonged to the Capucin convent in Besançon (*Ad usum Capucinorum conventus Vesuntionensis*); *La Belle Dame a mercy* appears on fols 79^{v}–87^{r} and is called *Une complainte d'amours que l'on dit autrement la Belle dame a mercy faicte par maistre Alain Charretier*.

Qb — Carpentras, Bibliothèque Imguibertine, MS 390; 15th c.; contemporary binding in calfskin; heavy paper; watermark of an ox head (Briquet 14329–40, dating from 1440–1480); several worm holes; 79 folios, numbered 11–39, 41–90; first quire missing (fols 1–10^{v}); 310 × 230 mm; 25 long lines; justification 170 × 103 mm; collation 2^{10}, 3^{10} (tenth lost), 4–8^{10} (first quire of 10 sheets, signed 'a' lost); catchwords; signatures b–h; brown ink; no rubrics; regular handwriting, bastard gothic; contemporary foliation in Roman numerals, xi–xc; no decoration, but space left for initials; manuscript belonged to M. René de Castellane, son of Caspar de Castellane, Lord of Andon et Mazaingnes (cf. Barrois, Append. 2289), whose signature (on fol. 52^{v}) and those of other members of the family (François, Gaspar, Henry) appear often; on the back board is the name of Pierre Parent, bachelier en loys; the poem appears on fols 61^{r}–68^{v} with the simple rubric *L'amant*, but is listed as *La belle dame qui eut mercy* in the library catalogue.

Qd — Toulouse, Bibliothèque municipale, MS 826 (formerly 161); early 15th c.; title *Alain Chartier*; parchment binding; paper; three watermarks of an ox-head, a gloved hand, and a paschal lamb (Briquet 14313, 11084, and 39 respectively, dating from 1419–1435); 107 folios; 295 × 210 mm; 32 long lines for verse, 34–36 for prose; catchwords; cursive hand with corrections; although *Qd* contains some irregular lines and has been copied carelessly, Laidlaw considered it one of the two best collected manuscripts of Chartier's works (*Poetical Works*, p. 123); *La Belle Dame qui eust mercy* appears on fols 57^{v}–63^{v}, under the title *Complainte*.

Qh — Copenhagen, Kongelige Bibliotek, MS Ny. kgl. S. 1768.2 (formerly Barrois 355); late 15th c.; title *La belle dame sans mercy et d'autres oeuvres d'Alain Chartier. Man. du 15^{e}*; binding in yellow leather decorated with 19th-c. blind tooling; paper, although fol. 1 is parchment; no visible watermarks; 308 folios; 288 × 198 mm; 24–26 lines per folio; justification 200 × 110 mm; catchwords trimmed; no signatures; brown ink; no rubrics; at least three cursive hands; modern foliation in Arabic numerals; no decoration, except on fol. 1 with framing of page in fine gold leaf swirls and sprays of little flowers; space left blank for a miniature; one lettrine, four lines in height, in gold on blue and purple background, in a white design; the manuscript belonged to the Ashburnham collection and contains the poem on fols 16^r–23^r, which is called *La belle dame a mercy* in the manuscript and in the library catalogue.

Qn — New Haven, Yale University, Beinecke Library, MS 1216; *c.* 1490; title *Chartier (Alain) Oeuvre*; binding in 18th-c. French red morocco gilt, back fully tooled; vellum; 136 folios; 311 mm × 210 mm; two columns with 43 long lines written in *lettres bâtardes*; eight large and eleven small miniatures, painted by an artist of superior ability, seven of the large miniatures within borders of birds, beasts, monsters, insects, flowers, fruit, foliage and acanthus decoration, all on gold grounds; twelve other folios with full borders of flowers, fruit, gold ivy leaf and acanthus, some birds, beasts and grotesques; fourteen large and many smaller initials painted in colours on gold grounds, rubrics; executed in France for a lady whose initials AA, conjoined by a widow's girdle, appear in every border, which may have been Anne de Beaujeu, daughter of Louis XI and wife of Pierre de Bourbon, Lord of Beaujeu, who was Dauphin of Auvergne; manuscript owned until 1769 by Louis-Jean Gaignat, then by Louis César de La Baume Le Blanc, duc de la Vallière until 1784, when it was purchased by the Abbé Lécuy; it was then part of the library of the Seventh Duke of Newcastle, Henry Pelham Archibald Douglas Newcastle (1864–1928), but was removed from Clumber, Worksop, and sold at the Sotheby auction on 6 December 1937 (Lot #941) for £1600 to Maggs Brothers book dealers in London for Maurice Burrus of Strasbourg; the manuscript was sold in 2017 by Christie's Auction House of London to Yale University's Beinecke Library; the poem appears on fols 102^r–104^r; a multifaceted miniature precedes *La Belle Dame qui eust mercy* (reproduced on the cover of this edition); the top frame presents two events: to the left, a nobleman (dressed in a belted blue tunic, rose-coloured tights, black collar with gold necklace, a black chaperon, and a small dagger on his belt) and another remove their hats as they enter a luxurious room, to be greeted by a noblewoman wearing a flowing, belted dress of burnt gold and blue brocade with tight bodice, a steeple headdress or hennin with white lace veil, and a necklace; they clasp hands and the man leans in to buss her cheek; to the right, the same nobleman and lady, as well as a maiden in a similarly styled gown of less ornate fabric, are each holding what looks to be small ruby-coloured boxes with gold trim; the bottom frame has a single image, showing the nobleman and his lady seated in a walled garden, facing one another (with the same or another maiden, but in a different gown, seated behind the lady); here, the lady is gently holding the man's right hand while placing a ring on the middle finger of his left hand; the poem is called *La belle dame ou mercy*.

Qp — Turin, Biblioteca Nazionale e Universitaria, MS L.II.12 (formerly 473); mid-16th c.; title *Oeuvres de Maistre Alain Chartier*; on the last folio, fol. 165^r, *Fin des oeuvres maistre Alain Chartier*; this manuscript and thousands of others were damaged in a fire in 1904; parchment; 295 × 105 mm; certain folios are distorted (shrunk due to heat) or the ink bleeds through, rendering some texts difficult to decipher; the title appearing before the poem is *Comment l'amoureux deprie sa dame et est fort repugnant la Belle Dame sans mercy selon maistre Alain.chartier*, but listed as *La belle dame a mercy* in the catalogue; the poem appears on fols 103ra–105vb ; *Le Dialogue* is found on fols 150vb–154ra.

Qq — Rome, Bibliotheca Apostolica Vaticana, MS 4794/4798; 15th c.; binding in white parchment with the pontifical arms; shield watermark with three lilies and a crown (Briquet 4895, 4899, or 4902, dating from late 15th c.); 218 folios; 297 × 198 mm; 32 long lines per folio; the first line of several poems missing; justification 215 × 110 mm, marked by folds; regular quires with catchwords; no signatures; black ink that has reddened the paper; cursive writing; manuscript belonged to 'Maistre Bertran H…met, secretaire du roy, acheté à Paris au Palays le ven. 5 oct. MCCCCLXIIII'; *La Belle Dame ou a mercy* is found on fols 25^r–30^v, and is called *La belle dame a mercy* in the catalogue.

Qr — Vienna, Österreichische Nationalbibliothek, MS 2619; mid-15th c.; parchment; 148 folios; 42 long lines per folio; catchwords; miniature with a decorated border at the beginning of each piece; *La Belle Dame qui eust mercy* appears on fols 143^d–146^a and is labeled simply *Balade* .

Qx — London, Westminster Abbey Library, MS 21; mid-15th c.; executed in France, but brought to England at the beginning of the 16th c.; modern binding in brown leather; paper; 79 folios; 275 × 200 mm; about 30 long lines per page, but irregular; a few folios with double columns; fols 1–7 are mutilated; scribbling in English, Greek and Latin on some folios; neither catchwords nor signatures; brown ink; no rubrics; regular handwriting, but with a few corrections and words crossed out; modern foliation in Arabic numerals; no decoration; cover in vellum, bearing the name of Robert Acland; *La Belle Dame qui eust mercy* appears in fragments on fols 80^r–80^v (Stanzas XV, XVIII, XIX, XX, XXII, and XXIV only).

Xa — Bibliothèque nationale de France, Paris, Ye 30–31; *CIBN*[32] C-267, *GKW*[33] 6557, Bechtel[34] C-270, *ChL*[35] 1467, Claudin[36] II 75–76, Copinger[37] 4912, *CRF*

---

[32] *Catalogue des incunables: Bibliothèque nationale*, 2 vols (Paris: Bibliothèque nationale, 1981–2006).
[33] *Gesamtkatalog der Wiegendrucke*, 8 vols (Leipzig, Stuttgart: Hiersemann, 1928–).
[34] *Printed Books and Manuscripts: Featuring the Kenneth K. Bechtel Collection of Californiana and Fine Books* (Los Angeles: Christie's, Thursday, 31 January 2002).
[35] Ada Thurston and Curt F. Buhler, *Check List of Fifteenth-Century Printing in the Pierpont Morgan Library* (New York: Pierpont Morgan Library, 1939).
[36] Anatole Claudin, *Histoire de l'imprimerie en France au XIVe et au XVe siècles*, 4 vols (Paris: Imprimerie nationale, 1900–1905).
[37] Walter A. Copinger, *Supplement to Hain's* Repertorium Bibliographicum (London: Sotheran, 1895–1902).

V^{38}-261, *CRF* XCII^{39}-180, Delisle^{40} 415, Goff^{41} Ce^3 C-425, *ISTC*^{42} ic00425000, Morgan 1467; Pellechet^{43} 3529 and 3529A; <http://gallica.bnf.fr/ark:/12148/bpt6k70118r>; 5 September 1489, published by Pierre Le Caron in Paris, making it the earliest collected edition of Chartier's (and others') works; title on binding *Oeuvres*; title page: *Les fais maistre Alain Chartier, notaire et secretaire du Roy Charles VIe* (1385?–1430?); the edition is divided into twenty *livres*, with two parts presented in one volume; 78 folios in Part 1; 84 folios in Part 2; gothic type; double columns; 36 long lines per folio; woodcut initial on title page; on the next page, a woodcut table to both Parts I and II depicts three characters: a pensive lover reclining on a bed gazing away from the other figures and with the rubric *Entendement* written on a ribbon overhead, a squire standing behind the bed holding back the bedcurtains with a white ribbon added for a missing rubric, and a lady standing to the right of the squire with the ribbon above her reading *Merencolie*; folios are signed with small and capital letters, and with Roman numerals; this edition had two printings with only minor differences between them; the colophon (fol. 161^v) reads: ... *ce present livre ... des fais maistre alain chartier ... imprime en la ville de paris par honnourable home ... maistre pierre le caron ... demourant en la grant rue du temple ... Le V. iour de septembre, Lan mil. iiij^e, iiijxx. et noef.* The Belle Dame poem begins on fol. Ciii^r, in 'le x. livre' in Part 1, with the rubric *[C]omment l'amoureux deprie la dame et est fort repugnant a la belle dame sans mercy selon maistre alain,* and ends on fol. Cvi^r; *Le Dialogue* begins on fol. Iviii^{ra} with the rubric *Dun amoureux parlant a sa dame par amours* and ends on fol. Kiii^r; copies of Le Caron's *editio princeps* of Alain Chartier's works (and those of others) are held in the following institutions: the Musée Condé, Chantilly; the Foundation Bodmer, Cologny; the Bibliothèque municipale, Le Havre; the Rylands Library at the University of Manchester; the Musée Dobrée, Nantes; the Morgan Library, New York; the Bibliothèque municipale, Rouen; the National Library, Saint Petersburg; and the Austrian National Library, Vienna. The text in the Parisian *Xa* was compared to Morgan Library PML 23214, as well as copies from Cologny, Manchester, and Vienna,

---

^{38} Louis Torchet, *Catalogues régionaux des incunables des Bibliothèques publiques de France*, 20 vols, Bibliothèques de la Région des Pays de la Loire (Bordeaux: Société des Bibliophiles de Guyenne, 1987), V.

^{39} Valérie Neveu, *Catalogues régionaux des incunables des Bibliothèques publiques de France,* 20 vols, Bibliothèques de la région Haute Normandie (Geneva: Droz, 1979), XVII.

^{40} Léopold Delisle, *Chantilly, Le Cabinet des livres: imprimés antérieurs au milieu du XVIe siècle* (Paris: Plon-Nourrit, 1905).

^{41} Frederick R. Goff, *Incunabula in American Libraries: A Third Census of Fifteenth-Century Books Recorded in North American Collections* (New York: Bibliographical Society of America, 1964).

^{42} *Incunabula Short Title Catalogue* (London: British Library), <www.bl.uk/catalogues/istc>.

^{43} Marie Léontine Catherine Pellechet, *Catalogue général des incunables des bibliothèques publiques de France*, 3 vols (Paris: Picard, 1905; Paris: Kraus-Thomson Reprint, 1970).

all of which contained only variations in the style (or lack) of the hand-drawn decorated capitals added post-printing.

Xd — Bibliothèque nationale de France, Imprimé 705 (formerly 226); <http://archive.org/stream/OeuvresDeMaistreAlainChartier2/Oeuvres_d_Alain_Chartier#page/n709/mode/2up>; 1617, published by André Du Chesne Tourangeau; printed in Paris by Samuel Thiboust 'au Palais en la Gallerie des Prisonniers'; parchment binding; on the front, the gold interlaced initials of DG, an original copy of Denis Godefroy (1615–1681), annoted in his hand with an engraved ex-libris in his name; title on binding *Alain Chartier*; title page: *Les Oeuvres Maistre Alain Chartier, clerc, notaire et secretaire des Roys Charles VI et VII. Contenans l'Histoire de son Temps, L'Esperance, le Curial, le Quadriloge, et autres pieces, Toutes nouvellement reveues, corrigées, et de beaucoup augmentées sur les exemplaires escrits à la main*; paper; 888 pages; justification 220 × 170 mm; later owned by Antoine Moriau until 1757, then by the library of the city of Paris until the end of the eighteenth century, at which time it became the property of the Bibliothèque de l'Institut de France; the Belle Dame poem is found on pp. 684–94 (fols RRrriii^v–SSssiii^v), and is labelled *Complainte d'Amours et Response*; *Le Dialogue* begins on p. 782 and ends on p. 792 (fols FFFffiii^v–GGGggiv^v).

Xe — Bibliothèque nationale de France de France, Réserve P. Ye 137; *GKW* 6569, Bechtel C-494, *CIBN* C-276, Dalbanne-Droz 7, *ISTC* ic00794550, Pellechet 3526, Thierry-Poux[44] XXVII, 1–2; *c.* 1478–1480; published by Johannes Solidi (Schilling) in Vienne; title *La complainte d'ung amoreux et la repsonce* [sic] *de la dame*; paper; 8 folios devoted exclusively to *La Belle Dame qui eust mercy*; gothic type; single column; 20–27 long lines per folio; no signatures; the poem begins *Cy commence la complainte dung amoreux et la repsonce* [sic] *de la dame* on fol. Ai^r and ends on fol. Aviii^v with *Explicit deo gracias*; *Xe* is the only known copy of this printed book.

Xn — *Le Thrésor des joyeuses inventions du paragon des poésies, contenant épistres, balades, rondeaux, dizains, huictains, épitaphes, et plusieurs lettres amoureuses fort récréatives*; <http://gallica.bnf.fr/ark:/12148/bpt6k3158436>; 124 pages; published in Paris for La Veuve Jean Bonfons, Catherine Sergent, rue Neuve Notre-Dame in 1568 (other early editions were published by Etienne Groulleau in 1554, Etienne Denise in 1556–1558, and by Abraham Cousturier in Rouen in 1599); this edition was also part of the Duc de La Vallière's library (see above) and can also now be found in the Bibliothèque de l'Arsenal in Paris, Rés. 8-BL-9919. The fragments of *Le Dialogue* appear on pp. 39–42.

---

[44] Olgar Thierry-Poux, *Premiers monuments de l'imprimerie en France au XVe siècle* (Paris: Hachette, 1890).

✳   ✳   ✳   ✳   ✳

In the introduction to their 2003 edition of poems in the Belle Dame cycle, Hult and McRae commented that 'les textes poétiques du XVe siècle qui ont survécu en copies multiples se prêtent mal à un classement traditionnel par stemma' (p. lxxi). This is certainly true for the manuscripts and *incunabula* containing *La Belle Dame qui eust mercy* and *Le Dialogue*. Evidence of contamination in the copying of the poems is clear, due to scribal errors (a result of inattention, drowsiness, poor sight, haste, bad lighting, not to mention haphazard organization of copied materials) and/or borrowing of readings from multiple sources. One scribe, puzzled by a given text, may have tried to correct perceived errors, only to pass on imperfections to subsequent copyists. Pairs and groups of manuscripts may share readings, but may also contain readings which align with manuscripts from a seemingly different tradition. And the bipartite structure of both poems attests to substantial contamination in the copying of the works. Nevertheless, affinities between certain manuscripts and early printed editions can be detected and these are outlined below (using their *sigla* to identify them).

Pc presents a complete, legible text of *La Belle Dame qui eust mercy* and a near complete one of *Le Dialogue*, and thus was chosen as the base manuscript for this edition and translation. *Pc*, *Pp*, and *Qr* share many readings, some of them unique. These three manuscripts, for example, are the only ones to contain the reading at lines 133–35, wherein the lady states that if it please God, she will find her true love and husband, just as he will find her. In the other manuscripts, the lady uses the future tense to say that she will never love anyone but her *espoux et amy*, suggesting that she may already be married. *Pp* is missing line 149, thus may have been copied from *Pc* and/or *Qr*.

Hult and McRae suggested that a link existed between *Pc* and *Pk* (p. lxxii). While these manuscripts show some affinities, there are more examples of *Pk* following *Pd*, with significantly different readings from those found in *Pc*. At line 17, for example, *Pd* and *Pk* read *cherement vous prie*, whereas *Pc*, *Pp*, *Qr*, and others read *humblement vous prie*. *Pc* and *Pd/Pk* also diverge in a significant manner at lines 25–27 (see Variant Readings at the end of this edition).

The reading at the start of Part 2 (Stanza XIX) places the manuscript witnesses into two distinct groups. The first group includes *Pc* and *Pk*, but their readings are not identical: *Pc*, *Pl*, and *Qn* alone read *Mer de doulchour source de riviere*; *Pp* is similar (*Ma doulceur …*); while *Pa*, *Pk*, *Qp*, *Qr*, *Xa*, and *Xd* give a variation using *Cueur de doulceur*. The remaining manuscripts form a second group, with variations on *Jeune gente source de riviere* (although *Qq*'s reading stands somewhat apart, reading *Jeune gente fresche et entiere*).

Pa, *Pk* and *Qp* are very similar manuscripts, and share readings with Le

Caron's 1489 printed edition (*Xa*),[45] but there are lines where the group splinters into sub-groups. *Pa*, *Qp*, and *Xa* for example, are all missing lines from Stanza II (*Pa* and *Xa* are missing lines 9–12, *Qp* lacks lines 9–16), which is a good indication that they were copied from *Pk*, which contains all of those lines. *Pk* and *Xa* share several of the same readings, and even contain the same errors at the rhyme (in line 205, by inverting the penultimate and ultimate word, and in line 263, by putting *grant douleur* instead of *douleur mainte* when a rhyme in *–ainte* was required). These errors are not found in *Pa* or *Qp*. At line 56, however, *Pa*, *Qp*, and *Xa* share the same reading (*Nadoulcist mon cueur et refraint*), which differs from that in *Pk* (*Madoulcist mon mal et refrain*). The end of Stanza XXX is interesting in that line 299 is missing completely from *Pk* and *Xa*, whereas it appears in *Pa*, *Qp*, and *Xd*, but in a totally unique reading. This suggests that the copyist of one of these three realized a line was missing and added a new one with the correct rhyme. *Pa*, *Qp*, and *Xd* add a faulty fourteenth line to the stanza (line 299bis), while *Pa*, *Qp*, *Xa*, and *Xd* present another unique reading at line 300. *Pk* and *Xa* alone are missing line 305. Finally, *Pa*, *Qp*, and *Xa* contain the same long title (*Comment lamoureux deprie sa dame et est fort repugnant a la belle dame sans mercy selon maistre alain chartier*), whereas *Pk*'s title is simply *Complainte damant a amye*.

Pb and *Qh* exhibit kinship, as both are missing lines 175, 183, 240, 254, 264, and 325; they invert several of the same lines; and they alone add a new line (180bis), which hides the fact that line 183 is missing in terms of line count in the stanza. Only *Pb*, however, is missing line 273, which may indicate that it was copied from *Qh* (rather than the reverse, suggested by McRae). *Qq* is also related to these two.

Pe was one of the main manuscripts used in the making of Du Chesne's 1617 printed edition *Xd*, but it is alone in missing lines 134–35, 155–57, 309 and 332 (in those lines and others, *Xd* often aligns with *Qp*). *Pe* has similar readings to *Pf*, *Pj*, *Qa*, *Qb*, and *Qr*, but in many instances it contains unique readings.

Pf and *Pj* appear to be in the same hand and they present almost identical copies of the works that appear in them. They align occasionally with other manuscripts, but no pattern is evident. They are the only two manuscripts that present an extra, 37th, stanza in *La Belle Dame qui eust mercy*, in which the lover acknowledges his lady's acceptance of his love. They are both missing line 323, so it is hard to know which manuscript was copied from which, or if they are both simply copies of a lost master copy. McRae suggested that *Pf* was

---

[45] Laidlaw noted in his edition of Alain Chartier's poetry that Paulin Paris had seen similarities between *Pa* and Galliot du Pré's 1529 printed edition, but that Piaget showed that *Pa* had been copied from Le Caron's second edition (*Poetical Works*, pp. 100–01).

copied from Pj,[46] and thus used the latter as a primary base manuscript in her edition.

Pl, Po, and Pp share many readings, but their relationship is hard to determine. Whereas Pl and Po (along with several others) invert lines 356–57, Pp does not. Po, however, is alone in lacking lines 158–83, 231, and 376–77. The relationship between Pl and two others, Qn and Xe, is closer and more interesting, as they share most, sometimes unique, readings, and they often present the same lacunae and inversions (relative to the base manuscript Pc). Both Pl and Qn are missing lines 278–80, which appear in Xe. This latter, however, is missing lines 210–22 and 294–300, so it cannot have served as the sole base for Pl and Qn. Pl and Xe alone invert lines 154–55 (creating a bad rhyme); these lines are correct in Qn. All three manuscripts invert Stanzas XVII–XVIII and lines 226–27, 356–57, and 376–77, but Xe does not invert stanzas XXIII–XXIV as the two others do. And only Pl and Qn contain a unique extra stanza before the *explicit*, in which the lover continues to lament his lady's recalcitrance (even though she clearly agreed to his suit in the three previous stanzas).

Qa is missing line 188, but the text of this line is placed after line 196. Qa shows no special relationship to any other witness; it occasionally aligns with Pe and Xd, but more often than not has its own unique readings. Qb loosely follows the reading found in Pc, but also contains several unique readings. It alone is missing lines 166–68, and so could have been copied from Pc, which is complete. Qd is complete and shares readings and inversions with Pl and Po, among others. As mentioned above, Qp is akin to Pa. Laidlaw states that Qp was likely to have been copied from collected editions based on Xa (*Poetical Works*, p. 95). Qx is highly fragmented, lacking roughly three-quarters of the poem, and many of its variant readings are unique.

Xa and Xd are the 1489 printed edition by Pierre Le Caron and the 1617 printed edition by André Du Chesne respectively. As mentioned earlier, Le Caron's edition was reprinted and reworked by other editors, who seemed not to have questioned the blanket attribution of all poems to Chartier. Du Chesne produced his edition of these works primarily by consulting Pe and Galiot Du Pré's 1529 edition.

In terms of their relationship to the manuscript witnesses, both Xa and Xd contain La Belle Dame sans mercy, Le Dialogue, and other poems of that ilk, so they are akin to manuscripts under Laidlaw's *sigla* P and Q. In his edition of Chartier's poetry, Laidlaw notes that Xa often agrees with, but cannot have depended 'solely on a manuscript in the tradition of Pc, for Xa often agrees with other manuscripts and contains works, for example, the *Lai de plaisance*, which are not found in Pc or kindred manuscripts' (p. 144). He went on to say that he judged Xa to be inferior in quality to Pc.

---

[46] Joan McRae, ed. and trans., *The Quarrel of the Belle Dame sans mercy* (New York; London: Routledge, 2004), p. 31.

Xa aligns most often with *Pa*, *Pd*, *Pk*, and *Qp*, while *Xd* is most similar to *Pe* (which is the only manuscript that has the *explicit* that Du Chesne cites and marks with an asterisk). In Stanza XXXI, for example, lines 299 and 305 are missing in both *Pk* and *Xa*, but are present in *Pa* and *Xd* (in a reading unique to them). And in line 74, *Pe* and *Xd* (as well as *Qa*) align in reading *Perdries vous et labour et peine*, while *Pa*, *Pk*, and *Xa* give variations of the line found in the base manuscript *Pc*, *Perdriés et langaige et paine*. Line 309, however, is missing in *Pe*, but is present in all other manuscripts, suggesting that Du Chesne consulted more than just *Pe* in preparing his edition. Indeed, the following line, *Comme en qui de joye n'abonde*, is unique to *Qp* and *Xd*, suggesting that Du Chesne had access to this manuscript, along with *Pe*.

The 1478–1480 self-contained print edition of *La Belle Dame qui eust mercy* (*Xe*) is unique in missing lines 210–22 and 294–300. Along with *Pl*, it inverts lines 154–55, while it aligns with *Pl* and *Qn* in inverting lines 226–27, 356–57, and 376–77. In the first and last of these, the rhyme is disrupted at the inversion. As mentioned earlier, three new lines are added to Stanza XIX in *Xe* (145bis, 147bis, 152bis) in an effort to regularize the stanza length.

The final early printed edition used in this edition (*Xn*) dates from 1568, published by La Veuve Jean Bonfons, Catherine Sergent, in Paris. The full title of this compilation of love poetry is *Le Thrésor des joyeuses inventions du paragon des poésies, contentant épistres, balades, rondeaux, dizains, huictains, épitaphes & plusieurs lettres amoureuses fort recreatives*. The fragment of *Le Dialogue* that is presented here contains only six stanzas from the poem, with several unique readings: three stanzas spoken by the lover (Stanzas XIX–XXI), labelled *Epistre d'un amant a sa dame*; followed by three by the lady (Stanzas XXII–XXIV), called *Rescrit de la dame au dit amant*. This exchange is followed by a four-line envoi, which repeats two lines from an earlier stanza (XVII).

§8. Modern Editions

Nearly three centuries went by after Du Chesne's 1617 print edition of *La Belle Dame qui eust mercy* and *Le Dialogue* before any more attention was paid to these poems. Then, in 1901–1905, Piaget published his series of articles in *Romania* on the imitations of Chartier's *La Belle Dame sans mercy*. Among those works were poems by Baudet Herenc, Achille Caulier, Pierre de Hauteville, Henri Anctil, and Franci, as well as a number of anonymous poems, including *La Belle Dame qui eust mercy* and *Le Dialogue*. The so-called imitation poems range in length from 300 to 1400 lines. They are found in nearly four dozen late medieval manuscripts and numerous *incunabula*. Many of them have multiple manuscript witnesses, and they total over 3,500 folios of text. In his 1904–1905 articles, Piaget provided an inventory of the manuscripts known then to contain *La Belle Dame qui eust mercy* and *Le Dialogue*, as well as an overview of the poems, but he did not edit them.

David Hult and Joan McRae's 2003 critical edition of Chartier's *La Belle Dame sans mercy* and other poems in the Belle Dame cycle, using BnF, MS f. fr. 1131 as the base manuscript, shed valuable new light on these poems and the context in which they were written. *La Belle Dame qui eust mercy* and *Le Dialogue*, which are found in the same manuscript, were mentioned in this collection, but were not edited there. In 2004, McRae published *Alain Chartier: The Quarrel of the Belle Dame sans mercy*, which included an edition and English translation of *La Belle Dame qui eust mercy* based primarily on BnF, MS f. fr. 20026 (*Pj*). Both of these manuscripts are missing one line and include a unique, thirty-seventh stanza at the end of the poem. McRae's edition documents variant readings from eight more of the twenty extant manuscript witnesses to the poem, but none of the *incunabula* or early printed editions. *Le Dialogue* has never been edited.

§9. Establishment of the Text

Accuracy and readability have been the guiding principles in the making of this edition, conforming to practices advocated in *Editing Old French Texts* by Alfred Foulet and Mary Blakely Speer, as well as the *Conseils pour l'édition des textes médiévaux* by Pascale Bourgain and Françoise Vieillard. The text of the poem in the base manuscript has been altered as little as possible; unique readings therein have not been rejected for that reason alone. Where the base manuscript is clearly defective, it has been emended using the best reading from the other manuscript witnesses. An asterisk at the end of a line indicates an endnote. These are presented according to the number of the line referenced. When a variant reading (letter, word, or phrase) is borrowed, it is set off in square brackets within the poem, with the original text provided in the endnote, along with the *siglum/a* of the provenance of the correction. When an erroneous and superfluous word or letter is removed from the text, there is no indication in the text itself, but details on the change appear in the endnote. A very limited number of editorial corrections have been made when the text is clearly defective and no variant reading is found; these are also fully documented in the endnotes.

In general, the spelling in the base manuscript has been respected. A distinction is made between the letters *i* and *j* and between *u* and *v*, although the spelling of *pouez* from *pouoir* is used for the modern verb *pouvoir*, following the recommendation of Omer Jodogne.[47] The differences between *sf* / *ff* and

---

[47] Omer Jodogne, 'Povoir ou pouoir? le cas phonétique de l'ancien verbe *pouvoir*', in *Mélanges de linguistique et de philologie romanes offerts à Monseigneur Pierre Gardette*

ct / *tt* not always being obvious, I have opted for *sf* and *ct* when these letter combinations are ambiguous. The typical inversions in Old and Middle French of *que* for *qui*, and *qui* for *que* and for *que il/z*, as well as the lack of distinction between *se*, *si*, and *ce*, have not been corrected. Also left unchanged are words and letters that were often interchangeable in this era (i.e. *car/que, par/pour, non/nom/mon, en/a, que/quand, sur/suz, et/en/ne, e/a, ai/oi, s/z*).

Hypometric and hypermetric lines (indicated by -1 or +1 respectively in the endnotes) are only corrected when there is significant support from other manuscript witnesses. All such corrections are documented in an endnote. Corrections to the rhyme were made according to the same principle.

Abbreviations have been resolved according to modern usage. Punctuation, which was non-existent, irregular, or faulty in the manuscripts, has been established using modern standards. The apostrophe has been used in those places where an article, a pronoun, or a possessive adjective is elided before a word beginning with a vowel (*j'ay, m'ame*), even if the words are conjoined in the manuscript. Accents, almost totally absent from the manuscripts, have been added in a limited way. The trema is used to separate the pronunciation of adjoining vowels (for reasons of metre) and/or to give a word the syllabic value that it had in Middle French. The cedilla is used to show that the *c* is sibilant. The grave accent is not used. The acute accent is used for a final tonic *e*, an *e* followed by an *s* in the second person plural of a verb (*sachés* for 'sachez'), and for a masculine plural past participle ending in an *s* or a *z* to distinguish it from the feminine plural past participle.

A list of variant readings found in the manuscript witnesses and a selection of *incunabula* for each poem is located at the end of the edition, grouped and ordered by stanza. Only the variants that significantly modify the verse are documented; ones that are purely orthographical in nature are not (e.g. *panser / penser*). In citing more than one witness to a variant reading, the *sigla* are given in alphabetical order and the spelling is that of the first text. Tables at the end of the edition provide information on missing, inverted, and added lines, as well as on the rhyme types and quality in the poems. Finally, a glossary is provided.

All translations in this edition are my own, unless otherwise noted. The English translations of *La Belle Dame qui eust mercy* and *Le Dialogue* use the primary base manuscript, BnF, MS f. fr. 1131, and reflect the editorial emendations and/or corrections made to it. The goals of this translation included being true to the original Middle French texts, interpreting and conveying idiomatic expressions particular to late medieval culture so that they are comprehensible to a modern reader, being sensitive to the structure and flow of the poem, and presenting a translation that reads as smoothly as possible in English, with a hint of the courtly register in which the poems were written.

(Paris: Klincksieck, 1966), IV, pp. 257–66.

§10. Language

The language of the base manuscript, BnF, MS f. fr. 1131, most closely resembles Picard, the language spoken in the historical region of Picardy, north of Paris, into the modern Belgian region of Wallonia (along the France–Belgium border). *La Belle Dame qui eust mercy* and *Le Dialogue* were written during a transitional phase in the history of the French language, between Old and Modern French, thus inconsistencies in spellings, conjugations, and agreement are frequent. The spelling of the scribes has been maintained, except when the reading clearly has errors or when the misspelling could lead to a misreading of the text (such cases are documented in endnotes). A few linguistic particularities are noted below, giving some evidence of the language of the author(s) and the scribe of the base manuscript, of poetic licence possibly taken by the author(s), and/or of scribal errors. Line numbers are in parentheses, with either a B or a D to indicate the poem from which the example is taken.

The spelling variations found in the base manuscript are typical of the late fourteenth and fifteenth centuries. Without a dot over the letter *i*, it is sometimes difficult to distinguish this letter from the strokes of an *n*, *m*, or *u*. A *y* is often used where an *i* would be used today: *vray* (B60) or *joye* (D135) and it is also used where the consonant ending is not vocalized, as in *Je vous dy* ('dis' from 'dire') (B193). Some plurals are indicated by a *z* instead of an *s*, as in *motz* for *mots* (B6), but the spelling *mos* (B3) is also used. Single words in Modern French are often broken into their component parts: *pour quoy* (D48) for *pourquoi*, *puis quil* (B49) for *puisqu'il*. In other cases, words are contracted that would not be so today: *m'amour* (B149) for *mon amour* and *S'ainsy* (D220) for *Si ainsi*. Elision, however, is common (*j'ay, qu'il, n'en, m'estoit*).

Interchangeability in spelling between like-sounding endings is common, e.g. *ay/é* as in *Je ne fus pas nay* (B229) and *és/ais* as in *jamés* for *jamais* (D153). Within a single poem, different vowels can be used in the spellings of a verb's conjugation: *Et qui scet combien je vous ayme* (D346) and *Ne garison ne scay trouver* (D370). There is also a certain amount of fluidity between words that are more strictly governed in modern times, including *Se* used in place of *Si* (*Se vo beaulté*, B54); *Si* used as a short form of *ainsi* (*Si sera pour vous ung beau fait*, D363); and *Ce* used as a short form of *ceci* (*Que de ce plus ne parlissez*, B270).

Requirements of the rhyme and/or metre also resulted in spelling modifications. In B172, *recueul* is used instead of the normal first person singular, present indicative *recue(i)lle* (from *recueillir*) to maintain the rhyme scheme (*eul : recueul : deul : seul*). And alternative spellings of certain adverbs are undoubtedly related to metre: *fort* (D405) or *forment* (B264), *ja* (B64) or *jamaiz* (B95) / *jamés* (D153).

Typical of other works in Middle French, the poem shows some fluctuation between the use of the epicene adjective, without gender distinction, and the analogue adjective, whose form is determined by the noun to which it is attached, probably in the service of the metre. Common epicene adjectives can be found in the base manuscript, modifying feminine nouns: *grant merveille* (B129); and *tel grevance* (D100), but analogue forms are also present, e.g. *mainte doulour* (D82) and *telle ardure* (B125). There is a single error in number among the analogue adjectives when speaking of the lover, but this could have been scribal or made simply to maintain the metre: 'Vous serviray, jeunes et vieulx' (B159). There is also an example of inclination (*enclise*), where the definite article *les* before *dangiers* is absorbed into the preposition *en* to form *es*: *Voulés vous me mectre es dangiers* (B288).

The scribe of the base manuscript had a regular, generous handwriting style, almost completely free from abbreviations commonly found in manuscripts of this era, indicating that economy of space was not a priority. Here, only the tilde is used, to indicate either the doubling (*fēme* for *femme*) or the addition (*cōgnois* for *congnois* [*connais*]) of a consonant. No other abbreviations or contractions are present. Punctuation is absent from the manuscript. Decorated initials and capital letters, however, serve as a kind of punctuation or organizing tool. An indented, five-line-high space is left blank at the start of *La Belle Dame qui eust mercy*, presumably for decoration, rather than a large initial, since outside of this space there is a two-line-high decorated initial B marking the first letter of the poem. An initial of this same size is used to indicate the start of each three-stanza speech by the lady and the lover. A single-line-high decorated initial begins each new stanza within their speeches. The first letter of each subsequent line in every stanza is capitalized and is set off slightly from the following letter(s). When *belle* is used to address the lady, the word is not capitalized in the manuscript (B113). Personifications such as *Amours* (B228) or *Pitié* (D205) are also not capitalized.

Placement of direct and indirect objects in Middle French can vary from modern usage in that the object pronoun may be placed before the auxiliary verb rather than the infinitive, regardless of the tense or mood of the auxiliary verb. This is a relatively rare occurrence in these two poems, but an example from each illustrates the point: *Si ne me veulliés escondire* (B69) and *Qui bien vos peust remectre en joye* (D412). It should be noted that if the object pronouns in the first example had been placed according to modern usage, a hypometric line would have resulted, which may or may not have been a consideration for the poet or scribe.

The order of the object pronouns may also differ from current usage. In the following example, the pronoun *me* would have preceded *la* in Modern French: *Quant il la me fist choysir telle* (B108). In B22, the imperative *pardonnés* is preceded by the direct object *me*, rather than followed by the disjunctive pronoun form *moy*, whereas in B9, the disjunctive pronoun is used in place of the direct object pronoun in order to maintain the metre (*Veulliés moy ouÿr humblement*).

§11. Versification

Skill in rhyme and metrical forms was cultivated by late medieval poets and *La Belle Dame qui eust mercy* and *Le Dialogue* both exhibit elements of the formal complexity so appreciated at the time. All of the lines in *La Belle Dame qui eust mercy* and *Le Dialogue* are octosyllabic. Of the 378 total lines in the first poem, there are two hypermetric lines (B145, 174) and five hypometric lines (B67, 121, 123, 257, 309), or just under 2% of the total. In *Le Dialogue*, there is a single instance of a hypermetric line (D28); there are three hypometric lines (D57, 136, 368). There are no cases in either poem in the base manuscript of non-elision of the non-accented *e* to preserve the metre, as was seen in line B72 in other witnesses (*Je suis vostrë ou que je soye*).

The conjunction of coordination *si/se* often elides when necessary for the metre, as in *S'elle est en droit honneur comprise* (B45). In all instances, the conjunction of subordination, *que*, elides with the vowel that follows, as in *Ce n'est que ung poy de plaisant paine* (D408), and is never in hiatus. The poet uses the weak form of the pronoun *moy* in a strong position instead of *me* when the metre demands it, as in *De moy amer en verité* (D44), but also when *me* could have been used with no elision required, as in *A moy requerir de cest point* (B73). And *chevilles*, short phrases of little semantic importance (*ainsy m'aist dieu, par mon ame, se dieu plaist*), are frequently used as filler, making up the required number of syllables in a metrical line.

Metrical considerations regarding the cæsura generally do not apply to the eight-syllable line, although one occasionally senses a hiatus after the fourth syllable in lines like *Tout ung mesmes / vouloir ayon* (B373). Examples of possible hiatus after the second, third, and fifth syllables can also be found, respectively, in the following lines: *Et que / pour pire ou pour meillour* (B354); *Se Dieu plaist, tant que je vivray* (D322); and *Vostre beau parler / m'a vaincue* (B344).

The rhyme schemes used in these poems are outlined in Table 2 and the rhyme gender, quality, and frequency in Table 3. Both poems can be situated clearly within the late medieval lyric tradition in that they contain a wide variety of rhymes. Alliteration is found in the very first line of *La Belle Dame qui eust mercy* (*Belle que bon renom et los*), as well as at the start of the lady's final speech in which she grants her love to her suitor: *Mon cueur tressault, tremble et tressue* (B340).

Richer levels of rhyme quality are represented, in both masculine and feminine forms, including assonant, consonant, leonine (simple, perfect, and pluperfect), and equivocal (*rime du même au même*) rhymes. Stanza XXII in *La*

Belle Dame qui eust mercy is especially noteworthy, containing an impressive range in rhyme quality in its thirteen lines: masculine assonant (*tous : vous*), masculine consonant (*maintient : appartient : tient*); feminine leonine simple (*sauvage : langage : sage : courage*), and feminine leonine pluperfect (*folie : amolie : mirencolie*). Stanza VIII in *Le Dialogue* has a nice pluperfect feminine leonine rhyme (*dame belle : rebelle*), while examples of masculine leonine perfect rhymes can be seen in Stanza XXVII (*tressaillir : assaillir : saillir*) and Stanza V (*requerir : enquerir*). And there is an ironic masculine leonine rhyme in Stanza VII between *aimer* (transitive verb, 'to love') and *amer* (adjective, 'bitter').

Two studies on rhyming in late medieval French poetry also help to situate *La Belle Dame qui eust mercy* and *Le Dialogue* amongst works by contemporary poets relative to the use of the masculine assonant rhyme. John Fox calculated the frequency of this rhyme type by the fifteenth-century nobleman-poet, Charles d'Orléans, and compared that to several of his predecessors. To this list, I have added data from the two poems edited here:[48]

Charles d'Orléans:	
First ten *balades*	70.11%
Balades 90–100	67.47%
La Retinue d'Amour	64.18%
Le Songe en complainte	41.27% [49]
Oton de Granson	56.36%
Jean de Garencières	54.79%
Eustache Deschamps	53.33%
Le Dialogue d'amoureux et de sa dame	43.3%
	(Poem 1, 49.3% / Poem 2, 39%)
Henri Baude	36%
Guillaume de Machaut	30.14%
Guillaume Coguillart	29.49%
Jean Régnier	24.64%
La Belle Dame qui eust mercy	20.4%
	(Poem 1, 18.2% / Poem 2, 21.7%)
Jean Lemaire de Belges	19.18%
François Villon	15.74%
Alain Chartier	13.81%
Christine de Pizan	12.82%
Jean Molinet	4%
Guillaume Crétin	3.7%

While Fox's study focuses on a relatively limited aspect of late medieval

---

[48] Fox calculated his percentages based on all of the masculine rhymes taken from a sampling of texts from each author, often the first ten *balades* in a collection, or the first 40 lines of a longer poem.

[49] This percentage may be lower because this more rigorous poetic schema demanded six rhymes per stanza.

versification, he does show that Charles d'Orléans, Granson, Deschamps, and Machaut made substantially more frequent use of simple masculine assonant rhyme than the author(s) of *La Belle Dame qui eust mercy* and Alain Chartier, with *Le Dialogue* midway between these two groups.

Georges Lote's study of early French poetry underscores the prevalence of feminine rhymes, in general, in order to strengthen the sound of the preceding consonant, and of multi-syllabic feminine leonine rhymes, in particular.

> Au XVᵉ siècle, le léonisme fait fureur; il se manifeste chez tous les poètes et est prôné par tous les traités de versification ... La rime léonine est abondante; mais il s'en faut de beaucoup qu'elle soit toujours de bon aloi. Souvent on s'occupe fort peu de ce qu'elle vaut, pourvu qu'on obtienne l'accord de deux syllabes, condition qu'on réalise à n'importe quel prix (pp. 147–48).[50]

In this, *La Belle Dame qui eust mercy* and *Le Dialogue* are no exceptions, with feminine rhyme words making up one third of the total. Fox attributed this increased development of the feminine rhyme to a desire on the part of the poets to increase 'the ornateness of verse [which] makes the composition of poetry a greater challenge, a more esoteric discipline, following the pattern of evolution manifested by most art forms, particularly in their decadence, when difficulty is sought for its own sake and when the balance between detail and overall effect is lost'.[51]

Finally, a study of the words used at the rhyme can be helpful in revealing the phonemic rapport between orthography and pronunciation at the time of a poem's composition. Assonance between a vowel and a diphthong was acceptable, as seen in *comparer : muser : gaignier : penser* (D331–32, 334–35) and *ayme : reclame* (D346, 349). Rhyming with different vowels is also found, providing evidence of the fluidity in Middle French in the speech / spelling relationship, as in *regretz : faiz* (D225–26). Spelling variations involving consonants at the rhyme are also typical in this period, including *entente : comtempte* (D294, 297), *ame : blasme* (B22, 24), *quicte : despite* (B154, 157), *fine : digne* (B271, 274), *touche : doulce* (B34, 36), and *ung : commun* (B321–22).

§12. Stylistics

Labels used for medieval poetic works were, as Fourrier noted, 'assez vagues et assez vastes pour englober des formes et des contenus très divers'.[52] What to call *La Belle Dame qui eust mercy* and *Le Dialogue*? In the titles found in the manuscripts, they are called a complaint, a treatise, a dialogue, a prayer, and a

---

[50] George Lote, *Histoire du vers français*, 6 vols (Paris: Boivin, 1949–1955), II, pp. 147–48.

[51] John Fox, *The Lyric Poetry of Charles d'Orleans* (Oxford: Clarendon Press, 1969), p. 135

[52] Jean Froissart, *Dits et débats*, ed. by Anthime Fourrier (Geneva: Droz, 1979), p. 13.

lamentation, whereas the term 'debate' is often used today to label the poems in the Belle Dame cycle.[53] The term *pastourelle* is not entirely appropriate, because the context is not one where a shepherd or a knight makes 'une requête amoureuse' of a shepherdess;[54] the interlocutors in *La Belle Dame qui eust mercy* and *Le Dialogue* are both members of courtly society. The *dit* could be considered as a designation, as it was 'an elastic construction allowing the association of multiple distinct formal units, as well as the mingling of several kinds of content',[55] but the narrative framing and didactic elements common to the *dit* are not present in either poem. And to call them *complaintes*, as Du Chesne did, acknowledges the pleas of the lover, but fails to take into account the lady's voice and the discussion that takes place between the two speakers.

In his work on the medieval debate poem, Pierre-Yves Badel suggested that the uncertainty about the label 'debate' came from the fact that 'aucun texte mediéval n'énonce les règles auxquelles aurait à se conformer le débat' (p. 95). He added that only a limited number had been edited; moreover, he judged that literary history had not paid enough attention to the genre to clarify the issue. For his part, Badel tried to distinguish debate and dialogue by saying that the term 'dialogue' implied a mode of representation related to the direct discourse found in a discussion between two people, whereas a 'debate' denoted an event, a conflictual or litigious scenario, often resembling a kind of parlour game, in which a judgment or decision was expected or promised.

---

[53] Piaget, however, called *La Belle Dame qui eust mercy* a dialogue ('Imitations', *Romania*, 33, p. 201).
[54] Joël Blanchard, *La Pastourelle en France aux XIVe et XVe siècles* (Paris: Champion, 1983), p. 17.
[55] Altmann, p. 12. The classic definition of the *dit* as simply a 'lyrico-narrative genre' may be inadequate, but it expresses the elastic nature of the form. Pierre-Yves Badel called it a half-narrative, half-didactic genre, but many *dits* lack the didactic or the narrative element, or both. See 'Le Débat', in *La Littérature française aux XIVe et XVe siècles. Grundriss der romanischen Literaturen des Mittelalters*, 8.1, ed. by Jean Frappier, Daniel Poirion, and Aurelio Roncaglia (Heidelberg: Winter, 1988), pp. 95–110. Paul Zumthor said simply that the *dit* was not definable either on the thematic or the formal plan. Cf. 'Rhétorique et poétique latines et romanes', *Grundriss der romanischen Literaturen des Mittelalters* (Heidelberg: Winter, 1972), p. 88. Paul Imbs, too, found that the *dit* was simply the common name to designate a literary form that did not follow strict rules and which grouped together diverse elements based on the nature of the subject matter alone. Cf. '*Le Voir-dit*' de Guillaume de Machaut: étude littéraire (Paris: Klincksieck, 1991), p. 213. In her article on the *dit*, Jacqueline Cerquiglini proposed that three characteristics distinguish it from other forms: it operates on a principle of discontinuity; it has an engaged, first-person narrator speaking in the present tense and working within a *mise en présence* or staging; and the narrator is a writer-clerk, resulting in the work having a didactic nature. See 'Le Dit', in *La Littérature française aux XIVe et XVe siècles. Grundriss der romanischen Literaturen des Mittelalters*, 8.1, ed. by Jean Frappier, Daniel Poirion, and Aurelio Roncaglia (Heidelberg: Winter, 1988), pp. 86–94. Using these criteria, it would be hard to label either *La Belle Dame qui eust mercy* or *Le Dialogue* as a *dit*.

He allowed for overlap or nesting between forms, citing Christine de Pizan's *Le Livre du débat de deux amans*, which contained an overheard debate, but which was otherwise not itself a debate poem. The stanzaïc nature of many debate poems, in Badel's opinion, provided discrete, isolated, and 'natural' frames for comments and replies ('nouvelle strophe, nouveau locuteur') that suited the oppositional elements of the debate genre and extended the tête-à-tête of two opposing views by fragmenting it (p. 104). Using Badel's classification, therefore, *La Belle Dame qui eust mercy* and *Le Dialogue* could be considered to incorporate elements of both the dialogue and the debate, being more than just a discussion, but less than a formal litigation with an adjudicator.

More recently, Laëtitia Tabard[56] has looked at the medieval debate genre through the lens of poetic structures defined in contemporary rhetorical studies such as Pierre Fabri's *Le Grand et Vrai Art de pleine rhétorique*. She focused especially on the large corpus of *dits* which contain 'un combat verbal élégamment mené' based on an opposition between the characters, seeking an 'identifier' for the genre exhibiting 'une dominante formelle qui permet d'accéder au sens de la "matière" propre à une série de textes'. Recalling the violence at the heart of the early medieval juridical term 'debate' (designating the combat between a falcon and its prey), she examined what she saw as the violence at the heart of the 'discours policé' [civilized discourse] of the debate genre, and the way in which the literary scenes of trial and arbitration ultimately tried to mitigate those tensions. Lacking the trial *mise en scène* and dynamic, however, no part of *La Belle Dame qui eust mercy* nor *Le Dialogue* seems to fit comfortably into this version of the debate poem.

If, however, we consider the debate to be, at its core, a discussion involving opposing viewpoints, with the possibility of a judgment or a determination of a winning argument, then the two poems can clearly be called debate poems. In each, there is an exchange between the lover and the lady about whether she should take him as her *amy*. The lover initiates the discussion, but each interlocutor has a chance to argue his/her point of view in alternating sets of three stanzas. Each lover attempts to persuade his lady to agree to his suit by professing his undying love, pledging his loyalty and discretion, assuring her of the God of Love's approval of their union, and by expressing the suffering he has endured due to his lovesickness. As for the lady, she deflates and/or deflects each of the lover's arguments. To her mind, no one can be forced to love, no one can fault her if he misread the way she looked at him, no one can blame her if she wants to safeguard her reputation, and no one dies of lovesickness.

---

[56]Laëtitia Tabard, '"Bien assailly, bien deffendu": le genre du débat dans la littérature française de la fin du Moyen Âge' (doctoral dissertation, Université Paris Sorbonne, 2012), *Perspectives médiévales*, 34 (2012) <http://peme.revues.org/561?lang=en> [accessed 17 September 2017].

While there is no narratorial framework, no poet-narrator, and no judge in *La Belle Dame qui eust mercy* or *Le Dialogue*, there are winners and losers. The lady's unwavering and adamant rejection of the lover's pleas for her love at the end of Poem 1 in each poem, as well as at the end of *Le Dialogue*, can be seen as the lady 'winning' the debate by not being forced into a love relationship that she does not want. In contrast, by the end of Poem 2 in *La Belle Dame qui eust mercy*, as the title explains, the lady is overwhelmed by the lover's sweet words and is ready to start their happy life together. Clearly, the victory here goes to the lover.

§13. Rhetorical Elements

La Belle Dame qui eust mercy and *Le Dialogue* display several of the rhetorical elements common to lyric poetry of their period. The apostrophe to the lady that begins the first poem (*Belle, que bon renom et los*) prefigures others, relating both to the lady and her lover: *Sire, du los que me donnés* (B25); *Belle, de beaulté bien eureuse* (B97); and *Certes, Belle, a ce que je voy* (B113). *Le Dialogue* begins with a similar apostrophe to the lady: *M'amour, ma dame souveraine, mon bien, et ma seule plaisance* (D1–2) and also includes: *Amis, se je vouloye avoir* (D91) and *Biau sire, ce est bien mon gré* (D151). And the force of the apostrophe is also felt at the start of the second part in each poem: *Mer de doulchour source de riviere* (B145) and *Hellas! Ma dame et ma maistresse* (D181), arguing in favour of their being separate poems.

Amplificatio can be seen when the lover enumerates the many pains he claims that his heart has endured and the many times he has cried out in frustration over his condition: *Hellas! mon douloureux cueur sent | Mieulx que la bouche ne peust dire | Des doulours dont j'ay plus de cent | De quoy je ne congnoiz la pire* (B65–68). The lady uses amplification in *Le Dialogue* when she suggests that her suitor seek love from a lady who would be far more worthy: *Aussy avés vous aultre amye | Qui bien vos peust remectre en joye | Cent foyz mieulx que je ne feroye* (D411–13). And the lovers in both poems exaggerate the suffering they experience from their unrequited love, although both ladies are merciless in their dismissal of what they consider to be trifles.

The lovers frequently use enumeration to convince the ladies of their sincerity, as in *Seray joyeux, cointe, et secret* (B62), and of their suffering: *Croistre dor en avant mes plains | Et mes souppirs dont je me plains | De la durté qui me fait plaindre | Souppirer et gemir et taindre* (D212–15). Pairs of synonyms are often used for emphasis, as well as for metrical demands: *Ou vous estes maulvés et faulx* (B286) and *Or soyés secret et privé* (B363). And an alliterative cluster of verbs marks the point at which the lady decides to grant her suitor's wishes: *Mon cueur tressault, tremble et tressue | Et suis presque toute esperdue*

(B340–41). In a similar way, antithesis is used for emphasis, here to accentuate the reversals one experiences in love: *Faictes moy ou plorer ou rire* (B71) and *En ce point vueil vivre et mourir* (B150). And the lover's mourning of the death of his own joy, marked by his wearing black, is juxtaposed with the evocation of springtime and the month of May, the traditional season of love and happiness: *Je prendray drap de noyre sorte | Ce may ou toute joye habonde | En signe que ma joye est morte* (B309–11).

Anadiplosis, or the repetition of a prominent word in the first part of a line that is also found at the end of the preceding line albeit with a change or an extension of meaning, is used to good effect in the pair *folie / Fol* in Stanza XXII of *La Belle Dame qui eust mercy*. Here, the substantive form of a word ends one line and the adjectival form of the same word starts the next line, underscoring the high degree of foolishness that the lady sees in the lover's stubborn request for her love (reiterated in the same stanza).

One strategy used by both lovers, similar to that used in a trial setting, is to pose a series of semi-rhetorical questions to the lady, in an effort to gain her sympathy, as in: *Est ce donques vostre vouloir | De faire ainsy tousjours douloir?* (D259–60). This is also seen in Stanza XXVII of *La Belle Dame qui eust mercy* when the lover tries to get the lady to imagine herself in his situation. He even sums up his argument in the manner of a barrister when he states: *Et pour ce je dys et conclus | Qu'en ce point ne me tenés plus | Maiz me faictes en cas pareil* (B259–61). *Le Dialogue* also places a proverb, *Bien assailly, bien deffendu*, in the lady's speech, and then immediately inverts it in the lover's response: *Bien deffendu, bien assailly* (D120–21).[57]

Not surprisingly, both poems contain the kind of courtly language and images that are typical of poetry of the period. Using *La Belle Dame qui eust mercy* to demonstrate the point, the lover asks the lady to pardon him if he has aimed too high in seeking her love (*Ne me tenés pour mal apris | Se j'ay trop hault fait entrepris*, B20–21) and if his speech is too coarse (*mon tresrude parler*, B5). He seeks her love, however, because he claims that *tout bien* (B16) will come from her alone, *Des aultres belles l'exemplaire* (B98). The God of Love is to be blamed for his condition (*Cha fait Amours, qui m'a espris | C'est tout par luy s'il y a blasme*, B23–24) by enflaming his heart with love only for this lady. The lover has been captured in the snare of her goodness and beauty, beauty which has blossomed because of her honour and joyful countenance. He now suffers lovesickness that only she can cure. He pledges to be a *humble et petit servant* (B58) and a *vray amant* (B60), and if granted her love, he will live out his life,

---

[57] Hassell documents the presence of this proverb in works by Charles d'Orléans, Georges Chastellain, Jean Lemaire de Belges, and others in the fifteenth and early sixteenth centuries. Cf. James Woodrow Hassell, *Middle French Proverbs, Sentences, and Proverbial Phrases* (Toronto: Pontifical Institute of Medieval Studies, 1982), p. 44.

jeunes et vieulx (B159), serving her. If she remains unmerciful, however, he will be the most miserable man in the world and will die of his pains and his grief. She controls all, able to make him *ou plorer ou rire* (B71).

Finally, the personifications appearing here are familiar to readers of this type of poetry. The God of Love has a benevolent side (*Amours* [...] | *Vous doint dame en amours parfaicte*, B219–20), but is also a cruel matchmaker (*Amours qui me livre l'assault*, D287) who fails to give succour to the unfortunate lover (*Il est temps qu'Amours me sequeure*, B228). *Espoir* urges the lover to continue his suit, in the hope that *Grace* will be his (D295–97), although *Dangier* is a formidable protector of the lady's virtue (D80). *Desir* (D203) and *Esperance* (D204) are optimistic that *Pitié* (D205) will come to the lover's aid. Somewhat ironically, the only reference to Mercy appears in *La Belle Dame qui eust mercy*, in the lover's final speech to the lady (*Et Mercy ne me reconforte*, B308), just prior to her mercifully accepting his advances.

Works Consulted

Other Editions

ANDRÉ LE CHAPELAIN, *Traité de l'amour courtois*, ed. and trans. by C. Buridant (Paris: Klincksieck, 1974)

CHARLES D'ORLÉANS, *Poésies*, ed. by Pierre Champion, 2 vols (Paris: Champion, 1923–1927)

CHARTIER, ALAIN, '*La Belle Dame sans merci* d'Alain Chartier: texte français et traduction catalane', ed. by Amadée Pagès, *Romania*, 62 (1936), 481–531

—— *La Belle Dame sans mercy et les poésies lyriques*, ed. by Arthur Piaget (Paris: Droz, 1945; Lille: Girard, 1949)

—— *Les Fais maistre Alain Chartier, notaire et secretaire du roy Charles VI* (Paris: Pierre Le Caron, 1489, with reprints for Anthoine Vérard 1493–1494; Michel Le Noir 1514; Veuve feu Jean Trepperel and Jean Jeannot *c.* 1515; Philippe Le Noir *c.* 1520 and 1523; and Galliot du Pré 1529)

—— *Les Œuvres de Maistre Alain Chartier, clerc, notaire et secretaire des Roys Charles VI et VII, contenans l'histoire de son temps, l'Esperance, le Curial, le Quadrilogue, et autres Pieces, Toutes nouvellement reveues, corrigées et beaucoup augmentées sur les Exemplaires escrits à la main*, ed. by André Du Chesne Tourangeau (Paris: Triboust, 1617)

—— *Poèmes*, ed. by James C. Laidlaw (Paris: Union générale d'éditions, 1988)

—— *The Poetical Works of Alain Chartier*, ed. by James C. Laidlaw (Cambridge: Cambridge University Press, 1974)

CHASTELLAIN, GEORGES, *Œuvres*, ed. by Kervyn de Lettenhovem, 8 vols (Brussels: Heussner, 1863–67)

CHAUCER, GEOFFREY, *The Riverside Chaucer*, ed. by Larry D. Benson, 3rd edn (Boston: Houghton Mifflin, 1987)

CHRISTINE DE PIZAN, *La Cité des dames*, ed. and trans. by Thérèse Moreau and Eric Hicks (Paris: Stock, 1986)

—— *The Love Debate Poems of Christine de Pizan*, ed. by Barbara K. Altmann (Gainseville: University Press of Florida, 1998)

—— *Œuvres poétiques*, ed. by Maurice Roy, 3 vols (Paris: Didot, 1886–96; repr. New York: Johnson, 1965)

—— *The Treasure of the City of Ladies or The Book of the Three Virtues*, ed. and trans. by Sarah Lawson (New York: Penguin, 1985)

FROISSART, JEAN, *Dits et débats*, ed. by Anthome Fourrier (Geneva: Droz, 1979)

—— *Œuvres*, ed. by Kervyn de Lettenhove, 28 vols (Brussels: Devaux, 1867–1877)

GARENCIÈRES, JEAN DE, *Le Chevalier poète Jehan de Garencières (1372–1415): sa vie et ses poésies complètes*, ed. by Young Abernathy Neal (Paris: Nizet, 1953)

GUILLAUME DE MACHAUT, *Le Jugement du roi de Navarre*, ed. and trans. by R. Barton Palmer (New York: Garland, 1988)

—— *Le Jugement du roy de Behaigne and Remede de Fortune*, ed. and trans. by James I. Wimsatt and William W. Kibler (Athens: University of Georgia Press, 1988)

—— *Le Livre du voir dit*, ed. and trans. by Paul Imbs (Paris: Librairie générale de France, 1999)

—— *La Louange des dames*, ed. by Nigel Wilkins (New York: Barnes and Noble, 1973)

—— *Œuvres*, ed. by Ernest Hoepffner, 3 vols (Paris: Didot, 1908–1921; repr. New York: Johnson, 1965)

—— *Poésies lyriques*, ed. by V. Chichmaref, 2 vols (Paris: Champion, 1909)

HULT, DAVID F., and JOAN E. MCRAE, eds, *Le Cycle de 'La Belle Dame sans mercy': une anthologie poétique du XVe siècle (BNF Ms. Fr. 1131)* (Paris: Champion, 2003)

JEAN LE SENESCHAL (with Philippe d'Artois, Comte d'Eu; Boucicaut le Jeune; Jean de Crésecque), *Les Cent Ballades: poème du XIVe siècle*, ed. by Gaston Raynaud (Paris: Didot, 1905)

LE FRANC, MARTIN, *Le Champion des dames*, ed. by Robert Deschaux, 5 vols (Paris: Champion, 1999)

MAROT, CLÉMENT, *Œuvres complètes*, ed. by Pierre Jannet, 4 vols (Paris: Picard, 1868)

MCRAE, JOAN, ed. and trans., *The Quarrel of the Belle Dame sans mercy* (New York; London: Routledge, 2004)

MONTAIGLON, ANATOLE DE, and JAMES DE ROTHSCHILD, eds, *Recueil de poésies françoises des XVe et XVIe siècles*, 13 vols (Paris: Jannet, 1876)

OTON DE GRAN(D)SON, 'A Critical Edition of the Poetry of Oton de Grandson, MS. L', ed. by Caroline A. Cunningham (unpublished doctoral dissertation, University of North Carolina, Chapel Hill, 1987; Ann Arbor: UMI, 1988)

—— *Oton de Grandson, sa vie et ses poésies*, ed. by Arthur Piaget (Lausanne: Payot, 1941)

—— 'Oton de Granson et ses poésies', ed. by Arthur Piaget, *Romania*, 19 (1980), 237–59

—— *Poems*, ed. and trans. by Peter Nicholson and Joan Grenier-Winther (Kalamazoo: Medieval Institute Publications, Western Michigan University, 2015)

—— *Poésies*, ed. by Joan Grenier-Winther (Paris: Champion, 2010)

PIAGET, ARTHUR, ed., *Le Miroir aux dames: poème inédit du XVe siècle* (Neuchâtel: Attinger Frères, 1908)

VITALE–BROVARONE, ALESSANDRO, ed., *Recueil de galanteries (Archivio di Stato di Torino, J.b.IX.10)* (Montreal: CERES, 1980)

WILKINS, NIGEL, ed., *One Hundred Ballades, Rondeaux and Virelais from the Late Middle Ages* (Cambridge: Cambridge University Press, 1969)

Studies on Late Medieval Poets and Poetry

ANGELO, GRETCHEN V., 'A Most Uncourtly Lady: The Testimony of the *Belle Dame sans mercy*', *Exemplaria*, 15.1 (2003), 133–57

ALTMANN, BARBARA K., and CARLETON W. CARROLL, eds, *The Court Reconvenes: Courtly Literature across the Disciplines* (Cambridge: Brewer, 2003)

ANGENOT, MARC, *Les Champions des femmes: examen du discours sur la supériorité des femmes 1400–1800* (Montreal: University of Quebec Press, 1977)

ARDEN, HEATHER, 'Othon de Grandson and Christine de Pizan: Love's Martyrs', in *Othon de Grandson, chevalier et poète*, ed. by Jean-François Kosta–Théfaine, *Medievalia*, 63 (Orléans: Paradigme, 2007), pp. 103–21

ARMSTRONG, ADRIAN, *Technique and Technology: Script, Print, and Poetics in France, 1470–1550* (Oxford: Clarendon Press, 2000)

—— *The Virtuoso Circle: Competition, Collaboration, and Complexity in Late Medieval French Poetry* (Tempe, AZ: Arizona Center for Medieval and Renaissance Studies, 2012)

——, and MALCOLM QUAINTON, eds, *Book and Text in France 1400–1600: Poetry on the Page* (Aldershot: Ashgate, 2007)

——, and SARAH KAY, *Knowing Poetry: Verse in Medieval France from the 'Rose' to the Rhétoriqueurs* (Ithaca: Cornell University Press, 2011)

ATTWOOD, CATHERINE, 'La Dialectique amoureuse chez Othon de Grandson', in *Othon de Grandson, chevalier et poète*, ed. by Jean-François Kosta-Théfaine, *Medievalia*, 63 (Orléans: Paradigme, 2007), pp. 85–101

—— *Dynamic Dichotomy: The Poetic 'I' in Fourteenth- and Fifteenth-Century French Lyric Poetry* (Amsterdam: Rodopi, 1998)

BADEL, PIERRE-YVES, 'Le Débat', in *La Littérature française aux XIVe et XVe siècles. Grundriss der romanischen Literaturen des Mittelalters*, 8.1, ed. by Jean Frappier, Daniel Poirion, and Aurelio Roncaglia (Heidelberg: Winter, 1988), pp. 95–110

BASSO, HÉLÈNE, 'L'Envol et l'ancrage: la quête amoureuse comme épreuve de soi dans *Le Dit de l'alérion* de Guillaume de Machaut et *Le Livre messire Ode* d'Othon de Grandson', in *Othon de Grandson, chevalier et poète*, ed. by Jean-François Kosta-Théfaine, *Medievalia*, 63 (Orléans: Paradigme, 2007), pp. 137–63

BECKER, KARIN, 'La Mentalité juridique dans la littérature française (XIIIe-XVe siècles)', *Moyen Âge*, 103.2 (1997), 309–27

BETEMPS, ISABELLE, '*Les Lais de plour*: Guillaume de Machaut et Oton de Grandson', in *Guillaume de Machaut: 1300–2000*, ed. by Jacqueline Cerquiglini–Toulet and Nigel Wilkins (Paris: Presses de l'Université de Paris–Sorbonne, 2002), pp. 95–106

BLANCHARD, JOËL, *La Pastourelle en France aux XIVe et XVe siècles* (Paris: Champion, 1983)

BOURDIEU, PIERRE, *Le Sens pratique/The Logic of Practice*, trans. by Richard Nice (Cambridge: Polity Press, 1990)

BRADDY, HALDEEN, *Chaucer and the French Poet Graunson* (Baton Rouge: Louisiana State University Press, 1947)

——'Messire Oton de Graunson, Chaucer's Savoyard Friend', *Studies in Philology*, 35 (1938), 515–31

BRANDIN, LOUIS M., and WILLIE GUSTAVE HARTOG, *A Book of French Prosody: With Specimens of French Verse from the Twelfth Century to the Present Day* (Glasgow: Blackie, 1904)

CALIN, WILLIAM, 'Intertextual Play and the Game of Love: The *Belle Dame sans mercy* Cycle', *Fifteenth-Century Studies*, 31 (2005), 31–46

CARDEN, SALLY TARTLINE, '*Le Livre messire Ode* d'Oton de Grandson: un interrogatoire poétique', *Moyen Français*, 35–36 (1996), 79–89

——'Oton de Grandson', in *Literature of the French and Occitan Middle Ages: Eleventh to Fifteenth Centuries*, ed. by Deborah Sinnreich-Levi and Ian S. Laurie, *The Dictionary of Literary Biography* (Detroit, MI: Gale, 1999), pp. 141–48

CARTIER, NORMAND R., 'Oton de Grandson et sa princesse', *Romania*, 85 (1964), 1–16

CAYLEY, EMMA, *Debate and Dialogue: Alain Chartier in his Cultural Context* (Oxford: Oxford University Press, 2006)

——'Drawing Conclusions: The Poetics of Closure in Alain Chartier's Verse', *Fifteenth-Century Studies*, 28 (2003), 51–64

CERQUIGLINI, JACQUELINE, 'Le Dit', in *La Littérature française aux XIVe et XVe siècles. Grundriss der romanischen Literaturen des Mittelalters*, 8.1, ed. by Jean Frappier, Daniel Poirion, and Aurelio Roncaglia (Heidelberg: Winter, 1988), pp. 86–94

CERQUIGLINI-TOULET, JACQUELINE, *The Colour of Melancholy: The Uses of Books in the Fourteenth Century: 1300–1415*, trans. by Lydia G. Cochrane (Baltimore: Johns Hopkins University Press, 1997)

CHAUBET, DANIEL, 'Le Duel Othon de Grandson — Gérard d'Estavayer du 7 août 1397: une conséquence des événements qui agitèrent la Savoie dans les dernières années du XIVe siècle', in *Othon de Grandson, chevalier et poète*, ed. by Jean-François Kosta–Théfaine, *Medievalia*, 63 (Orléans: Paradigme, 2007), pp. 11–42

CONNOLLY, MARGARET, and YOLANDA PLUMLEY, 'John Shirley and the Circulation of French Lyric Poetry', in *Patrons, Authors and Workshops: Books and Book Production in Paris around 1400*, ed. by Godfried Croenen and Peter Ainsworth (Leuven: Peeters, 2006), pp. 311–32

DELOGU, DAISY, EMMA CAYLEY, and JOAN MCRAE, eds, *A Companion to Alain Chartier (c. 1385–1430): Father of French Eloquence* (Leiden: Brill, 2015)

DESCHAUX, ROBERT, 'Le Lai et la complainte', in *La Littérature française aux XIVe et XVe siècles. Grundriss der romanischen Literaturen des Mittelalters*, 8.1, ed. by Jean Frappier, Daniel Poirion, and Aurelio Roncaglia (Heidelberg: Carl Winter, 1988), pp. 70–85

DULAC, LILIANE, 'Christine de Pisan et le malheur des "vrais amans"', in *Mélanges de langue et de littérature médiévales offerts à Pierre Le Gentil* (Paris: SEDES, 1973), pp. 223–33

DWYER, R. A., 'Je meurs de soif auprès de la fontaine', *French Studies*, 23 (1969), 225–28

FABRI, PIERRE, *Le Grand et Vrai Art de pleine rhétorique*, 1521, ed. by Alexandre Héron, 3 vols (Rouen: E. Cagniard, 1889–1890)

FERRANTE, JOAN M., 'Male Fantasy and Female Reality in Courtly Literature', *Women's Studies*, 11 (1984), 67–97

Fox, John, *The Lyric Poetry of Charles d'Orléans* (Oxford: Clarendon Press, 1969)

——, and Mary-Jo Arn, eds, *Poetry of Charles d'Orléans and his Circle: A Critical Edition of BnF Ms. Fr. 25458, Charles d'Orléans's Personal Manuscript* (Tempe, AZ: Arizona Center for Medieval and Renaissance Studies, 2010)

Galway, Margaret, 'Chaucer, Graunson, and Isabel of France', *Review of English Studies*, 24 (1948), 273–80

Gilbert, A. J., 'Chaucer, Grandson, and the "Turtil Trewe"', *Notes and Queries*, 19 (1972), 165

Grenier-Winther, Joan, 'On Authorship of *La Belle dame qui eut mercy*', in *Othon de Grandson, chevalier et poète*, ed. by Jean-François Kosta–Théfaine, *Medievalia*, 63 (Orléans: Paradigme, 2007), pp. 33–64

Hassell, James Woodrow, *Middle French Proverbs, Sentences, and Proverbial Phrases* (Toronto: Pontifical Institute of Medieval Studies, 1982)

Imbs, Paul, *Le 'Voir-dit' de Guillaume de Machaut: étude littéraire* (Paris: Klincksieck, 1991)

Jodogne, Omer, 'Pouvoir ou pouoir? Le cas phonétique de l'ancien verbe *povoir*', in *Mélanges de linguistique et de philologie romanes offerts à Monseigneur Pierre Gardette* (Paris: Klincksieck, 1966), IV, pp. 257–66.

Jung, Marc René, 'Répertoire des poèmes d'Oton de Grandson', in *Moyen Âge et Renaissance: Hommage au Professeur François Rouy* (Nice: Faculté des Lettres, Arts et Sciences Humaines, 1995), pp. 91–125

Kelly, Douglas, *Medieval Imagination: Rhetoric and the Poetry of Courtly Love* (Madison: University of Wisconsin Press, 1978)

Kelly, Henry Ansgar, *Chaucer and the Cult of Saint Valentine* (Leiden: Brill, 1986)

Kelly, Joan, 'Early Feminist Theory and the *Querelle des femmes*, 1400–1789', *Signs*, 8 (1982), 4–28

Kibler, William W., 'The Narrator as Key to Alain Chartier's *La Belle Dame sans mercy*', *French Review*, 52.5 (1979), 714–23

——, and James I. Wimsatt, 'The Development of the Pastourelle in the Fourteenth Century: An Edition of Fifteen Poems with an Analysis', *Medieval Studies*, 45 (1983), 22–78

Kosta–Théfaine, Jean-François, 'De la Continuité à l'innovation: *Le Livre messire Ode* d'Othon de Grandson et *Le Livre du duc des vrais amans* de Christine de Pizan', *Quires de recherches médiévales*, 11 (2004), 239–51

—— 'Du Chant d'amour au chant du désespoir, ou l'écriture d'une poétique de la tristesse dans la lyrique d'Othon de Grandson', *Romanistische Zeitschrift für Literaturgeschichte*, 23 (1999), 297–310

—— 'L'État de la recherche sur Othon de Grandson', in *Othon de Grandson, chevalier et Poète*, ed. by Jean-François Kosta–Théfaine, *Medievalia*, 63 (Orléans: Paradigme, 2007), pp. 183–94

—— '*Le Livre messire Ode* d'Othon de Grandson, ou l'écriture fragmentaire d'un discours amoureux', *Germanisch–Romanische Monatsschrift*, 53 (2003), 355–61

—— ed., *Othon de Grandson, chevalier et poète*, *Medievalia*, 63 (Orléans: Paradigme, 2007)

Kruger, Roberta, *Women Readers and the Ideology of Gender in Old French Verse Romance* (Cambridge: Cambridge University Press, 1993)

Laidlaw, James C., 'André Du Chesne's Edition of Alain Chartier', *Modern Language Review*, 63 (1968), 569–74

—— 'The Manuscripts of Alain Chartier', *Modern Language Review*, 61 (1966), 188–98

LAURIE, IAN, 'Les Amitiés métriques: Othon de Grandson et Eustache Deschamps', in *Othon de Grandson, chevalier et poète*, ed. by Jean-François Kosta–Théfaine, *Medievalia*, 63 (Orléans: Paradigme, 2007), pp. 123–36

LLOYD, JAMES, and VIRGINIA LEON DE VIVERO, 'The Artful Rejection of Love from Ovid to Andreas to Chartier', *Modern Language Studies*, 9.2 (1979), 46–52

LOTE, GEORGES, *Histoire du vers français*, 6 vols (Paris: Boivin, 1949–55)

MACKEY, LOUIS, 'Eros into Logos: The Rhetoric of Courtly Love', in *The Philosophy of (Erotic) Love*, ed. by Robert C. Solomon and Kathleen M. Higgins (Lawrence: University Press of Kansas, 1991), pp. 336–51

MARCHELLO-NIZIA, CHRISTIANE, *Histoire de la langue française aux XIVe et aux XVe siècles* (Paris: Bordas, 1979)

MASSÓ I TORRENTS, JAUME, 'Oto de Granson ì les balades de Lluis de Vilarasa', in *Mélanges de linguistique et de littérature offerts à M. Alfred Jeanroy* (Paris: Droz, 1928), pp. 403–10

NEWMAN, BARBARA, *God and the Goddesses: Venus, Poetry, and Belief in the Middle Ages* (Philadelphia: University of Pennsylvania Press, 2003)

OLSON, GLENDING, 'Towards a Poetics of the Late Medieval Courtly Lyric', in *Vernacular Poetics in the Middle Ages*, ed. by Lois Ebin (Kalamazoo, MI: Medieval Institute Publications, 1984), pp. 227–48

ORUCH, JACK B., 'St Valentine, Chaucer, and Spring in February', *Speculum*, 56 (1981), 534–65

PAGÈS, AMÉDÉE, *La Poésie française en Catalogne du XIIIe siècle à la fin du XVe siècle* (Toulouse: Privat, 1936)

—— 'Le Thème de la tristesse amoureuse en France et en Espagne du XIVe au XVe siècle', *Romania*, 58 (1932), 29–43

PASTOUREAU, MICHEL, *Figures et couleurs: études sur la symbolique et la sensibilité médiévales* (Paris: Léopard d'Or, 1986)

PHILLIPS, HELEN, '*The Complaint of Venus*: Chaucer and de Graunson', in *Medieval Translator*, 4, ed. by Roger Ellis and Ruth Evans (Binghamton, NY: Medieval and Renaissance Texts and Studies, 1994), pp. 86–103

PIAGET, ARTHUR, '*La Belle Dame sans merci* et ses imitations', *Romania*, 30 (1901), 22–48, 317–51; 31 (1902), 315–49; 33 (1904), 179–208; 34 (1905), 375–428, 559–97

—— '*Le Chemin de vaillance* de Jean de Courcy et l'hiatus de l'*e* final des polysyllabes aux XIVe et XVe siècles', *Romania*, 27 (1898), 582–607

—— 'La Cour amoureuse dite de Charles VI', *Romania*, 20 (1891), 417–54

—— 'Notice sur le ms. 1727 du fond français de la Bibliothèque nationale', *Romania*, 23 (1894), 192–208

POIRION, DANIEL, 'Lectures de *La Belle Dame sans mercy*', in *Mélanges de langue et de littérature médiévales offerts à Pierre le Gentil* (Paris: SEDES, 1973), pp. 691–705

—— *Le Poète et le prince: l'évolution du lyrisme courtois de Guillaume de Machaut à Charles d'Orléans* (Paris: Presses Universitaires de France, 1965)

PREISIG, SARA, review of JANE H. M. TAYLOR, *The Poetry of François Villon*, in *Modern Language Notes*, 117.4 (2002), 932–36

RIQUER, MARTÍN DE, 'La Canción de san Valentín del poeta Pardo', *Revista de la filología española*, 39 (1955), 338–44

Sansone, Giuseppe E., '*La Belle Dame sans merci* et le langage courtois', *Moyen Français*, 39–41 (1997), 513–26

Scattergood, John, 'Chaucer's *Complaint of Venus* and the "Curiosité" of Graunson', *Essays in Criticism*, 44 (1994), 171–89

Solterer, Helen, *The Master and Minerva: Disputing Women in French Medieval Culture* (Berkeley: University of California Press, 1995)

Stuip, R. E. V., 'Je meurs de soif et suy à la fontaine', in *Mélanges de linguistique et de littérature offerts à Lein Geschiere par ses amis, collègues et élèves*, ed. by A. Dees, A. Kibédi Varga, and R. E. V. Stuip (Amsterdam: Rodopi, 1975), pp. 25–36

Swift, Helen, *Gender, Writing, and Performance: Men Defending Women in Late Medieval France (1440–1538)* (Oxford: Oxford University Press, 2008)

Tabard, Laëtitia, '"Bien assailly, bien deffendu"': le genre du débat dans la littérature française de la fin du Moyen-Âge' (doctoral dissertation, Université Paris Sorbonne, 2012), *Perspectives médiévales*, 34 (2012) <http://peme.revues. org/561?lang=en> [accessed 17 September 2017]

Taylor, Jane H. M., 'Courtly Gatherings and Poetic Games: "Coterie" Anthologies in the Late Middle Ages in France', in *Book and Text in France 1400–1600: Poetry on the Page*, ed. by Adrian Armstrong and Malcolm Quainton (Aldershot: Ashgate, 2007), pp. 13–30

—— 'Embodying the Rose: An Intertextual Reading of Alain Chartier's *La Belle Dame sans Mercy*', in *The Court Reconvenes: Courtly Literature across the Disciplines*, ed. by Barbara K. Altmann and Carleton W. Carroll (Cambridge: Brewer, 2003), pp. 325–33

—— 'Inescapable Rose: Jean le Seneschal's *Cent Ballades* and the Art of Cheerful Paradox', *Medium Ævum*, 67 (1998), 60–84

—— *The Making of Poetry: Late Medieval French Poetic Anthologies* (Turnhout: Brepols, 2007)

—— *The Poetry of François Villon: Text and Context* (Cambridge: Cambridge University Press, 2001)

Tison, Frédéric, ed., *Charles d'Orléans et les poètes de sa cour: 'Je meurs de soif auprès de la fontaine', Les Onze Ballades du Puy de Blois vers 1457–1460* (Paris: Lulu, 2011)

Wack, Mary F., *Lovesickness in the Middle Ages: The 'Viaticum' and its Commentaries* (Philadelphia: University of Pennsylvania Press, 1990)

Willard, Charity Cannon, 'Lovers' Dialogues in Christine de Pizan's Lyric Poetry from the *Cent ballades* to the *Cent ballades d'amant et de dame*', *Fifteenth Century Studies*, 4 (1981), 167–80

Wimsatt, James I., 'Chaucer and Deschamps: Natural Music', in *The Union of Words and Music in Medieval Poetry*, ed. by Rebecca A. Baltzer, Thomas Cable, and James I. Wimsatt (Austin: University of Texas Press, 1991), pp. 132–50

—— *Chaucer and his French Contemporaries: Natural Music in the Fourteenth Century* (Toronto: University of Toronto Press, 1991)

—— *Chaucer and the French Love Poets: The Literary Background of the 'Book of the Duchess'* (Chapel Hill: University of North Carolina Press, 1968)

—— *Chaucer and the Poems of 'Ch'* (Kalamazoo, MI: Medieval Institute Publications, 2009)

—— 'Froissart, Chaucer, and the *Pastourelles* of the Pennsylvania Manuscript', *Studies in the Age of Chaucer: Proceedings,* 1 (1984), 69–79

WIND, BARTINA, 'Ce Jeu subtil, l'amour courtois', in *Mélanges offerts à Rita Lejeune,* 2 vols (Gembloux: Duculot, 1964), II, pp. 1257–61

WINDEATT, BARRY, *Chaucer's Dream Poetry: Sources and Analogues* (Woodbridge: Brewer, 1982)

ZUMTHOR, PAUL, 'Rhétorique et poétique latines et romanes', in *Grundriss der romanischen Literaturen des Mittelalters,* 1 (Heidelberg: Winter, 1972), pp. 57–91

Manuscript / *Incunabula* Catalogues and Studies

ABRAHAMS, N. C., *Description des manuscrits français du Moyen Âge de la Bibliothèque Royale de Copenhague* (Copenhagen: Thiele, 1844)

ARLIMA (Archives de littérature du Moyen Âge), *La Belle Dame qui eut merci,* <http://www.arlima.net/mp/oton_de_grandson.html#bel> [accessed 17 September 2017]

BARROIS, JEAN, *Bibliothèque protypographique ou librarie des fils du roi Jean, Charles V, Jean de Berri, Philippe de Bourgogne, et les siens* (Paris: Treuttel et Wurtz, 1830), no. 1304, Appendix 2289

BAUDRIER, HENRI LOUIS, *Bibliographie lyonnaise: recherches sur les imprimeurs, libraires, relieurs, et fondeurs de lettres de Lyon au XVIe siècle,* 12 vols (Lyon: Brun; Paris: Picard, 1904), XI, pp. 474–75

Bibliothèque impériale: catalogue des manuscrits français, ancien fonds, 4 vols (Paris: Didot, 1868), I

BOURGAIN, PASCALE, and FRANÇOISE VIEILLARD, *Conseils pour l'édition des textes médiévaux: Textes littéraires,* III (Paris: École nationale des chartes, 2002)

BRIQUET, C. M., *Les Filigranes: dictionnaire historique des marques du papier,* 4 vols (Leipzig: Hiersemann, 1923)

Catalogue des incunables, Bibliothèque nationale, 2 vols (Paris: Bibliothèque nationale, 1981–2006)

Catalogue général des livres imprimés de la Bibliothèque nationale, 231 vols (Paris: Imprimerie nationale, 1897–1981)

Catalogue général des manuscrits de bibliothèques publiques de France: Paris, Bibliothèques de l'Institut: Musée Condé de Chantilly, Bibliothèque Thiers, Musées Jacquemart-André (Paris and Chaalis) (Paris: Plon, 1928), pp. 357–58

Catalogue général des manuscrits des bibliothèques publiques de France, 66 vols (Paris: Plon, 1897), XXXII, Besançon, pp. 322–24

Catalogue général des manuscrits des bibliothèques publiques de France, 66 vols (Paris: Plon, 1901), XXXIV, Carpentras, pp. 193–95

Catalogue of Books Printed in the XVth Century now in the British Museum [British Library], 13 vols (London; 't Goy-Houten, 1963–2007)

Catalogue of Manuscripts and Early Printed Books from the Libraries of William Morris, Richard Bennett, Bertram, fourth Earl of Ashburnham, and other sources, now forming Portion of the Library of J. Pierpont Morgan, 4 vols, Early Printed Books, Italy and Part of France (London: Chiswick, 1907), II, no. 519, pp. 226–27

Catalogue of the Magnificent Library of the Late 7th Duke of Newcastle removed from Clumber, Worksop: The Third Portion including Twenty-Nine Highly

Important Illuminated Manuscripts to be Sold by Auction by Sotheby & Co. on Monday, 6 December 1937, 4 vols (Lot 941), III, pp. 231–32

Catalogue of the Portion of the Famous Collection of Manuscripts of the Rt Hon. the Earl of Ashburnham known as the Barrois Collection to be Sold by Auction by Sotheby, Wilkinson & Hodge on Monday, 10 June 1901 (Lot 103), pp. 40–41

CLAUDIN, ANATOLE, *Histoire de l'imprimerie en France au XIV*^e *et au XV*^e *siècles*, 4 vols (Paris: Imprimerie nationale, 1900–1905)

COATES, ALAN, and OTHERS, eds, *A Catalogue of Books Printed in the Fifteenth Century now in the Bodleian Library, Oxford*, 6 vols (Oxford: Oxford University Press, 2005)

COPINGER, WALTER A., *Supplement to Hain's 'Repertorium Bibliographicum'* (London: H. Sotheran, 1895–1902)

DALBANNE, CLAUDE, and EUGÉNIE DROZ, *L'Imprimerie à Vienne en Dauphiné au XV*^e *siècle* (Paris: Droz, 1930)

DELISLE, LÉOPOLD, *Chantilly, Le Cabinet des livres: imprimés antérieurs au milieu du XVI*^e *siècle* (Paris: Plon-Nourrit, 1905)

DI STEFANO, GIUSEPPE, *Dictionnaire des locutions en moyen français* (Paris: Klincksieck, 1969)

Dictionnaire du Moyen Français, version 2015 (DMF 2015), ATILF–CNRS and the Université de Lorraine < http://www.atilf.fr/dmf> [accessed 17 September 2017]

FOULET, ALFRED, and MARY B. SPEER, *On Editing Old French Texts* (Lawrence: Regents Press of Kansas, 1979)

GARDNER, ROSALYN, and MARION A. GREENE, *A Brief Description of Middle French Syntax* (Chapel Hill: University of North Carolina Press, 1958)

Gesamtkatalog der Wiegendrucke, 8 vols (Leipzig, Stuttgart: Hiersemann, 1928–)

GODEFROY, FRÉDÉRIC, *Dictionnaire de l'ancienne langue française et de tous ses dialectes du IX*^e *au XV*^e *siècles*, 10 vols (Paris: Vieweg; Paris: Bouillon, 1881–1902)

GOFF, FREDERICK R., *Incunabula in American Libraries: A Third Census of Fifteenth-Century Books Recorded in North American Collections* (New York: Bibliographical Society of America, 1964)

GREIMAS, ALGIRDAS JULIEN, *Dictionnaire de l'ancien français*, 3rd edn (Paris: Larousse, 2004)

GREIMAS, ALGIRDAS JULIEN, and TERESA MARY KEANE, *Grand Dictionnaire moyen français*, 2nd edn (Paris: Larousse, 2007)

GUIRARD, PIERRE, *Le Moyen Français* (Paris: Presses Universitaires de France, 1963)

HAIN, LUDWIG, *Repertorium Bibliographicum*, 4 vols (Stuttgart: Cotta, 1826–1838)

Incunabula Short Title Catalogue (London: British Library) <www.bl.uk/catalogues/istc> [accessed 17 September 2017]

JAMMES, BRUNO, *Catalogues régionaux des incunables des Bibliothèques publiques de France*, 20 vols, Bibliothèque de l'Institut de France, Bibliothèque Thiers (Paris: Klincksieck, 1990), VII

LABORDE, ALEXANDRE DE, *Les Principaux Manuscrits à peintures conservés dans l'ancienne Bibliothèque Impériale Publique de Saint-Petersbourg*, 2 vols (Paris: Pour les membres de la Société française de reproductions de manuscrits à peintures, 1938), II, pp. 140–41

LAMBERT, C. G. A., *Catalogue des manuscrits de la Bibliothèque de Carpentras* (Carpentras: Rolland, 1862), pp. 218–21

MACFARLANE, JOHN, *Antoine Vérard* (London: Chiswick, 1900; repr. Geneva: Slatkine, 1971)

MARTIN, HENRY, *Catalogue des manuscrits de la Bibliothèque de l'Arsenal*, 7 vols (Paris: Plon, 1885–1899), III, pp. 415–17

MASSÓ I TORRENTS, JAUME, and JORDI RUBIÓ I BALAGUER, *Catàleg dels manuscrits de la Biblioteca de Catalunya* (Barcelona: Biblioteca de Catalunya, 1989), pp. 24–29

MERRYWEATHER, F. SOMNER, and WALTER A. COPINGER, *Bibliomania in the Middle Ages: Being Sketches of Bookworms, Collectors, Bible Students, Scribes, and Illuminators, from the Anglo-Saxon and Norman Periods to the Introduction of Printing into England*, ed. by Harold B. Copinger (London: Woodstock Press, 1933; repr. New York: Blom, 1972)

MEYER, PAUL, 'Notice d'un recueil manuscrit de poésies françaises du XIIIe au XVe siècle appartenant à Westminster Abbey', *Bulletin de la Société d'Anciens Textes Français*, 1 (1875), 25–36

NEVEU, VALÉRIE, *Catalogues régionaux des incunables des Bibliothèques publiques de France*, 20 vols, Bibliothèques de la Région Haute Normandie (Geneva: Droz, 1979), XVII

PÄCHT, OTTO, and DAGMAR THOSS, *Die illuminierten Handschriften und Inkunabeln der Österreichischen Nationalbibliothek: Franzöische Schule*, 2 vols (Vienna: Verlag de Österreichischen Akademie der Wissenschaften, 1974), I, pp. 26–27

PARIS, PAULIN, *Les Manuscrits françois de la bibliothèque du roi*, 7 vols (Paris: Techener, 1845), VI-VII

PARQUEZ, GUY, *Catalogues régionaux des incunables des Bibliothèques publiques de France*, 20 vols, Bibliothèques de la Région Rhône-Alpes: Ain, Ardèche, Loire, Rhône (Paris: Aux amateurs de livres, 1991), XI

PASINI, GIUSEPPE, *Codices manuscripti bibliothecae regii taurinensis athenai*, 2 vols, Cod. XXXVII (Turin: Ex. typ. regia, 1749), II, pp. 473–74

PELLECHET, MARIE LÉONTINE CATHERINE, *Catalogue général des incunables des bibliothèques publiques de France*, 3 vols (Paris: Picard, 1905 ; repr. Paris: Kraus-Thomson, 1970)

PEYRON, BERNARDINO, *Catalogo dei manoscritti francesi della Biblioteca Nazionale di Torino* (Turin: Biblioteca Nazionale di Torino, 1904)

PICOT, ÉMILE, *Catalogue des livres composant la Bibliothèque de feu M. le Baron James de Rothschild*, 2 vols (Paris: Morgand, 1884; repr. New York: Franklin, 1967), I, pp. 244–46

POLAIN, MARIE-LOUIS, *Catalogue des livres imprimés au quinzième siècle des bibliothèques de Belgique* (Bruxelles: Société des Bibliophiles, 1932)

Printed Books and Manuscripts: Featuring the Kenneth K. Bechtel Collection of Californiana and Fine Books (Los Angeles: Christie's, 31 January 2002)

PROCTOR, ROBERT, *An Index to the Early Printed Books in the British Museum from the Invention of Printing to the Year MD, with Notes of those in the Bodleian Library*, 2 vols (London, 1898; 4 supplements, 1899–1902; Part 2, MDI–MDXX, Germany, London, 1903)

REY, ALAIN, *Dictionnaire historique de la langue française*, 2 vols (Paris: Robert, 1993)

SPEER, MARY B., 'Editing Old French Texts in the Eighties', *Romance Philology*, 45 (1991), 7–43.

STILLWELL, MARGARET BINGHAM, *Incunabula in American Libraries: A Second Census of Fifteenth-Century Books Owned in the United States, Mexico, and Canada* (New York: Bibliographical Society of America, 1940)

THIERRY-POUX, OLGAR, *Premiers Monuments de l'imprimerie en France au XVe siècle* (Paris: Hachette, 1890)

THURSTON, ADA, and CURT F. BUHLER, *Check List of Fifteenth-Century Printing in the Pierpont Morgan Library* (New York: Pierpont Morgan Library, 1939)

TORCHET, LOUIS, *Catalogues régionaux des incunables des Bibliothèques publiques de France*, 20 vols, Bibliothèques de la Région des Pays de la Loire (Bordeaux: Société des Bibliophiles de Guyenne, 1987),

UNIVERSITY OF OXFORD, BODLEIAN LIBRARIES, Bod-Inc Online, <http://incunables.bodleian.ox.ac.uk/record/C-408> [accessed 17 September 2017]

VIEILLARD, FRANÇOISE, and OLIVIER GUYOT-JEANNIN, eds, *Conseils pour l'édition des textes médiévaux: Conseils généraux, I* (Paris: Ecole Nationale des Chartes, 2001)

VINGTRINIER, AIMÉ, *Histoire de l'imprimerie à Lyon de l'origine jusqu'à nos jours* (Lyon: Storck, 1894)

WALRAVENS, C. J. H., *Alain Chartier: études biographiques, suivies de pièces justificatives, d'une description des éditions et d'une édition des ouvrages inédits* (Amsterdam: Meulenhoff-Didier, 1971), pp. 223–29

WALSH, JAMES E., *A Catalogue of the Fifteenth-Century Printed Books in the Harvard Library*, 5 vols (Binghamton, NY; Tempe, AZ, 1991–1995); supp. by David R. Whitesell, *Harvard University Bulletin*, XVI, nos. 1–2 (2005)

La Belle Dame qui eust mercy
(The Beautiful Lady Who Had Mercy)

Based on Paris, Bibliothèque nationale
de France, MS f. fr. 1131 (*Pc*)

Poem 1

[La Belle Dame qui eut mercy de son amant]   fol. 184^r

[L'Amant]

I.

Belle, que bon renom et los
Font saige de tous appeller,
Vers vous vieng pour dire a briefz mos
4   Ce que je ne puis plus celler.
Et se mon tresrude parler
N'est mie de doulx motz enté,
Prenés en gré, sans regarder
8   Fors a la bonne voulenté.

II.

Veulliés moy ouÿr humblement
Et par vo courtoisie entendre,
Vous m'alegerés grandement
12   Sans que vostre honneur en soit mendre.
Car, ainsy m'aist Dieu que mesprendre
Ne veul vers vous, ja ne m'adviengne
Que vers celle fache a reprendre
16   Dont il fault que tout bien me viengne.

III.

Toutesfoys, humblement vous prie,
Ains que sachés comme il m'est pris.
Quant ma requeste aurés ouÿe,
20   Ne me tenés pour mal apris
Se j'ay trop hault fait entrepris,
Ains me pardonnés car, par m'ame,
Cha fait Amours, qui m'a espris.
24   C'est tout par luy s'il y a blasme.

[La Dame]

IV.

Sire, du los que me donnés,
Vous mercy, c'est de vostre bien,
Car largement me blasonnés
28   Sans qu'il y ait que poy du mien.

Poem 1

[The Beautiful Lady Who Had Mercy on her Lover]

[The Lover]

I.

Beautiful lady, whom good reputation and praise
Cause to be called wise by all,
I come to you to say in just a few words
4   What I can no longer hide.
And if my very rough speech
Is not adorned with sweet words,
Receive it favourably, seeing nothing there
8   But goodwill.

II.

Please listen to me with kindness,
And through your grace, hear me,
For you will comfort me greatly
12   Without tarnishing your honour.
For, so help me God, I do not wish
To do you any harm, nor may it ever happen
That I do anything deserving reproach
16   To the one from whom all of my well-being must come.

III.

In any case, I humbly beg you,
Above all, to understand what has taken hold of me.
When you have heard my request,
20   Do not think me ill-bred
If I have aimed too high,
But pardon me because, by my soul,
Love has done this, he has taken me captive.
24   It's all due to him if there is any blame.

[The Lady]

IV.

My lord, for the praise you bestow upon me,
I thank you, but it comes from your own worthiness,
For you flatter me greatly
28   Without there being much to do with me.

Vous parlés doulcement et bien,
Et mieulx qu'entendre ne vous puis,
Maiz tieulx mos ne servent de rien
32   A si nice comment je suis.

V.

Se vous m'avés a dire chose   fol. 184^v
Qui a bien et a honneur touche,
Comme je le croy et suppose,
36   Je l'orray de voulenté doulce,
Car je vous tieng si sans reprouche
Et nay de si haulte noblesse
Que ja n'ystra de vostre bouche
40   Ung mot qui l'onneur d'aultry blesse.

VI.

Je ne congnois vostre pensee
Ne vostre celee entreprise,
Aussi suis je poy apensee
44   Et de l'entendre mal aprise.
S'elle est en droit honneur comprise,
El n'est oultrageuse ne haulte.
Maiz sans ce que je vous mesprise,
48   Ce poyse moy s'il y a faulte.

[L'Amant]

VII.

Puis qu'il vous plaist moy escouter,
Sachés je veul user mes jours
A vous amer, servir, doubter,
52   Combien que j'aye des doullours.
[Mais tous] mes plaisirs seront cours[*]
Se vo beaulté, qui me contraint
A vous requerir par amours,
56   Ne les adoulchist et reffraint.

VIII.

Et s'il vous plaist moy retenir
Pour vostre humble et petit servant,
A toujours vous vouldray servir,
60   Comme doibt faire ung vray amant,

You speak sweetly and well,
And better than I can understand you,
But such words serve no purpose
32   To one as naïve as I am.

V.

If you have something to say to me
That touches upon virtue and honour,
Just as I believe and suppose,
36   I will hear it with kind goodwill,
For I hold you to be so above reproach
And born of such high nobility
That never will spring from your mouth
40   A single word that might harm another's honour.

VI.

I know not your thoughts
Nor your hidden intent,
For I am simple
44   And unschooled in such matters.
If it is comprised of true honour,
Then it is neither excessive nor bold.
But without wishing to disparage you,
48   It troubles me if there is any wrongdoing here.

[The Lover]

VII.

Since you agree to listen to me,
Know that I want to spend my days
Loving, serving, and revering you,
52   Regardless of the number of pains I have.
But all of my pleasures will be fleeting
If your beauty, which compels me
To pursue you out of love,
56   Does not ease and alleviate my suffering.

VIII.

And if it pleases you to retain me
As your humble and lowly servant,
I will dedicate myself to serving you forever,
60   As a true lover ought to do,

Car en vostre honneur bien gardant
Seray joyeux, cointe, et secret.
Et de bien servir feray tant
64   Que vous n'y aurés ja regret.

IX.

Hellas! mon douloureux cueur sent   fol. 185^r
Mieulx que la bouche ne peust dire
Des doulours dont [j'ay] plus de cent,[*]
68   De quoy je ne congnoiz la pire.
Si ne me veulliés escondire;
Que vostre grace n'y pourvoye.
Faictes moy ou plourer ou rire –
72   Je suis vostre quel que je soye.

[La Dame]

X.

A moy requerir de cest point,
Perdriés et langaige et paine,
Si ne vous en travailliés point.
76   Fol est qui pour si poy se paine.
S'Amours vous tient en son demaine,
Je ne sçay quant il vous advint.
C'est une plaisance soubdaine;
80   El s'en yra comme elle vint.

XI.

Se vous avés d'amours desir
Pour vivre en joyeuse plaisance,
Dame poués ailleurs querir
84   Qui plus que moy vous y advance.
Ostés de moy vostre fiance
Et veulliés ailleurs regarder,
Car je veul, sans vostre acointance,
88   A part moy, mon honneur garder.

XII.

Se vostre cueur a aporter
Des maulx plus qu'il n'ot onques maiz,
A vous est de le conforter,
92   Quant aultre que vous n'en peust maiz.

For in safeguarding your honour
I will be joyful, courteous, and discreet.
And I will do my best to serve so well
64   That you will never have a single regret.

IX.

Alas! My sorrowful heart feels,
More than a mouth can say,
The hundred or more pains that I have,
68   Of which I know not the worst.
So please do not reject me;
May your grace keep you from doing so.
Make me either cry or laugh —
72   I am yours, whatever else I may be.

[The Lady]
X.

To implore me on this account,
You waste both your words and your efforts,
So don't belabour the point.
76   Foolish is he who suffers for so little.
If Love holds you in his domain,
I have no idea when this came about.
It is just a fleeting pleasure;
80   It will go away as quickly as it came.

XI.

If you have a desire to love
In order to live in joyous delight,
You can seek a lady elsewhere
84   Who will favour you more than I do.
Withdraw your vows of love
And kindly look elsewhere,
For I prefer to preserve my honour,
88   On my own, without your involvement.

XII.

If your heart has to bear
Far more suffering than ever before,
It is up to you to comfort it,
92   Since no one but you can ever do that.

Si ne croy je pas que vous trayz
Tant de doullours comme vous dictes.
Or ne vous en plaigniés jamaiz,
96   Car je croy qu'ilz sont bien petites.

[L'Amant]

XIII.

Belle, de beaulté bien eureuse,   fol 185^v
Des aultres belles l'exemplaire,
Vostre simple chiere joyeuse
100   Fait a vous mon cueur si actraire
Que je vous ayme sans retraire,
Et l'ay celé par pluseurs moys.
Se j'en meur, puis qu'a faire faire,
104   Mourir me fault il une foys.

XIV.

Onques maiz Amours ne m'esprist,
Pour aultre dame ou demoyselle,
Maiz, a mon gré, pas ne m'esprist
108   Quant il la me fist choysir telle.
Ne me parlés d'amour nouvelle.
Il est de moy tout ordonné,
Car a vous, comme a la plus belle,
112   Ay mon cueur tout entier donné.

XV.

Certes, Belle, a ce que je voy,
Vous ne congnoissiés qu'amours monte.
Et Dieu scet se je l'aperchoy.
116   Maintes foys que je n'en tiens compte,
J'ay souvent de souppirer honte
Quant je m'entroublie en mains lieux.
Il m'est pis que je ne vous compte.
120   Maiz quant vous plaira, j'aray mieulx.

[La Dame]

XVI.

Se mon maintien [vous] avés veu,[*]
Que vous loés oultre mesure,
Et vos yeulx vous [y] ont deceu[*]

Moreover, I do not believe that you are afflicted
By as many pains as you claim.
Now, cease your complaints, once and for all,
96   For I believe that they are but trifles.

        [The Lover]
XIII.

Fair lady, graced with such beauty,
The paragon of all other lovelies,
Your pure, joyful countenance
100   Beguiles my heart so much
That I love you without reserve,
And I have hidden it for several months.
If I die from this, since it must happen,
104   Well, I have to die once.

XIV.

Never before has Love ensnared me,
For any other lady or damsel,
But, as I wished, he did not enflame me
108   When he made me choose another.
Do not speak to me of a new love.
I have set everything to rights,
Because it is to you, as the most beautiful lady,
112   That I have given my heart, fully and absolutely.

XV.

Surely, Beauty, from what I can see,
You do not know what love amounts to.
And God knows if I even know.
116   On many occasions, so often that I don't realize,
I am ashamed when I forget myself
And heave a great sigh, regardless of where I am.
It is even worse than what I am telling you here.
120   But when it pleases you, I will have relief.

        [The Lady]
XVI.

If you observed my countenance,
Which you praise beyond measure,
And your eyes deceived you

124   Par mal adviser ma figure,
             Si n'avés vous pas telle ardure
             Que vous en perdés le mengier.
             Maint plus malade vit et dure.
128   On ne meurt pas si de legier.

XVII.
             Je me donne trop grant merveille   fol. 186^r
             Que je vous voy tant enquerir,
             Car mainte aultre vostre pareille
132   En beaulté poués acquerir,
             Vous ne l'avés pas a querir.
             Car il est legier a savoir
             Que homs qui scet si bel requerir
136   N'est pas sans belle amye avoir.

XVIII.
             Vous dirés ce qu'il vous plaira
             Et voulentiers l'escouteray,
             Maiz ja nulz homs mon cueur n'ara,
140   Ne ja par amours n'ameray,
             Fors ung a qui je garderay
             Ma foy comme espoux et amy.
             Se Dieu plest, je le trouveray
144   Au tel que si fera il my.

Poem 2

                   [L'Amant]
XIX.
             Mer de doulchour, source de riviere*
             D'onnour et de joyeuse chiere,
             Qui font en vous beaulté flourir,
148   Vous estes ma dame premiere,
             Vous estes m'amour toute entiere.
             En ce point veul vivre et mourir.
             Et se ne voulés secourir
152   Mon cueur, dont je vous ay fait don,
             Or en faictes a vostre bon,
             Comme du vostre, franc et quicte.
             J'espereray, veulliés ou non,

124   By misreading my expression,
       Well, you cannot have such a burning desire
       That you lose your appetite over it.
       Many who are sicker live and endure.
128   One does not die of something so slight.

XVII.

       I am truly astonished
       When I see you beseech me to this extent,
       For you can attract many other ladies
132   Your equal in beauty,
       You have only to seek one out.
       For it is easy to see
       That a man who is skilled in courtship
136   Is never without a beautiful lady.

XVIII.

       You will say whatever you please
       And I will gladly listen,
       But no man will ever possess my heart,
140   Nor will I ever truly love anyone,
       But the one to whom I will remain faithful
       As my husband and lover.
       If it pleases God, I will find him
144   Just as he will find me.

Poem 2

       [The Lover]
XIX.
       Sea of sweetness, source of a river
       Of honour and of joyous countenance,
       Which make beauty blossom in you,
148   You are my lady above all,
       You are my absolute love.
       In this state I want to live and die.
       And if you do not wish to console
152   My heart, which I have gifted to you,
       Then do with it as you please,
       For I am yours, willing and free.
       I will remain hopeful, whether you wish it or not,

156 Car vous n'avés pas le renon
   D'estre orguelleuse ne despite.

XX.

   En espoir qu'il m'en soit de mieulx,
   Vous serviray, jeunes et vieulx,
160 Et je m'en tieng moult honnouré.
   Et se je faiz trop l'ennuyeulx,   fol. 186^{v}
   C'est signe de cueur poy joyeulx,
   Triste, dolent, et esplouré,
164 Et largement en amouré.
   Maiz, s'il est ainsy qu'il vous plaise
   Moy commander que je me tayse
   De vous demander reconfort,
168 A tout le mains, ne vous desplaise
   Se j'ayme en souffrant ma mesaise.
   En ce ne vous faiz je nul tort.

XXI.

   Je congnoiz bien et voy a l'eul
172 Que les maulx que d'amer recueul
   Sans mort n'auront point grant duree.
   Neantmains j'ayme mieulx vivre en deul,*
   Trop plus d'assés que je ne seul,
176 Que aultre dame avoir procuree.
   Et eussiés vous ma mort juree,
   Ce qui vous plaist m'est agreable.
   Et ne me verrés variable
180 Pour assault que doulour me livre.
   Se vous ne m'estes amyable,
   Combien que mort m'est profitable,
   Si veul je en vostre mercy vivre.

     [La Dame]
XXII.
184 Quant femme en honneur se maintient
   Et respont ce qu'il appartient
   A qui la requiert de folie,
   Fol est qui despite la tient.
188 Pourtant s'elle se contretient
   Que beau parler ne l'amolie.

156   For you do not have the reputation
Of being arrogant or spiteful.

XX.

In the hope that my condition improves,
I will serve you, throughout my life,
160   And I consider myself most honoured to do so.
And if I am too bothersome,
It is a sign of a heart without joy,
Sad, dejected, and tearful,
164   And deeply in love.
But if it is the case that you prefer
To order me to be silent,
To stop seeking comfort from you,
168   At the very least, don't be irritated
If I continue to love while enduring my discomfort.
In this, I do you no wrong.

XXI.

I am well aware and can see with my own eyes
172   That the pains that I reap from loving
Will not last long before death intervenes.
Nonetheless, I prefer to live in grief,
Even more than I am already accustomed to doing,
176   Than to acquire another lady.
And even if you had sworn my death,
Whatever pleases you is agreeable to me.
And you will not find me to be inconstant,
180   Regardless of the assault that sorrow wages against me.
If you are not sympathetic toward me,
However much death might be beneficial,
I still want to live in your mercy.

[The Lady]

XXII.
184   When a lady conducts herself honourably
And responds in an appropriate manner
To one who foolishly pursues her,
He is a fool who judges her to be disdainful.
188   Moreover, she behaves in such a manner
So that sweet talk will not weaken her resolve.

Si n'ayés ja mirencolie
Que je vous soye trop sauvage,
192   Car apprés assés de langage
Je vous dy bien ung mot pour tous —
Qui que m'en tiengne folle ou sage —   fol. 187^r
Que je n'aray ja le courage
196   De me faire blasmer pour vous.

XXIII.

Se vous voulés, vous aymerés,
Et se non, vous le laisserés.
Je ne vous y puis pas contraindre.
200   Maiz quant d'amer me parlerés,
Ja par moy haÿ n'en serés —
Cela ne debvés vous ja craindre.
Ung amant peust prier et plaindre,
204   Et puis qui veult si, si consente.
Bien sçay que pas ne vous contempte
Et que vostre doulleur vous griefve.
Ce poyse moy, j'en suis dolente;
208   Maiz se j'eusse eu d'amer entente,
J'eusse fait responce plus briefve.

XXIV.

Vous n'avés gardé que je face
Nulle rien que mort pourchace
212   Ne de quoy vostre cueur se deulle,
Car onques encor que je sache,
Ne me faistes, en nulle place,
Nulle chose que bien ne veulle.
216   C'est rayson que bel vous accueulle,
Pour l'onneur que vous m'avés faicte.
Vous avés mainte paine traycte.
Amours, qui scet bien qu'il vous fault,
220   Vous doint dame, en amours parfaicte,
Ainsy comme je le souhaycte
Et que vostre gent corps le vault.

So, don't ever feel melancholy
Should I be too cruel toward you,
192   For after so much talking
I say to you, once and for all —
Whether I am judged to be foolish or wise —
That I will never be disposed to
196   Bring blame upon myself because of you.

XXIII.

If you want, you will love,
And if not, you will forsake it.
I cannot force you, one way or the other.
200   But when you speak to me of love,
I will never hate you for that —
That you shouldn't fear.
A lover may beg and plead,
204   And whoever wishes to do so, may consent.
I am sure that this does not make you happy,
And that your sorrow pains you.
This troubles me, I am saddened by it;
208   But if I had intended to love,
I would have given a much shorter answer.

XXIV.

You need not worry that I will do
Anything that will bring about your death
212   Nor that will make your heart suffer,
For you have never, to my knowledge,
Done anything to me, anywhere,
That was, in any way, against my wishes.
216   It is only fair that I want the best for you,
For the honour that you have done me.
You have endured much pain.
May Love, who is well aware of what you need,
220   Grant you a lady perfect in love,
Just as I wish
And just as your noble body deserves.

[L'Amant]

XXV.

Se ma requeste me cassés,
224   Je tieng mes bons jours pour passés,
Quant nul plaisir ne me demeure.
Je suis a moytié trespassés —   fol. 187ᵛ
N'ay je pas eu des maulx assés ?
228   Il est temps qu'Amours me sequeure.
Je ne fus pas nay de bonne heure,
Quant je n'ay d'Amours nul solas,
Combien c'onques je ne fus las
232   Ne ne brisay ma loyaulté.
Puis que je suis pris en ces lacs,
S'en la fin m'en fault dire, Hellas !
Je n'en blasme que vo beaulté.

XXVI.

236   Si vous suppli a jointes mains,
Belle dame, qu'a tout le mains,
De tout points ne me deboutés,
Et se les maulx dont je me plains
240   Sont de vous assés petit plains,
Au mains que vous les escoutés.
Il pert que de moy vous doubtés,
Qui suis vostre, comme qu'il soit,
244   Et qui suis celluy qui feroit
Ce que vous commanderiés.
Se desplaisir vous sourvenoit,
Mon cueur tresdolent en seroit,
248   Au tant comme vous seriés.

XXVII.

S'ainsy estoit qu'il advenist
Que vostre cueur tant devenist
Amoureux comme je fus onques,
252   Et que par force convenist
Que de doullours tant soubstenist
Comme moy ou aultre quelconques,
Il vous desplairoit moult adonques?
256   Que ung amant feist de vous reffus,
Que feriés [vous] en sourplus?*

[The Lover]

XXV.

If you spurn my request,
224   I consider my happy days at an end,
For no pleasure remains for me.
I am half dead —
Haven't I suffered enough?
228   It is time for Love to come to my aid.
I was not born at a fortunate hour,
For I have no solace at all from Love,
Even though I was never weary of serving
232   Nor did my loyalty wane.
Since I am caught in these snares,
I must end by saying, Alas!
I can only blame your beauty.

XXVI.

236   So, with hands joined, I beseech you,
Beautiful lady, if nothing else,
Do not reject me completely.
And if the pains that I lament
240   Are but minor grievances to you,
Please listen to them at least.
It seems that you are wary of me,
Though I am yours, come what may,
244   And I am the one who would do
Whatever you commanded.
And if you were overcome with displeasure,
My heart would be deeply saddened,
248   Just as you would be.

XXVII.

If it were to happen
That your heart became
As filled with love as mine,
252   And it were forced to sustain
As many sorrows
As I or others have had to bear,
Would that displease you?
256   Were a lover to refuse you,
What more would you do?

Vous ne sariés nul consceil.
Et pour ce je dys et conclus   fol. 188^r
260   Qu'en ce point ne me tenés plus,
Maiz me faictes en cas pareil.

[La Dame]

XXVIII.

  Se vraye estoit vostre complainte,
Enduré avés douleur mainte
264   Et vostre cueur forment se deult.
Maiz on n'ayme pas par contrainte,
Aultrement l'amour seroit fainte.
Nul n'ayme qui amer ne veult.
268   Laisse chacun ce qu'il ne peust.
Il me pleust, se vous voulsissiés,
Que de ce plus ne parlissiés
Et que la chose en ce point fine;
272   Lors aultre dame choisissiés
Dont mieulx que de moy vaulsissiés,
Car d'amer ne suis je point digne.

XXIX.

  Il me desplaist moult qu'il conviegne
276   Qu'en parler longuement vous tiegne,
Maiz c'est par vous, vous le savés,
Car oncques maiz qu'il me souviegne
Ne vys nul qui si ferme se tiegne
280   Son propos comme vous avés.
Je ne sçay se vous recepvés
Pour moy ou pour aultres vos maulx.
Se vous avés desirs nouveaulx
284   De jour en jour, ce seroit mal.
Maiz veu vos diz joyeulx et beaulx,
Ou vous estes maulvés et faulx,
Ou tresparfaictement loyal.

XXX.

288   Voulés vous me mectre es dangiers
De ces faulx parlans losengiers
Dont rien fors que mal n'est rectraict?
Ilz parlent assés voulentiers   fol. 188^v

You would have no idea.
So, for this reason, I say in conclusion that,
260   On this point, you can no longer fault me,
But treat me as a similar case.

[The Lady]

XXVIII.
If your complaint were true,
Then you have endured many sorrows
264   And your heart suffers grievously.
But one cannot be compelled to love,
Otherwise, love would be false.
No one loves who does not wish to love.
268   Stop trying to force what is not possible.
I would prefer, if you agreed,
That you cease talking about this
And that this discussion end right now;
272   Then that you choose another lady
More deserving of your attention than me,
For I am not worthy of loving.

XXIX.
It really irritates me that it has been necessary
276   To discuss this with you at such length,
But it is your own doing, as well you know,
For never, to the best of my recollection,
Have I seen anyone hold to his purpose
280   As firmly as you have done.
I do not know if your suffering
Comes from me or others.
If you have new desires
284   From one day to the next, that would hurt.
But given your joyous and lovely words,
Either you are cruel and false,
Or most perfectly loyal.

XXX.
288   Do you want to put me in danger
Of those false-speaking gossipmongers
From whom nothing comes but harm?
They speak very freely

292   Et dient du mal plus du tiers
        Qu'oncques ne fu pensé ne fait.
        Si ne veul rien faire de fait
        Qui soit a mon honneur nuysans.
296   Vous en seriés desplaisans
        Se vous estes de moy amys.
        Gens sont sans cause mesdisans,
        Et qui les feroit voir-disans,
300   Encores seroit ce du pis.

            [L'Amant]

XXXI.

        Se mon service en gré prenés,
        Et vostre amy me retenés,
        Vous me ferés grant amitié.
304   Et s'aultrement l'entreprenés,
        Il me semble que mesprenés
        Et qu'estes dame sans pitié.
        Se je suis par vous mal traictié
308   Et Mercy ne me reconforte,
        Je prendray [drap] de noyre sorte*
        Ce may ou toute joye habonde,
        En signe que ma joye est morte
312   Et comme celuy qui se porte
        Pour le plus maleureux du monde.

XXXII.

        Et se je devieng vostre acointe,
        Sans ce qu'aultre m'en desacointe,
316   Je pourray dire sans mentir
        Que j'ayme la belle et la cointe,
        Et tant que la mort nous despointe,
        Vous ne m'en verrés repentir.
320   Et pour ce veulliés consentir
        Que nos deulx cueurs soient tout ung,
        Qui a nos deulx sera commun,
        Sans que jamés nul aultre y parte.
324   L'un ayme l'autre et l'autre l'un,   fol. 189^r
        Et face son debvoir chacun,
        Jusqu'a ce que mort nous departe.

292   And say over a third more evil
        Than was ever thought or done.
        So I do not want to do anything at all
        That might be damaging to my honour.
296   You would be vexed by this
        If you were a friend of mine.
        People say wicked things for no reason,
        And whoever understands them to be truth-tellers
300   Well, that would be even worse.

[The Lover]

XXXI.

If you look favourably upon my service,
        And retain me as your lover,
        You will do a great kindness to me.
304   Yet if you do otherwise,
        It seems to me that you are mistaken
        And that you are a lady without pity.
        If I am mistreated by you
308   And Mercy brings me no comfort,
        I will dress in black
        This month of May, which brims with joy,
        As a sign that my joy is dead
312   And as one who considers himself
        As the most unfortunate man in the world.

XXXII.

But if I gain your favour,
        Without anyone breaking us apart,
316   I will be able to say truthfully
        That I love the most beautiful and gracious lady,
        And until death dispossesses us,
        You will never see me regret this.
320   So, for this reason, please consent
        To our two hearts being as one,
        Which the two of us will share,
        Without anyone ever coming between us.
324   May one love the other, and the other the one,
        And each be dutiful toward the other
        Till death do us part.

XXXIII.

       Si vous supply et derechief
328   Que me dictes, a ung mot brief
       De ce que je vous ay requis.
       Vivray je tousjours en meschief
       Ou se je vendray ja a chief
332   De ce que j'ay si long temps quis ?
       Onques aultre dame n'a[y] quis;*
       Ja ne me soit il reprouvé.
       Vous eussiés bien aultre trouvé
336   Trop plus gracieulx et plus bel,
       Maiz quant vous m'arés esprouvé
       Il sera bien par vous prouvé
       Qu'en loyaulté n'en est nul tel.

         [La Dame]

XXXIV.
340   Mon cueur tressault, tremble et tressue,
       Et suis presque toute esperdue.
       Je ne sçay plus nulle deffence,
       Car je me sens d'amours ferue.
344   Vostre beau parler m'a vaincue,
       Qui plus me plaist tant plus y pense.
       Dieu doint que ce soit sans offense
       Et la chose en bien se parface.
348   Je suis de vous reffuser lasse;
       Mon cueur plus ne se combatra.
       Jamés a nul jour ne cuydasse
       Que, pour rien, par amours amasse.
352   Je ne sçay comme il m'en prendra.

XXXV.

       S'il vous plaist garder mon honnour,
       Et que pour pire ou pour meillour,
       Jamés ne me veulliés changier.
356   Je veul oster toute rigour   fol. 189ᵛ
       Et vous octroyeray m'amour
       Sans en faire plus de dangier.
       Je ne vous veul pas estrangier.
360   Et combien que j'aye estrivé,
       De grace ne serés privé,

XXXIII.

     So I beseech you once again
328   To tell me, in a single word,
     Your answer to what I have asked of you.
     Will I live forevermore in distress
     Or will I obtain
332   What I have sought for so long?
     I have not pursued any another lady;
     I can never be reproached for that.
     You may well have found another lover
336   Far more gracious and handsome than me,
     But once you have put me to the test,
     You will have clear proof
     That, in loyalty, I have no peer.

       [The Lady]

XXXIV.

340   My heart shivers, shakes, and shudders,*
     And I am almost completely overwhelmed.
     I no longer know any defence,
     For I feel myself lovestruck.
344   Your beautiful words have vanquished me,
     And they please me the more I think about them.
     May God grant that this will be without offence
     And that everything will work out well.
348   I am tired of refusing you.
     My heart will no longer put up a fight.
     Never would I have believed, not for a single moment,
     Or for anything, that I would fall so much in love.
352   I don't know how it will affect me.

XXXV.

     Please safeguard my honour,
     And both for better and for worse,
     Please don't betray me.
356   I want to stop being obstinate,
     And will grant you my love,
     Without putting up any more resistance.
     I don't want to keep you at a distance.
360   And even though I refused you before,
     You will no longer be deprived of my grace,

Dont dame ne doibt estre large.
Or soyés secret et privé.
364   Si sera tout blasme eschivé.
Ce sont les poins que je vous charge.

XXXVI.
Puis que nous sommes aliés
Ainsy comme vous me priés,
368   Je vous supply de tresbon cueur
Qu'en ma loyaulté vous fiés
Et que jamés ne m'oubliés.
Je ne le vouldroye a nul feur.
372   Maiz ainsy, comme frere et seur,
Tout ung mesmes vouloir ayon,
Et pour chose que dire oyon,
Que nostre amour ne desassemble.
376   Maiz souvent nous entrevoyon
Affin que plus joyeulx soyon.
Ainsy pourrons nous vivre ensemble.

Explicit la dame qui eust mercy de son amant

Title: *This title is written by a modern hand.*
53 Tant que m. p.; *reading taken from majority of witnesses.*
67 (-1) *correction from several manuscripts.*
121 (-1) *correction from Pd, Po, Qp, Xd.*
123 (-1) *corrections from Pd, Xe.*
145 (+1)
174 (+1) *Pa, Pk, Qp, Xa read* Mais jay plus chier de vivre en duel *which corrects the metre.*
257 (-1) *correction from multiple manuscripts.*
309 drap *missing (-1), but found in all of the other manuscripts but Pe, which is missing the line.*
333 a. d. nay quis *in Pa, Pl, Qn, Qp, Xd.*

With which a lady must not be generous.
But be discreet and reserved;
364   In that way all blame will be avoided.
These are the requests that I make of you.

XXXVI.
     Since we are united,
     Just as you request,
368   I beseech you, with a pure heart,
To trust in my loyalty
And to never neglect me.
I would never want that, not for anything.
372   But rather, like brother and sister,
Let us have one and the same desire,
And regardless of what we may hear said,
May our love never be rent asunder.
376   But let us see each other often
So that we may be even more joyful.
Thus will we be able to live together.

So ends the Beautiful Lady who had mercy on her lover.

---

340 *The verb 'tressuer' means to perspire profusely, out of fear, anguish, pain, or passion, and could refer to either cold or hot sweats. When speaking of the heart, it can mean to be extremely agitated. While these may not seem to be courtly images, this verb is frequently found in medieval lyrics alongside 'trembler' (as well as 'fremir' – to shiver, and 'chaloir' –to burn) to describe the physical effects of an assault by love. In his* Remede de Fortune *(c. 1341), for example, Guillaume de Machaut includes trembling, sweating, and burning in his inventory of the joys and the pains of lovesickness: '...cuer d'amant qui aimme fort | Or a joie, or a desconfort, | Or rit, or pleure, or chante, or plaint, | Or se delite en son complaint, | Or tramble, or tressue, or a chaut, | Or a froit, et puis ne li chaut | D'assaut qu'Amours li puisse faire.' (lines 28–34). For this line in* La Belle Dame qui eust mercy, *I have chosen to translate the verbs as 'shivers, shakes, and shudders' in a twofold effort to express the suffering that the lady is experiencing and to retain the alliteration of the French.*

*Le Dialogue d'amoureux
et de sa dame*

*(The Dialogue between a Lover
and his Lady)*

Based on Paris, Bibliothèque nationale
de France, MS f. fr. 1131 (*Pc*)

Poem 1

[L'Amoureux]

I.

M'amour, ma dame souveraine,   195^r
Mon bien et ma seule plaisance,
Veulliés ouÿr ce qui me maine
4   Vers vous, et n'ayés desplaisance
Se je vous diz la penitance
Qu'Amours me font pour vous sentir,
A qui je suis, sans departir,
8   Vray servant. Car pour dire voir,
Vous et luy poués resjouÿr
Mon cueur ou le faire douloir.

II.

Ne nul aultre fors que vos deulx
12   N'a pouoir de le conforter
Ne de le faire doulereux
Pour chose que on luy peust donner.
Il vous ayme et vous veult doubter
16   Plus que nulle qui soit vivant,
Et vostre honneur garder autant
Comme pour moy mesmes feroit,
Sans en monstrer [tour ne] semblant,[*]
20   Ne pour riens aultre n'ameroit.

III.

Et si vous ay long temps amee,
Sans avoir eu le hardement
De vous avoir dist ma pensee
24   Ne mon vouloir aucunement
Si ay je porté humblement,
Et tant que vous plaira feray.
Les engoisses qu'en mon cueur ay
28   Pour vous servir maiz ou que soye.[*]
Loyaulment je vous aymeray,
Car mieulx faire je ne pourroye.

Poem 1

[The Lover]

I.

My love, my sovereign lady,
My happiness and my sole delight,
Please hear what brings me
4   To you, and do not be displeased
If I tell you of the pain
That Love makes me feel for you,
To whom I am, steadfastly,
8   A loyal servant. For to speak truthfully,
You and he can make my heart rejoice,
Or make it suffer.

II.

And no one else but the two of you
12   Has the power to comfort it
Or to make it miserable
Over what it can be given.
It loves you and wants to revere you
16   More than any other lady alive,
And to guard your honour just as much
As it would do for myself,
Without any deceit or falseness,
20   Nor for anything would it love another.

III.

Thus have I loved you for a long time,
Without having been bold enough
To tell you my thoughts
24   Nor anything of the desire
That I have borne humbly,
And that I will continue to bear as long as it pleases you.
The anguish that I have in my heart
28   To serve you is present wherever I may be.
I will love you loyally,
For I could not love any better.

[La Dame]

IV.

Vous avés bien pouoir de dire
32   Quant a moy ce qu'il vous plaira;   195^v
Je ne le veulz pas contredire.
Maiz, certes, mon cueur n'aymera,
Ne oncques ne fist, ne ne fera
36   Se ce n'est ung qu'il doye amer,
[Honnourer, cherir, et doubter].*
Et quant ung amoureux s'avance
De choisir dame, il doibt garder,
40   S'il peust, qu'elle y ayt sa plaisance.

V.

Quant a moy, je suis esbahie
Dont vous vient ceste voulenté
Ne comment il vous prent envye
44   De moy amer. En verité,
Je ne vous ay semblant monstré
Dont vous me deussiés requerir,
Ne je ne veul pas enquerir
48   Pour quoy vous m'alés requerant
Ne paroles vous en tenir,
Car ce n'est pas chose advenant.

VI.

On dist qu'a ung bon demandeur,
52   Qui est hardy de demander
Ne fault que ung bon escondisseur,
Qui le sache bien reffuser.
Je ne suis pas digne d'amer
56   Ne tenir ne veul cest party.
Mon cueur ne sera [ja] party*
Pour vous ne pour aultre. Et sachiés
Qu'aultres que vous y ont failly
60   Qui ne s'en sont gueres vantés.

[L'Amoureux]

VII.

Bien say que pas ne suis assés
Bon ne vaillant pour vous aimer,

[The Lady]

IV.

You may certainly say
32   Whatever you please about me;
I don't want to dispute that.
But, to be sure, my heart will not love,
Nor has it ever, nor will it,
36   Apart from the one that it must love,
Honour, cherish, and revere.
And when a lover comes forward
To choose a lady, he must ensure,
40   If he can, that she is pleased about this.

V.

As for myself, I am bewildered
As to the origin of your desire,
And how it makes you yearn
44   To love me. In truth,
I have not given you any sign
To encourage you to pursue me,
And I do not want to find out
48   Why you go about pursuing me
And insist on speaking to me like this,
For this is not welcome.

VI.

It is said that a good seeker,
52   One who boldly demands something,
Only needs someone capable of resisting,
One who really knows how to refuse.
I am not worthy of loving
56   And I do not wish to be part of this.
My heart will never be divided
For you or for anyone else. And you should know
That others besides you have failed in this
60   And they hardly boast about it.

[The Lover]

VII.

I am well aware that I am not
Good or worthy enough to love you,

Car je scay bien que vous avés
64   Des biens assés pour sourmonter
Toutes dames qui en amer   196^r
Ont leur cueur et leur gentillesse.
Si vous supplie, ma maistresse,
68   Que ne veulliés avoir regart
A ma doulleur, a ma rudesse,
Maiz m'envoyés ung doulx regart,

VIII.

Qui viengne de vos rians yeulx,
72   Pour moy conforter doulcement.
Je ne vous requerray pas mieulx,
Belle dame, quant a present.
Maiz se je suiz entierement
76   Vostre servant, a tousjours maiz,
Mon cueur, qui est entre vos laiz,
Vous servira, ma dame belle,
Esperant que ayés, de ses faiz,
80   Mercy sans Dangier, le rebelle,

IX.

Qui m'a grevé trop long temps a
Et fait souffrir mainte doulour.
Et si ne scay s'il vouldra ja
84   Consentir qu'aye vostre amour.
Se je vous fiz onques faulx tour,
Banissiés moy de vo service
Et vers vous n'aye point d'office.
88   Si seray de tous poins rusé,
Et vivray comme fol et nice,
Et comment homme reffusé.

[La Dame]
X.

Amis, se je vouloye avoir
92   Des serviteurs, bien en auroye
Qui auroyent bien le pouoir
[De faire ce que je vouldroie].[*]
Maiz mon cueur changier ne pourroye[*]
96   Car pieca je l'ay accordé

For I am sure that you have
64   More than enough good qualities to surpass
All ladies who dedicate their heart and their kind nature
To loving.
So I beseech you, my lady,
68   Please pay no heed
To my suffering or my rough manner,
But send me a sweet look,

VIII.

Which comes from your laughing eyes,
72   To comfort me gently.
I do not request more of you,
Beautiful lady, for the moment.
But if I am entirely
76   Your servant, forevermore,
My heart, which is caught in your snare,
Will serve you, my fair lady,
Hoping that you will have, for its efforts,
80   Mercy without the hostile Resistance,

IX.

Who has plagued me for far too long
And made me suffer much pain.
And I don't know if it will ever want
84   To consent to my gaining your love.
If I have ever done you a bad turn,
Banish me from your service
And remove any standing I have with you.
88   Thus I will be thoroughly beaten,
And will live like a fool and a dolt,
And like a man spurned.

[The Lady]
X.

Friend, if I wanted to have
92   Servants, I would certainly have some
Who would truly be able
To do what I wanted.
But my heart could not possibly change,
96   For long ago I granted it

Et a ung aultre l'ay donné,   196^v
Qui me suffist pour ma plaisance.
Si n'estes pas bien advisé
100   De luy pourchasser tel grevance,

XI.

Veu qu'il ne pense pas a vous.
Maintenant je le scay de voir,
Et si n'en est mie jalous,
104   Je m'en puis bien appercevoir.
Se vous le voulés decevoir,
Et moy aussy, c'est grant folie.
Ostés ceste mirencolie
108   De ce fait et plus n'y pensés!
Et alés choisir aultre amye,
Car vous en trouverés assés,

XII.

De bonnes et de gracieuses,
112   Plus belles que moy la moytié,
Et qui seront mains dangereuses
De faire vostre voulenté.
S'il eschiet que je n'ay esté,
116   Et suis encores de present,
Ne me tenés plus parlement
De ce qu'avés tant actendu.
Se dictes vous ou aultrement,
120   « Bien assailly, bien deffendu. »

[L'Amoureux]
XIII.

«Bien deffendu, bien assailly. »
Ma dame, vous m'ameriés
Et auriés de moy mercy
124   Ne ja dangier n'en feriés,
Pour ce que pas ne vouldriés
Se tieng je ma destruction.
Car vous avés le cueur si bon
128   Comme dame le peust avoir,
Et aussy vostre bon renon   197^r
Ne vauldroit ja mieulx du vouloir.

And did give it to another,
Who satisfies me.
So you are strongly advised
100   Not to pursue him over such a grievance,

XI.

Seeing that he doesn't give a thought about you.
Now I know this for a fact.
And so he is not a bit jealous,
104   Which is quite apparent to me.
If you want to deceive him,
And me as well, well that is pure foolishness.
Stop feeling melancholy about this
108   And give it no more thought!
Go and choose another lady,
For you will find many,

XII.

Both good and gracious,
112   Half of them prettier than me,
And who will be less resistant
To doing what you want.
Since it is clear that I have not done so,
116   And continue to refuse you,
Do not hold me in conversation any longer
Over what you have sought for so long.
So you might say something like this:
120   'Well attacked, well defended.'

[The Lover]
XIII.

'Well defended, well attacked.'
My lady, you should love me
And should have mercy on me,
124   And should never resist me,
Because you should not want
To bring about my destruction.
For you have as good a heart
128   As any lady can have,
And also your good reputation
Would never allow any such desire.

XIV.

Quant a mon pouoir vous chiery
132   Et vous ayme et crains comme celle
Que mon povre cueur a choisy
Entre les aultres la plus belle,
Pour luy donner joye nouvelle.
136   Se vous consentiés [a] ma mort*
Et qu[e] vous en fussiés d'acort,*
Par le moyen de vostre veul,
Seulement vous auriés tort,
140   Car j'ay pour vous assés de deul.

XV.

Et quant ce vient au fort aler,
Faictes en ce qu'il vous plaira,
Car je ne puis pas ordonner
144   Contre ce que vo cueur vouldra.
Neant mains, quant Amours commanda
Que vostre fusse entierement,
A tousjours maiz, sans partement,
148   Et que vous servisse et amasse,
Ne me conseilla nullement
Que vostre bon gré reffusasse.

[La Dame]
XVI.

Biau sire, ce est bien mon gré
152   Que vous en depportés atant,
Et qu'il n'en soit jamés parlé
De ce fait cy ne poy ne grant.
Ne me requerés plus avant.
156   Souffise vous, je vous en prie,
Car se, pour vostre maladie,
Venés cy pour mire querir,
Je vous promet bien qu'a ma vie,
160   Vous n'aultre n'en pense a guerir,

XVII.

Au mains de chose qui me touche
A deshonneur aucunement.
Et si n'ouvriray ja ma bouche,

197ᵛ

XIV.

For I absolutely cherish you,
132   And love and revere you as the one
Whom my poor heart has chosen
As the most beautiful of all others,
To give it new joy.
136   If you were to consent to my death
And you were to agree to that,
Of your own will,
You would be completely wrong,
140   And I feel great sadness for you.

XV.

But, in the end,
Do as you please,
For I cannot order anything
144   That goes against what your heart wants.
Nevertheless, when Love commanded me
To devote myself entirely to you,
Forevermore, never parting,
148   And to serve and love you,
He gave me no warning at all
That your good will might refuse me.

[The Lady]

XVI.

Noble lord, it is truly my desire
152   That you conduct yourself properly,
And that nothing ever be said
Of this situation, great or small.
Do not beseech me any longer.
156   Be satisfied, I beg you,
For if, because of your malady,
You have come here seeking a healer,
I promise you that, upon my life,
160   I don't intend to cure you or anyone else,

XVII.

At least of anything which involves me
Dishonourably in any way.
And so I will never open my mouth,

164   Pour amour ne pour mal talent,
             Que puisse a mon essient
             Pour rien qui soit vous accorder.
             Je suis ou je veul demourer;
168   J'ay affayre a qui bien me plaist.
             Prenés en gré le reffuser.
             Ce poyse moy, s'il vous desplaist,

XVIII.
             Car chose en vous, ne scay pour quoy,
172   Qui ne soit bonne et gracieuse.
             Et si vous jure, par ma foy,
             Se je vouloye estre amoureuse,
             Je seroye bien envyeuse
176   Que vous me voulsissiés amer
             [Et vostre amie reclamer],*
             Hors du parler des mesdisans.
             Maiz ce me pourroit trop grever
180   De les en faire voir-disans.

Poem 2

                    [L'Amoureux]
XIX.
             Hellas! ma dame et ma maistresse,
             Puis que vostre plaisant jonesse
             M'a mis en tel point que je suis,
184   Hors de toute joye et liesse,
             Pour moy donner deul et tristesse
             Si largement que je ne puis
             Avoir bons jours ne bonnes nuys,
188   Ne vivre fors en desplaisance,
             Et si n'est pas en ma puissance
             Que une heure puisse repposer,
             N'avoir ailleurs nulle esperance
192   D'avoir de mon mal allegance,
             Veuilliés moy garison donner!

XX.
             Qu[e] s'il ne vous plaist moy garir   198^r
             Et mon grief mal faire fenir

164   Out of love or evil intent,
           To say anything, knowingly or for any reason,
           Which would grant you my favours.
           I am where I wish to remain;
168   I am with someone who truly pleases me.
           Accept this refusal graciously.
           I am saddened, if this displeases you,

XVIII.

           For there is something in you, I do not know why,
172   Which seems good and courteous.
           And so I swear to you, by my troth,
           If I wanted to fall in love,
           I would long for you
176   To want to love me,
           And to claim me as your beloved,
           Far from the prattle of gossipmongers.
           But this would grieve me too much
180   To turn them into truth-tellers.

Poem 2

           [The Lover]

XIX.

           Alas! My lady and my mistress,
           Since your delightful youth
           Has put me into the state where I find myself,
184   Beyond all joy and happiness,
           Giving me grief and sadness
           So great that I cannot
           Have good days or good nights,
188   Nor live except in displeasure,
           And since it is not in my power
           To find any repose, even for one hour,
           Nor to have any hope at all
192   Of having a respite from my pain,
           Please, give me a cure!

XX.

           But if it does not please you to heal me
           And to bring an end to my grievous pain

196   Pour vostre beaulté amoureuse,
            Je vous jure et sans mentir
            Qu'il me convendra brief mourir
            Se vous n'estes de moy piteuse.
200   Par une doulceur savoureuse
            Qui me tient dont j'ay grant merveille,
            Car quant je me reppose ou veille,
            Desir de plus en plus m'assault,
204   Et Esperance me conseille
            Et dist que Pitié s'apareille
            Pour moy donner ce qui me fault.

XXI.
            Maiz je ne sçay quant ce sera,
208   Ne se vostre doulchour vouldra
            Entendre mes piteux reclaims.
            Je cuyde bien qu'il te fauldra,
            Selon ce que je voy desja,
212   Croistre dor en avant mes plains
            Et mes souppirs, dont je me plains,
            De la durté qui me fait plaindre,
            Souppirer et gemir et taindre.
216   Et si ne faictes nul semblant
            De ma doullour voulloir estaindre,
            Ne vostre voulenté reffraindre,
            Dont je languis en vous servant.

            [La Dame]
XXII.
220   S'ainsy est que vo cueur se deulle
            Et que bien largement recueulle
            Du desplaisir, qu'en puis je maiz?
            Est il donc force que je veulle
224   Vous allegier et que je acqueulle
            En mon cueur vos piteux [regretz]?*
            Par moy ne sont pensés ne [faiz],*
            Combien que assés vous m'ayés dist,
228   Que quant vous estes en vo lit
            Vostre cueur tressault tant est fade.
            Maiz je cuyde bien qu'il se rit,
            Ou, s'il a mal, il est petit,

198ᵛ

196   Through your loving beauty,
I swear to you, truthfully,
That it will suit me to die soon
If you are not merciful toward me.
200   With a delectable sweetness
Which captivates and dazzles me,
Whether I am at rest or awake,
Desire assaults me, over and over,
204   While Hope counsels me
And says that Pity makes ready
To give me what I need.

XXI.

    But I do not know when this will be,
208   Nor if your sweetness will agree
To hear my piteous suit.
I truly believe that you should,
Based on what I see thus far,
212   Strip my pleas, from this point forward,
And my sighs, which I deplore,
Of the harshness which causes me to complain,
To sigh and moan and grow pale.
216   And yet you don't seem to want
To alleviate my suffering,
Nor to restrain your will,
Which makes me languish, while still serving you.

    [The Lady]

XXII.
220   If it is the case, that your heart grieves
And is filled with despair,
What can I do about it?
Must I, therefore, choose
224   To soothe you and gather
Your pitiful complaints into my heart?
None of these were thought or done by me,
Regardless of the number of times you have told me all about them,
228   As when you are in your bed
And your heart trembles so much that it grows weak.
But I truly believe that it is really just laughing at itself,
Or, if it is in pain, it is slight,

232   Car vous n'estes pas si malade.

XXIII.

Que languissiés en me servant —
Ne me servés en languissant,
Il ne se pourroit pas bien faire.
236   Car oncques jour de mon vivant
Je ne vous monstray nul semblant,
Ne chose ne fiz, pour vous plaire.
Aussy suis je de rude affaire,
240   Poy sachant et mal amoureuse,
Et de moy garder envyeuse.
Cuyde chacun ce qu'il vouldra
S'on dist que je suis desdaigneuse
244   Ou que je soye poy piteuse
De vous ou d'aultre, on le verra.

XXIV.

Au bien fait doibt estre l'onneur
Et la largesse est au donneur,
248   Je l'ay aultre foyz ouÿ dire.
Je n'ay a nul homme faveur,
Ne pour amour ne pour cremeur.
Tienge soy qui vouldra de rire.
252   Ne je n'ay pas vouloir d'eslire
Servant a qui face largesse
Des biens qui viennent de noblesse.
Femme ne doibt pas estre large
256   Ne subjecte ou elle est maistresse.
Et qui la poursuit de promesse
Face de loyaulté sa targe.

[L'Amoureux]
XXV.

Est ce donques vostre vouloir   199^r
260   De faire ainsy tousjours douloir?
Mon cueur a amer loyaulment
Sans que je puisse appercevoir
Ung seul confort ne recepvoir
264   De vostre gracieux corps gent.
Puis qu'il vous plaist, j'en suis comptent.

232   For you are really not that sick.

XXIII.

That you were languishing while serving me –
Well, don't serve me while languishing,
It should be possible to not do.
236   For never once in my life
Did I give you a sign,
Neither thing nor deed, to try to please you.
So, I am in a difficult situation,
240   For I am naïve and inexperienced in love,
And only want to protect myself.
Let others believe what they want;
If someone says that I am disdainful
244   Or that I am pitiless
Toward you or anyone else, so be it.

XXIV.

Honour must be found in good deeds
And generosity in the giver,
248   I once heard it said.
I have no inclination toward any man,
Neither out of love nor fear.
No one should find that laughable.
252   And I have no desire to choose
A servant to whom I will be generous
With the rewards that come from privilege.
A woman must not be generous,
256   Nor subject where she is mistress.
And whoever pursues her with promises
Must make loyalty his shield.

[The Lover]

XXV.

Is it therefore your desire
260   To still cause suffering in this way?
My heart has to love loyally
Without my being able to feel
Or to receive a single comfort
264   From your gracious, noble body.
Since it pleases you, I am content with that.

Faictes en vostre voulenté,
Car j'ayme mieulx de vostre gré
268   Mourir que pour une aultre vivre.
Quant je n'ay de mon mal santé
N'estre je ne puis conforté,
J'ayme mieulx en estre delivre.

XXVI.
272   Car puis que Pitié ne consent,
Et que Francyse ne s'absent
Que vostre doulceur me sequeure,
Il me vault mieulx tout de present
276   Mourir qu'atendre longuement,
Quant je n'ay bon jour ne bonne heure.
Ne l'ardant desir qui demeure
En mon cueur ne peust estre estaint,
280   Tant est de vostre amour actaint.
Belle, veulliés y prendre garde
Et regarder bien s'il se faint,
Car il a dedens luy en paint
284   Vo semblant que tousjours regarde.

XXVII.
Et si grant doubte ay de faillir,
Que souvent me font tressaillir,
Amours qui me livre l'assault
288   Et qui me viennent assaillir
[Si fort que ne m'en puis saillir]*
Ne moy deffendre ains en soursault.
Ung souvenir de mon cueur sault
292   Qui me dist que je garde bien
L'onneur de vous et que pour rien
Je ne desceuvre mon entente.
Et Espoir me redist: « Cha! Viens,
296   Serfz tousjours et loyal te tien
Affin que Grace te comtempte. »

199ᵛ

[La Dame]
XXVIII.
Se bien loyaulment vous servés
Ou bien secrectement amés,

Do as you wish,
For I prefer, if you so desire,
268   To die rather than to live for another.
Since I have no relief for my pain
And I cannot be comforted,
I prefer to be delivered from it.

XXVI.

272   For, since Pity does not consent,
And Nobility does not allow
Your sweetness to comfort me,
It is better for me, at present,
276   To die rather than spend a long time waiting,
When I have neither a good day nor a good hour.
And the burning desire that resides
In my heart cannot be extinguished,
280   So much is it brimming with love for you.
Beautiful lady, please pay heed
And judge whether it dissembles,
For imprinted inside it is your image,
284   Which I gaze at constantly.

XXVII.

And I am so afraid of failing,
That Love often makes me tremble,
As it is he who launches this assault on me
288   And who comes to attack me
So forcibly that I cannot withstand him,
Nor can I defend myself except by trying to dodge him.
One thought bursts from my heart
292   Reminding me that I must safeguard
Your honour and that under no circumstances
Should I reveal my intent.
And Hope urges me on, saying: 'Here! Come,
296   Serve faithfully and remain loyal
So that Grace will comfort you.'

[The Lady]

XXVIII.

Whether you serve very loyally
Or love very discreetly,

300   Je n'en ay pas grantment affaire.
        Ne se bien en gré vous prenés
        Ou a mal ce que vous avés,
        Il ne me plaist ne doibt desplaire,
304   Car je n'ay pas pris a parfaire
        Ce qu'il fault de vostre pensee,
        Ne je n'en seray ja blasmee
        Pour nul homme qui n'aura tort.
308   Quelle que soit la renommee,
        Je seray loyalle trouvee
        Puis que mon cueur en est d'accord.

XXIX.

        Et parle qui parler vouldra,
312   Car ja nul ne se vantera
        A droit de moy, de nulle chose,
        Ne ja parolle n'en dira.
        Que quant ung noble cueur l'orra,
316   Qu'il ne die qu'elle est enclose
        En honneur, ou mon cueur reppose,
        Que j'ayme et tousjours aymeray;
        Ne oncques ne fus ne ne seray
320   Sans avoir en moy telle tache.
        Mon fait en ce point conduyray,
        Se Dieu plaist, tant que je vivray.
        Je veul bien que chacun le sache.

XXX.*

324   Ne je ne pense faire chiere   200^r
        Trop pesante ne trop legiere,
        Pour vous ne pour aultre qui soit.
        Je suis saine, nette et entiere.
328   Et s'en regardant ma maniere
        Vostre voulenté vous dechoit
        Et vostre cueur ne l'aperchoit,
        Je ne l'ay pas a comparer.
332   C'est folie a vous de muser
        Ne de me compter vos clamours,
        Car vous ne pouez n'en gaignier,
        A moy dire vostre penser
336   N'a moy requerir par amours.

300   This is really not my concern.
        And whether you accept graciously
        Or poorly what you have,
        It does not please me nor must it displease me,
304   For I have chosen to withhold
        What you think that you need,
        And I will never be blamed for that,
        Not for any man, even one who won't be seen as wrong.
308   Regardless of the reputation I gain,
        I will be found to be loyal
        Since my heart is in agreement.

XXIX.

        And let him speak who wishes to speak,
312   For no one will ever have just cause to boast
        About me, for any reason.
        And not a single word will be said about this.
        But should a man of noble heart hear of my reputation,
316   May he say only that it is enshrined
        In honour, in the place that I love and will always love,
        Where my heart finds repose.
        And never was I, nor will I ever be,
320   Without such a mark of honour inside of me.
        I will conduct myself in this way,
        If it pleases God, as long as I live.
        I want everyone to know this.

XXX.

324   And I do not make a point to look
        Either too dour or too cheery,
        For you or for anyone else.
        I am healthy, pure and whole.
328   And if, when you observe my manner,
        Your will plummets
        And your heart does not notice,
        This means nothing to me.
332   It is folly for you to waste your time
        Reciting your complaints to me,
        For you can gain nothing from this,
        Telling me all your thoughts
336   And pursuing me out of love.

[L'Amoureux]

XXXI.

Est ce droit que, pour bien amer
Et pour longuement endurer
Des doulleurs et des maulx foyson,
340   Vostre beaulté qui est sans per
Et vostre gracieux viz cler
Me face perdre ma sayson?
Je croy que ce n'est pas rayson.
344   Maiz Amours, qui [scet] la querelle[*]
De mon desir et de vous, belle,
Et qui scet combien je vous ayme,
Me veulle faire droit de celle
348   Qu'a tort je treuve ainsy rebelle.
Pour qui juge je le reclame,

XXXII.

Car il scet que tousjours endure
Une douleur qui est si dure.
352   Et que j'ay tousjours enduré
La paine, l'ennuy, et l'ardure
Qui asprement en mon cueur dure.
Et longuement y a duré,
356   Par ce que je suis aduré,
En desplaisir et en tristesse   200[v]
Par vous, ma dame et ma maistresse,
Ma chierté, mon bien, mon confort.
360   Se vous ne faictes que brief cesse
Ma tresdoulereuse destresse,
Je n'actens riens plus que la mort.

XXXIII.

Si sera pour vous ung beau fait
364   Quant vous arés ainsy deffait
Celuy qui vous a tant amee
Et quant rien ne vous a meffait,
Maiz ferme et sans nul forfait
368   De cueur, de corps, [et] de pensee,[*]
Tant que ma tristesse est doublee,
Ne garison ne scay trouver.
Amours, veulliés moy conforter.

[The Lover]

XXXI.

Is it fair, for having loved so well
And for having endured so long
The suffering and such a multitude of pains,
340   That your beauty, which is without equal,
And your gracious and lovely face,
Make me lose so much of this time in my life?
I believe that it is not right.
344   But Love, who is aware of the quarrel
Between my desire and you, beautiful lady,
And who knows how much I love you,
Wants me to do right by you
348   Who I find so unjustly contrary.
Thus I call upon him to be the judge,

XXXII.

For he knows that I constantly endure
Suffering that is so severe,
352   And that I have always endured
The pain, the anguish, and the ardour
That bitterly remain in my heart.
And this has gone on for a very long time,
356   Because I am hardened,
Both in displeasure and in sadness
Caused by you, my lady and my mistress,
My beloved, my well-being, my comfort.
360   If you grant only a short reprieve
Of my most painful distress,
Then I will await nothing more than death.

XXXIII.

This will be a sweet victory for you,
364   Defeating in this way
One who has loved you so
And has done nothing to wrong you,
But has remained steadfast, without a single offence
368   Of heart, of body, or of thought,
So much so that my sadness is doubled,
And I know not how to find a cure.
Love, please comfort me.

372 Regardés mon cueur, qui se pasme,
 Qui est tout fin prest de finer
 Et de mourir de deul amer
 Par vous et vous aymer, ma dame.

  [La Dame]

XXXIV.
376 N'a a pour quoy dictes vous, amys,
 Que par moy il vous est de piz
 Et qu'en perdés vostre sayson?
 Car onques mal je ne vous fiz,
380 En fait, n'en pensee, n'en diz,
 Ne je n'en eu entencion.
 Maiz se vostre condiction
 Est d'amer si legierement,
384 Sans avoir nul commencement,
 Je ose bien dire, devant tous,
 Que s'il vous vient soubdainement
 Du desplaisir bien largement,
388 Vous n'en devriez blasmer que vous.

XXXV.
 Je suis franche, de tous exempte   201ʳ
 Fors que d'un, et si est m'entente
 De acquerir bonne renommee.
392 Je ne veul que nul ait actente
 Que par moy ne pour mon fait sente
 Bien ne mal; j'en suis advisee.
 Je y ay ma voulenté fermee
396 Et mon cueur en est bien contempt.
 Si n'est ce pas par mal talent
 Que j'aye a vous, je le vous jure,
 Ne pour vous haÿr nullement.
400 Et aussy le mal est neant
 Car pas longuement il ne dure,

XXXVI.
 Ne onques je n'en vys nul mourir
 Par deffaulte de secourir.
404 Tant eust desplaisance haultaine,
 Ne point de si fort a garir

372 Look upon my heart, which grows weak
   And is on the point of succumbing
   And dying of bitter grief,
   Due to you and to loving you, my lady.

    [The Lady]

XXXIV.
376 And why do you say, friend,
   That because of me your condition has worsened
   And that you have lost this time of your life?
   For I have done you no harm,
380 Not in action, nor in thought, nor in speech,
   And I had no such intention.
   But if your manner
   Is to love so casually,
384 Without any foundation,
   I dare to say, in front of everyone,
   That if you suddenly experience
   A great deal of displeasure,
388 You have only yourself to blame.

XXXV.
   I am free, subject to only one,
   And it is my intention
   To assure myself of a good reputation.
392 I do not want anyone else to decide
   That I feel, for myself or for whatever I may do,
   Good or ill; I have given this much thought.
   My mind is made up
396 And my heart is very comfortable with it.
   So it is not out of malice
   That I turn you down, I swear to you,
   Nor do I hate you.
400 And also, pain is nothing
   For it does not last long,

XXXVI.
   And I have yet to see anyone die
   From lack of succour.
404 Many have had intense displeasure,
   But nothing so hard to cure

Que on ne feist bien resjouÿr
Et avoir santé toute plaine.
408   Ce n'est que ung poy de plaisant paine
Que Amours aucune foys envoye.
Maiz, quant a moy, je ne sauroye.
Aussy avés vous aultre amye
412   Qui bien vos peust remectre en joye,
Cent foyz mieulx que je ne feroye
Et oster vostre maladie.

Explicit

The title of this poem appears in all but one manuscript or printed edition as 'D'un amoureux parlant a sa dame par amours' [On a Lover Speaking to his Lady out of Love]. In the base manuscript, Paris, BnF, MS f. fr. 1131, this title appears at the start of the poem, but is written in a modern hand. The title used in scholarship related to this poem, however, is 'Dialogue d'amoureux et de sa dame' [Dialogue between a Lover and his Lady], which is only found in André Du Chesne's 1617 edition of Alain Chartier's works. Nevertheless, this is the title used here to conform to modern usage.

19 m. jour nul s.; *Pa is the sole witness to* tour ne; *all others follow Pc.*

28 m. ou ou q. (+1).

37 *This line is missing in the base manuscript; the reading is taken from Pa, Xa, and Xd.*

57 (-1) ja *appears in Pa, Qp, Xa, and Xd, and corrects the hypometric line in Pc.*

94 *This line is missing in base manuscript Pc; the reading is from Pa, Qp, Xa, and Xd.*

95 *A space is left after this line in Pc, presumably for a missing line, but line 94 was missing.*

136 (-1) *Pa and the incunabula read* a ma mort, *which repairs the hypometric line in Pc.*

137 *Editorial emendation.*

177 *This line is missing in the base manuscript; the reading is taken from Pa, Qp, Xa, and Xd.*

225 v. p. reffrains; *the reading of* regretz *from Pa and the others corrects the rhyme.*

226 p. n. stains; *the corrected reading is found in all other witnesses and maintains the rhyme.*

289 *This line is missing in the base manuscript Pc; the reading is taken from Pa, Po, Qp, Xa, and Xd.*

That one doesn't rejoice
And return fully to good health.
408   It is only a little bit of pleasant pain
That Love sometimes sends our way.
But, as for me, I would not know about that.
Therefore, you should find another ladylove
412   Who can make you happy again,
One hundred times better than I could,
And put an end to your malady.

The End

Stanza XXX *This stanza is missing in all witnesses except Pc.*
344 q. soit l.; scet *is found in the other manuscripts.*
368 (-1) *Without* et, *which appears in all other witnesses, this line is hypometric in Pc.*

VARIANT READINGS

La Belle Dame qui eust mercy

Title : Comment lamoureux deprie la dame et est fort repugnant a la belle dame sans mercy selon maistre Alain *Pa*; [...]a belle dame ou a mercy *Pb*; La belle dame a mercy *Pd*; Complainte damours et response faicte par maistre Alain Charretier secretaire du Roy *Pe*; Le Traittié de la belle dame a mercy *Pf*; Apres sensuit la dame a mercy *Pj*; Complainte damant a amye *Pk*; *title missing Pl, Po, Qb*; Cy ensuit ung traittie en maniere de prieres en amours *Pp*; Cy sensuit une complainte damours que lon dit autrement la Belle dame a mercy faicte par maistre Alain Charretier *Qa*; Complainte *Qd*; Cy commence la belle dame a mercy *Qh*; La Belle Dame ou mercy *Qn*; Comment lamoureux deprie sa [...]me et est fort repugnant [...]elle Dame sans mercy [...]lon maistre alain.chartier *Qp*; La Belle Dame ou a mercy *Qq*; Balade *Qr*; Cy commence le .x. livre, [...] omment lamoureux deprie sa dame et est fort repugnant a la belle dame sans mercy selon maistre alain *Xa*; Complainte d'amours et response *Xd*; Cy commance la complainte dung amoreux et la repsonce [sic] de la dame *Xe*

Stanza I

Rubric: Le dixieme livre *Pa*; Lamant parle *Pf, Pj*; Lamant *Po, Qb*; Le x. livre *Qp* — 1–112 *(Stanzas I-XIV) lines missing Qx* — 1 B. qui b. *Pa, Pb, Pe, Pf, Pj, Pk, Pl, Pp, Qb, Qh, Qn, Qr, Xa, Xe*; [...]elle qui b. *Qp*; *line missing Qq* — 2 Fait s. des bons a. *Pa, Pk, Qp, Xa*; Fait s. des vous a. *Pb, Qh, Qq*; Fait s. d. *Pd, Pl, Po, Qa, Qn, Xe*; Sont s. d. t. appellez *Pf, Pj*; d. t. apparler *Qb*; F. de tous saiges a. *Qr* — 3 d. en b. *Pd*; a *missing Qa*; [...] v. v. p. *Qp* — 4 q. ne vous p. *Pa, Pb, Pk, Qd, Qh, Qq, Xa*; plus *missing Pl*; [...] n. vous p. *Qp* — 5 [...] m. t. *Qp* — 6 m. des deux m. *Pe*; d. beaulx m. *Pp*; [...] m. d. *Qp*; d. tresbeaulx m. *Qr*; N. de gracieulx m. hante *Xe* — 7 g. s. retarder *Qa*; [...]ez e. g. *Qp*; Pour dieu ne vueillez r. *Xe* — 8 Si non ma b. v. *Pb, Qh, Qq*; F. que l. *Pe*; F. qua l. *Pf, Pj*; F. qua la seule v. *Qa*; a ma b. *Qb*; [...] l. b. *Qp*

Stanza II

9–12 *lines missing Pa, Xa*; 9–16 *lines missing Qp*; *lines contained in square brackets, with marginal note* Adiouste du Ms. *(likely Pe) Xd* — 9 Vueillez m. o. *Pb, Pd, Pf, Pj, Pl, Pp, Qd, Qq, Xd, Xe*; m. o. doulcement *Pk* — 10 E. de vostre grace mentendre *Pd*; p. vostre c. *Pl, Qn*; p. vostre douleur e. *Po* — 11 Et m. g. *Pb, Qh*; Si m. g. *Pd, Po, Qa, Qb, Qd, Qq, Qr, Xd, Xe*; Si mallegaes g. *Qn* — 12 en

missing *Pl*, *Qn*; S. ce q. *Qa*, *Qn* — 14 Vers vous ne vueil ne ja nadviengne *Pb*,
Pd, *Pe*, *Pf*, *Pj*, *Pk*, *Pl*, *Po*, *Qa*, *Qb*, *Qd*, *Qh*, *Qn*, *Xa*, *Xd*, *Xe*; Vers vous ne vueil j.
n. *Pp*; Vers vous ne ja m. *Qq*; Vers vous ne vueil ja m. *Qr* — 15 v. elle f. *Pd*, *Qh*;
Quenvers c. f. *Pe*, *Qa*, *Qb*, *Xd* — 16 t. mon bien v. *Pb*, *Pe*, *Pk*, *Pl*, *Po*, *Pp*, *Qb*, *Qd*,
Qh, *Qn*, *Qq*, *Qr*, *Xa*, *Xd*

Stanza III

17 T. chierement v. *Pa*, *Pb*, *Pd*, *Pe*, *Pk*, *Pl*, *Po*, *Qa*, *Qb*, *Qd*, *Qh*, *Qn*, *Qq*, *Xa*, *Xd*, *Xe*;
[…]esfoiz cherement je v. p. *Qp* — 18 q. sachiez comment mespris *Pb*; q. sachiez
c. *Pf*, *Pj*, *Po*, *Pp*, *Qa*, *Qb*, *Qd*; il missing *Qa*, *Qh*, *Xe*; s. comment m. *Qh*, *Xe*; […]
q. s. *Qp*; s. comment i. *Qq* — 19 m. complainte a. *Pe*, *Qa*; […]d m. r. *Qp* — 20
t. pas m. *Pd*, *Qr*; […]z pas m. a. *Qp* — 21 j. fait trop hault e. *Pa*, *Pb*, *Pk*, *Qp*, *Xa*;
j. si h. *Pe*, *Po*, *Qa*, *Xd*; fait missing *Pf*, *Pj*, *Qr* — 22 Me p. c. *Pa*, *Pk*, *Qp*; Vueillez
p. c. *Pb*; Mais m. p. *Pe*, *Qa*, *Qb*, *Xd*; Pardonnez moy c. p. mon a. *Pf*, *Pj*; Vueillez
moy p. c. *Pl*, *Po*; Vueillez moy p. p. m. *Qd*, *Qn*, *Xe*; Vueillez pardonner c. p. *Qh*,
Qq; A. que m. *Qr*; Me p. c. p. mon a. *Xa* — 23 f. lamour dont suis e. *Pb*, *Qh*, *Qq*;
q. m. apris *Pe*; C. a f. *Pp*; q. a e. *Qr* — 24 Tout vient de la s. *Pa*, *Pk*, *Qa*, *Qp*, *Xa*;
Tout vient de l. s. *Pb*, *Pd*, *Pe*, *Pf*, *Pl*, *Po*, *Qb*, *Qd*, *Qh*, *Qn*, *Xd*, *Xe*; Tout vient de l.
si s. *Pj* — Rubric at the end of stanza La dame *Qb*

Stanza IV

Rubric : La dame respond *Pa*, *Qp*; La dame *Pb*, *Pd*, *Pf*, *Pj*, *Po*, *Pp*, *Qa*, *Qb*, *Qq*,
Xe; Responce *Pe*, *Qd*, *Xd*; Response l'amye *Pk*; Responce de la dame *Qr*; La dame
luy respond *Xa* — 25 Les grans loz q. vous m. d. *Pa*, *Pb*, *Pd*, *Pe*, *Pk*, *Pl*, *Po*, *Qa*,
Qb, *Qd*, *Qh*, *Qn*, *Qp*, *Qq*, *Xa*, *Xd*, *Xe*; Des granz los q. vous m. *Pf*, *Pj* — 26 Sire
viennent d. v. *Pa*, *Pb*, *Pd*, *Pe*, *Pk*, *Pl*, *Po*, *Qa*, *Qb*, *Qd*, *Qh*, *Qn*, *Qp*, *Qq*, *Xa*, *Xd*;
Qui viennent d. v. *Pf*, *Pj*; Si vous viennent d. v. *Xe* — 27 Qui l. m. *Pa*, *Pk*, *Qp*,
Xa — 28 a. gueres d. *Pa*, *Pk*, *Po*, *Qp*, *Xa*, *Xd*; q. p. de bien *Pf*, *Pj*, *Pl*, *Pp*, *Qn*; a.
ung p. *Pb*; a. ung p. de bien *Qb*; a. ung pou de ^du mien^ bien *Qh*; S. ce q. y a. rien
d. *Qq* — 30 M. q. n. scay ou p. *Pa*, *Pb*, *Pd*, *Pe*, *Pk*, *Pl*, *Po*, *Qa*, *Qb*, *Qd*, *Qh*, *Qn*,
Qp, *Qq*, *Xa*, *Xd*; M. que dire n. scay ou p. *Pf*, *Pj*; M. q. n. soy nc p. *Xe* — 31 Et t.
m. naffierent d. *Pa*, *Pk*, *Qp*, *Xa*, *Xd*; m. naffierent d. *Pb*, *Pd*, *Pf*, *Pj*, *Pl*, *Qb*, *Qd*,
Qh, *Qn*, *Qq*, *Xe*; m. naffieray en r. *Pe*; m. affierent a r. *Qa*; m. naffierent en r.
Qr — 32 n. comme j. *Pa*, *Pb*, *Pd*, *Pe*, *Pk*, *Pl*, *Qa*, *Qb*, *Qh*, *Qn*, *Qp*, *Qq*, *Qr*, *Xa*, *Xe*;
A ainsi n. comme j. *Pf*, *Pj*

Stanza V

33 vous missing *Pl*, *Qn*; v. navez a d. *Qa* — 34 b. ou a h. *Pa*, *Pd*, *Pe*, *Pl*, *Po*, *Qa*,
Qb, *Qd*, *Qp*, *Xa*, *Xd*, *Xe*; b. et h. me t. *Pf*, *Pj*, *Pp*; b. ou h. *Pk*, *Qh*, *Qn* — 35 Ce
autrement je ne s. *Pa*; Si quautrement je ne s. *Pb*; Ce quautrement je ne s. *Pd*, *Pe*,
Pk, *Pl*, *Po*, *Qa*, *Qb*, *Qd*, *Qh*, *Qn*, *Qp*, *Qq*, *Qr*, *Xa*, *Xd*, *Xe*; Comme aultrement j.

n. *Pf, Pj* — 36 d. v. douche *Pp*; d. v. toute *Xe* — 37 v. voy s. *Pa, Pk, Qp, Xa*; v. sens s. *Pb, Pe, Qh, Xd, Xe*; v. scay s. *Qa, Qb, Qd, Qq, Qr* — 38 nay/ne *missing*, s. treshaulte n. *Pb, Pe, Pf, Pj, Qa, Qh, Qq, Xd*; n. d. telle gentillesse *Xe* — 39 Q. nystra ja d. *Pl, Qn, Xe* — 40 Chose q. l. *Pa, Pb, Pk, Pp, Qb, Qh, Qp, Qq, Xa*; m. que honneur d. *Qa*; Chose qui honneur d. b. *Qd*; q. dautruy lonneur b. *Qr*

Stanza VI

42 v. seule e. *Pf, Pj*; v. clere e. *Qa*; n. scay pas v. *Qr* — 43 j. p. enpensee *Po, Qa* — 44 Sotte et dentendre m. a. *Pa, Pd, Pf, Pj, Pk, Pl, Po, Qb, Qd, Qn, Qp, Xa, Xd*; Sotte et de tendre a. *Pb, Qh, Qq*; Sotte dentendre m. a. *Pe*; Sotte dentendre et m. a. *Qa, Xe*; l. m. comprise *Qr* — 45 droit *missing Pa, Pb, Pf, Pj, Pk, Pl, Po, Qa, Qb, Qd, Qh, Qn, Qn, Qp, Qq, Xa, Xd, Xe*; h. bien c. *Pb, Pd, Pe, Pf, Pj, Pl, Po, Qb, Qd, Qh, Qn, Qq, Xd, Xe*; e. a h. *Pl*; h. bien aprinse *Po*; Mais celle e. e. *Qa*; d. h. emprise *Qr* — 46 Qui n. o. *Pb, Qh, Xe*; Et n. o. *Pe, Po, Qa, Qr, Xd, Xe*; Ne est o. n. *Qq* — 47 j. v. desprise *Pb, Pd, Pe, Pf, Pj, Pl, Pp, Qb, Qd, Qh, Qn, Qq, Qr, Xd, Xe*; Sans quautrement v. desprise *Po*; Lourray sans ce que v. desprise *Qa* — 48 s. ny a f. *Pb*; p. a m. — *Rubric at the end of stanza* Lamant *Qb*

Stanza VII

Rubric: Lamant *Pa, Pb, Pd, Pf, Pj, Pk, Po, Pp, Qb, Qq, Xe*; Complaincte *Pe, Qd, Xd*; Lamoureux *Qa*; Lamy attendant *Qp, Xa*; Lamant respond *Qr* — 49 De ce q. v. *Pa, Pb, Pd, Pe, Pf, Pj, Pk, Pl, Po, Qa, Qb, Qd, Qh, Qn, Qp, Qq, Xa, Xd, Xe* — 50 Vous mercy sachez que mes j. *Pa, Pd, Pe, Pk, Pl, Po, Qd, Qh, Qn, Qp, Qq, Xa, Xd, Xe*; Vous mercy sachiez que mes j. *Pb, Pf, Pj, Qa, Qb*; S. que v. *Pp, Qr* — 51 Vueil user a vous redoubter *Pa, Pb, Pd, Pe, Pf, Pj, Pk, Pl, Po, Qa, Qb, Qd, Qh, Qn, Qp, Qq, Xa, Xd, Xe* — 52 Comme ma princesse en amours *Pa, Pb, Pk, Pl, Po, Qa, Qb, Qd, Qh, Qn, Qp, Qq, Xa, Xd, Xe*; Comme a ma princesse en amours *Pd*; Comme y ma princesse en amours *Pe*; Comme ma maistresse en amours *Pf, Pj*; Comme en ma princesse en amours *Po*; q. jen ay d. *Pp*; q. je yay d. *Qr* — 53 Mais tous m. p. *Pa, Pb, Pd, Pf, Pj, Pk, Pl, Po, Qa, Qb, Qd, Qh, Qn, Qp, Qq, Xa, Xd, Xe*; Maiz tous mes plains s. bien c. *Pe* — 54 S. vostre b. q. c. *Pa, Pe, Pf, Pj, Pk, Pl, Po, Qa, Qb, Qd, Qn, Qp, Xa, Xd, Xe*; v. loyaulte q. c. *Pb, Qh*; S. vostre b. q. constraint *Pd*; q. vous c. *Pp*; S. vostre loiaulte q. c. *Qq* — 55 Mon cueur a la servir tousjours *Pa, Pk, Qp, Xa, Xd*; Mon cueur a vous servir tousjours *Pb, Pf, Pj, Qb, Qh, Qq*; Mon cueur a vous aymer tousjours *Pd, Pe, Pl, Po, Qa, Qd, Qn, Xe* — 56 Nadoulcist mon cueur e. r. *Pa, Qp, Xa*; Nadoulcist mes maulx e. r. *Pb, Pd, Pf, Pj, Pl, Po, Qa, Qb, Qh, Qn, Qq, Xd, Xe*; Ma doulcist mes maulx e. restraint *Pe, Qd*; Madoulcist mon mal e. r. *Pk*; l. madoulcist e. *Qr*

Stanza VIII

58 e. loyal s. *Pf, Pj*; A v. h. et loyal s. *Pp* — 59 Vers vous me verrez maintenir *Pa,*

Pb, Pd, Pe, Pf, Pj, Pk, Pl, Po, Qa, Qb, Qd, Qh, Qn, Qp, Qq, Xa, Xd; Toujours m. verrez maintenir *Pp, Qr*; Vers vous me voyes maintenir *Xe* — 60 En lestat dun loyal a. *Pa, Pb, Pd, Pe, Pf, Pj, Pk, Pl, Po, Qa, Qb, Qd, Qh, Qn, Qp, Qq, Xa, Xd, Xe* — 62 Vivray preux courtois e. s. *Pa, Pb, Pd, Pk, Qd, Qp, Xa, Xd*; Vivray preuz c. e. *Pe, Qa, Qb, Qh, Qq*; Vivre j. c. *Pf, Pj*; Vivray piteux c. e. *Pl, Qn*; Vivray en paix c. e. *Po*; Vivray j. c. *Xe* — 63 b. amer f. *Pb, Qb, Qh, Qq* — 64 a. nul r. *Pa, Pb, Pe, Pf, Pj, Pk, Qa, Qh, Qp, Qq, Qr, Xa, Xd*; v. nen a. *Xe*

Stanza IX

66 n. scet d. *Pa, Pb, Pd, Pe, Pf, Pj, Pk, Pl, Po, Pp, Qd, Qh, Qn, Qp, Qq, Qr, Xa, Xd*; Mes que sa b. n. scet d. *Qa*; Plus que je ne sauroie d. *Qb*; q. ma b. n. soyt d. *Xe* — 67 d. jay p. *Pa, Pb, Pe, Pf, Pj, Pk, Qa, Qb, Qh, Qp, Qq, Xa, Xd*; d. a p. *Pd, Pl, Qd, Qn*; De d. d. a p. *Po*; Les d. d. jay p. *Pp*; De d. d. je p. *Qr*; Et d. d. a p. d. *Xe* — 68 Dont j. me c. l. *Pa*; j. me c. *Qp, Xa, Xd* — 69 m. vueillez e. *Pa, Pb, Pd, Pe, Pk, Pl, Pp, Qd, Qh, Qn, Qp, Qq, Qr, Xa, Xd, Xe* — 70 g. n. pourroye *Pe*; v. honneur ne me p. *Pf, Pj* — 71 F. mon cueur p. et r. *Pa, Pk, Qp, Xa* — 72 Qui pense a vous ou q. j. *Pa, Pk, Qp, Xa*; v. ou q. *Pb, Pd, Pe, Pl, Po, Qa, Qb, Qd, Qh, Qn, Qq, Xd*; v. ou que que j. *Xe* — *Rubric at the end of stanza* La dame *Qb*

Stanza X

Rubric: La dame *Pa, Pb, Pd, Pf, Pj, Po, Pp, Qa, Qb, Qp, Qq, Xa, Xe*; Lamie *Pk*; Responce *Pb, Qd, Xd* — 73 O m. r. *Pa* — 74 Perdez l. e. vostre p. *Pa, Pk, Qp, Xa*; Perdez e. l. *Pb, Qh, Qq*; P. l. e. p. *Pd*; P. vous et labour e. p. *Pe*; Vous p. l. *Pf, Pj*; P. vo l. e. *Pp*; Perdrez vous et labour e. p. *Qa, Xd*; Perderes e. l. *Qb* — 75 e. travaillez p. *Pa, Pb, Qn, Qp, Qq, Qr, Xd*; Et n. v. *Pl, Qd, Qn, Xe* — 76 p. neant s. *Pa, Qp, Xa, Xd*; e. cil q. p. neant s. *Pk*; q. p. aultruy s. *Qb* — 77 S. se t. *Qa*; e. sa d. *Qb* — 78 Oncques par moy ne v. a. *Pa, Pb, Pd, Pe, Pf, Pj, Pk, Pl, Po, Qa, Qb, Qd, Qh, Qn, Qp, Qq, Xa, Xd, Xe*; q. ce v. *Pp, Qr* — 79 Ceste vie plaisante mondaine *Pb, Qh*; u. p. mondaine *Pc, Pf, Pj, Qa, Qq, Qr, Xc*; u. pensce s. *Qb* — 80 Qui s. y. *Pa, Pd, Pe, Pk, Po, Pp, Qa, Qb, Qd, Qn, Qp, Qr, Xa, Xd, Xe*; Qui s. va ainsi quelle v. *Pb, Qh*; Qui s. ira dont e. *Pf, Pj*; Qui s. va c. *Pl*; s. va ce c. *Qq*; c. y v. *Qr*

Stanza XI

81 a. damer d. *Pa, Pb, Pd, Pe, Pf, Pj, Pk, Pl, Po, Qb, Qd, Qh, Qn, Qp, Qq, Qr, Xa, Xd, Xe* — 83 Autre amie p. choisir *Pa, Pd, Pe, Pf, Pj, Pk, Po, Qa, Qd, Qp, Xa, Xd*; Autre dame p. q. *Pb, Qh, Qq, Xe*; Autre amye pourrez choisir *Pl, Qn*; p. a. choisir *Pp, Qr*; Aultre dame p. choisir *Qb, Xe* — 84 Q. mieulx q. *Pb, Qh, Qq*; v. en a. *Pf, Pj* — 85 Si en ostez v. f. *Pa, Pb, Pd, Pe, Pk, Pl, Po, Qa, Qb, Qd, Qh, Qn, Qp, Qq, Qr, Xa, Xd, Xe*; Or en ostez v. f. *Pf, Pj* — 86 E. pensez dailleurs r. *Pa, Pb, Pd, Pe, Pk, Pl, Po, Qa, Qb, Qd, Qh, Qn, Qp, Qr, Xa, Xd, Xe*; E. pensez dailleurs requerir *Pf, Pj*; E. vueillez a. *Pp*; E. poures dailleurs r. *Qq* — 87 v. par v. *Pa, Pk, Qp, Xa*;

Ou j. v. *Pb, Qh, Qq* — 88 m. h. chairir *Pf, Pj*; Appert m. m. *Qa*

Stanza XII

89 a aporte *Xe* — 90 m. assez plus quoncques m. *Pa, Pb, Pd, Pe, Pf, Pj, Pk, Pl,
Po, Qa, Qb, Qd, Qh, Qn, Qp, Qr, Xa, Xd, Xe*; m. asses quoncques m. *Qq* — 91 d.
len c. *Pb, Pe, Qh, Qq*; e. len c. *Pp*; d. bien c. *Qa*; d. vous c. *Qr* — 92 Car a. q. *Pa,
Pk, Qd, Qp, Xa, Xd, Xe*; Puis quautre q. v. *Pf, Pj*; a. de v. *Qa*; Puys quautre de v.
Qr — 93 c. je p. q. v. ayais *Pa, Pd, Pk*; c. p. quait en vous t. *Pb*; Que vous aiez
si ne croy pas, *faulty rhyme Pf, Pj*; Je n. c. p. q. v. ayes *Po*; p. quen voz t. *Pp, Xe*;
Et s. n., q. voz t. *Qa*; p. quant en vous t. *Qh*; je *missing*, q. v. ayez *Qp, Xa, Xd*; je
missing, q. len v. *Qq*; je *missing*, q. v. trayais *Qr* — 94 De tant d. d. que v. d. *Pb,
Qh*; d. d. que v. me d. *Pe, Qa, Xd*; Ait tant douleurs c. v. *Pp*; d. grief douleur que
v. *Qq, Qr*; Ait tant d. d. que v. *Xe* — 95 e. plaignez j. *Pa, Pb, Pd, Pe, Po, Qn*; Quoy
que v. e. *Pf, Pj*; Si n. v. *Qr* — 96 c. quelles s. p. *Pa, Pb, Pe, Pk, Pl, Po, Qa, Qb, Qd,
Qh, Qn, Qp, Qq, Qr, Xa, Xd, Xe*; c. quelle s. *Pd*; Mais bien croy que bien s. p. *Pf,
Pj*; c. bien quilz s. *Pp* — *Rubric at the end of stanza* Lamant *Qb*

Stanza XIII

Rubric: Lamant *Pa, Pb, Pd, Pf, Pj, Po, Pp, Qb, Xe*; Lamy *Pk*; Complaincte *Pe,
Xd*; Lamoureux *Qa, Qp, Xa*; Lamant repplique *Qr* — 97 b. b. ~~trop~~ e. *Pe*; Celle
d. b., bien *missing Pk* — 98 a. b. exemplaire *Pb, Pl, Qh*; D. a. dames exemplaire
Xe — 99 V. simple ~~vostre simple~~ c. j. *Pe*; V. belle c. *Qa* — 100 F. m. c. a soy fort
a. *Pa, Pk, Xa*; F. a m. c. soy s. traire *Pb*; F. a m. c. soy s. a. *Pd, Pe*; A fait m. c. a
soy r. *Pf, Pj*; F. m. c. a soy s. a. *Pl, Po, Qb, Qd, Qn, Qq, Xd, Xe*; F. m. c. si a soy a.
Pp; M. c. f. a soy s. a. *Qa*; F. m. c. a soy s. traire *Qh*; Or f. m., a s. so[...] *Qp*; Scet
m. c. si a vous a. *Qr* — 101 Car j. v. *Pf, Pj, Xe*; a. s. retr[...] *Qp* — 102 p. p. foys
Po; l. celer p. *Qa*; p. p. m[...] *Qp*; l. telle p. *Xa* — 103 Et je m. p. *Pb, Qh*; p. quil
fault f. *Pf, Pj*; p. quil le fault f. *Pl, Qn, Xe*; S. je m. *Pp*; p. quil fault afaire *Qb, Qd*;
p. q. a [...] *Qp* — 104 M. faloit i. *Pp, Qr*; i. u. fo[...] *Qp*; Et je m. p. q. f. a faire *Qq*

Stanza XIV

105 a. ne me print *Pa, Pd, Pk, Po, Pp, Qd, Qq, Xa, Xe*; O. a. si ne me prinst *Pb, Pf,
Pj, Qh*; a. me m. *Pe*; a. ne me esprit *Qa*; a. n. [...] *Qp*; a. me m. *Qr* — 106 P. amer
d. *Pa, Pk, Qp, Xa, Xd*; P. dame ne pour d. *Pe, Qa*; d. o. damo[...] *Qp* — 107 Et
a m. g. *Pa, Pk, Qp, Xa, Xd*; Et a m. g. na pas mesprins *Po*; g. point n. *Qb*; p. n.
mespr[...] *Qp* — 108 i. me la f. *Po, Qn*; f. c. [...] *Qp*; f. c. belle *Xe* — 109 m. parler
d. *Pd*; d. ne belle *Pf, Pj*; p. d. nouve[...] *Qp* — 111 v. com a l. *Pk*; Que a v. c. *Qa*;
l. p. [...] *Qp* — 112 Sest m. c. *Pa, Qp, Xa, Xd*; Est m. c. *Pd, Pe, Pf, Pj, Pl, Po, Qa,
Qd, Qn*; Cest m. c. *Pk, Pp, Qr*; t. oultre d. *Po*; t. e. do[...] *Qp*

Stanza XV

113 Helas b. a *Pa, Pb, Pd, Pe, Pk, Pl, Qa, Qb, Qd, Qh, Qn, Qp, Qq, Qr, Xa, Xd, Xe*; je *missing Pb*; Helaz dame a. c. *Pf, Pj*; Ha ma dame a c. *Po*; q. j. vo[...] *Qp*; Ellas b. a *Qx* — 114 n. congnoissez q. *Pa, Pb, Pd, Pe, Pf, Pj, Pk, Pl, Po, Qa, Qn, Qp, Qq, Qr, Xd, Xe*; n. c. quamou[...] *Qp*; Que n. c. *Qx* — 115 s. bien que l. *Pb, Qh*; s. que j. *Pe, Pp*; Dieu le s. s. *Qa* — 116 je *missing*, n. tenes c. *Qa*; n. fay c. *Qb, Qq, Xe*; n. t. co[...] *Qp* — 117 J. de souspirer bien grant h. *Pa, Pb, Pd, Pe, Pk, Po, Qa, Qb, Qd, Qh, Qp, Qq, Xa, Xd*; J. de souppirer si grant h. *Pf, Pj, Xe*; J. de souspirer grant h. *Pl, Qn, Qx*; b. g. [...] *Qp* — 118 j. me treuve e. *Pb, Pe, Qa, Qh, Xd*; Que j. men trouble e. m. *Pl, Qn*; m. e. [...] *Qp*; j. me trouble e. *Qq*; j. suis en plusieurs l. *Qx*; Que men suis trouble e. m. *Xe* — 119 Qui m. p. *Pf, Pj*; p. que que j. *Qx* — 120 v. vouldrez j. *Pd, Pl, Po, Qa, Qd, Qn, Qr, Qx*; j. m. ~~Jauray mieulx~~ *Pe* — *Rubric at the end of stanza* La dame *Qb*

Stanza XVI

Rubric: La dame *Pa, Pb, Pd, Pf, Pj, Po, Pp, Qa, Qb, Qp, Xa, Xe*; Responce *Pe, Qd, Xd*; Lamie *Pk*; La dame repplique *Qr* — 121–36 *(Stanzas XVI–XVII) lines missing Qx* — 121 m. vous a. *Pd, Po, Qp, Xd*; m. ~~mon~~ m. *Pj*; S. vous avez mon maintien v. *Xe* — 123 y. v. aient d. *Pb, Qh, Qq*; y. v. v. y o. *Pd, Xe*; E. si v. *Qp, Xd* — 124 P. trop regarder m. *Qq* — 125 Le mal que vostre cueur endure *Pa, Pb, Pd, Pe, Pf, Pj, Pk, Pl, Po, Qa, Qb, Qd, Qh, Qn, Qp, Qq, Xa, Xd, Xe* — 126 Ne fait pas la vie abregier *Pa, Pb, Pd, Pe, Pf, Pj, Pk, Pl, Po, Qa, Qb, Qd, Qh, Qn, Qp, Qq, Xa, Xd, Xe*; Que point e. p. *Qr* — 127 m. v. endure *Pa*; Mais p. m. *Pb, Qh*; Mais p. maladie v. *Pf, Pj*; p. m. vie endure *Qp, Xa* — 128 m. point d. *Pa, Pk, Qp, Qr, Xa, Xd*; Que n. m. *Pb*; Qui n. m. *Qq*

Stanza XVII

129–36 *and* 137–44 *(Stanzas XVII and XVIII) inverted Pa, Pb, Pd, Pe, Pf, Pj, Pk, Pl, Po, Qa, Qb, Qd, Qh, Qn, Qp, Qq, Xa, Xd, Xe; variants from inversions like this are presented according to the line number from the base manuscript Pc* — 129 Mais j. ill., trop *missing Pa, Pb, Pd, Pe, Pf, Pj, Pk, Pl, Po, Qa, Qb, Qd, Qh, Qn, Qq, Xa, Xd, Xe*; [...]is j. m., trop *missing Qp*; Or me donneroie g. m. *Qx* — 130 Dont tant v. v. moy seurquerir *Pa, Pk, Xa*; Quant j. v. *Pb, Qd, Qh, Qn, Xe*; Q. tant v. v. moy requerir *Pe, Qa, Xd*; Quant j. v. v. t. acquerir *Pl, Qn*; [...] v. v. moy seurquerir *Qp* — 131 C. une dame a vous p. *Pa, Pb, Pd, Pe, Pf, Pj, Pk, Pl, Po, Qa, Qb, Qd, Qh, Qn, Qp, Qq, Qx, Xa, Xd, Xe* — 132 E. b. vous deussiez querir *Pa, Pk, Qp, Xa*; Deussiez en b. requerir *Pb, Qh*; b. deussiez a. *Pd*; E. b. deussies vous choisir *Pe, Qa*; E. tous biens deussiez a. *Pf, Pj*; E. b. deussiez requerir *Pl, Po, Qb, Qd, Qn, Qq, Qx, Xe*; [...]aulte vous deussiez querir *Qp*; b. pourriez a. *Qr*; E. b. deussiez vous querir *Xd* — 133 l. mie a q. *Pd, Pf, Pj, Pl, Qb, Qd, Qn, Qq, Xe*; En laquelle prinssies plaisir *Po*; [...] n. l. *Qp* — 134–35 *lines missing Pe* — 134 C.

chascun peut assez s. *Pa, Pb, Pd, Pf, Pj, Pk, Pl, Po, Qa, Qb, Qd, Qh, Qn, Qq, Qr, Qx, Xa, Xd, Xe*; [...] chascun peult assez s. *Qp* — 135 homs *missing Pa, Pb, Pk, Qa, Qh, Qr, Xa*; homs *missing*, s. bien r. *Pd, Pj, Po, Qb, Qh, Qp, Xd, Xe*; homs *missing*, s. beau r. *Pf, Pl, Qd, Qn, Qq, Qx*; s. bien r. *Pp*; [...] q. s. *Qp* — 136 b. dame a. *Pa, Pb, Qb, Qh, Qp, Xa, Xd*; N. mye s. b. dame a. *Pd*; Il n. p., belle *missing Pe, Qa, Qx*; [...] p. s. *Qp*

Stanza XVIII

137 q. v. vouldrez *Pb, Qh*; q. v. voudries *Qq* — 139 M. croiez ja m. c. naurez *Pb, Qh*; Ne j. n. *Po*; ja *missing Pp*; j. homme m., nulz *missing Qb, Xe*; M. certes ja m. c. naures *Qq* — 140 ja *missing*, a. je n. *Pf, Pj*; [...] j. p. *Qp* — 141 F. a u., je *missing Pk, Xa, Xe*; j. pour a. *Qa, Qh*; [...]s a u., je *missing Qp*; Si non a q. j. donray *Qq* — 142 c. a e. *Pl, Qn*; [...] f. c. *Qp* — 143 Ja s. d. p. vouloir nauray *Pa, Pb, Pd, Pe, Pf, Pj, Pk, Pl, Qa, Qb, Qd, Qh, Qn, Xa, Xd*; p. ja vouloir naray *Po*; [...] d. p. vouloir nauray *Qp*; Ja s. d. vouloir nauray *Qq*; Et s. d. p. vouloir nauray *Xe* — 144 De departir mon cueur par m. *Pa, Pb, Pd, Pf, Pj, Pl, Po, Qa, Qb, Qd, Qh, Qn, Qq, Xa, Xd*; De departir cuer parmy *Pe*; Tel comme s. f. *Pp*; [...]epartir mon cueur parmy *Qp*; Tel q. s. sera i. *Qr*; De mespartir mon cueur par m. *Xe* — *Explicit at bottom of page 343* Et ho *Po* — *Rubric at the end of stanza* Lamant *Qb, with duplication of rubric ending at stanza XVIII in Qb.*

Stanza XIX

Rubric: Lamant *Pa, Pb, Pd, Pf, Pj, Po, Pp, Qb, Xe*; Lamoureux *Qa, Qp, Xa*; Lamy *Pk*; Complainte *Pe, Qd, Xd* — 145 *Stanza XIX marks a shift from eight-line octosyllabic stanzas to thirteen-line octosyllabic stanzas. In manuscripts Pb, Pd, Po, Qa, Qb, and Qh, this stanza starts on a completely new folio, but the handwriting is unchanged into the new folio. In all other manuscript witnesses, this stanza flows quite unremarkably from the previous one.* Cueur d. d. s. r. *Pa, Pk, Xa, Xd*; Jeune gente s. et r. *Pb, Pf, Pj, Qh, Xe*; Jeune et gente s. r. *Pd*; Jeune gente s. r. *Pe, Qx*; s. et r. *Pl, Qn*; Jeune et gente demourant sur r. *Po*; Ma doulceur s. et r. *Pp*; Jeune gente sourdant reviere *Qa*; Joyne gente s. et r. *Qb*; Jeune et gente s. et r. *Qd*; [...]eur d. d. s. r. *Qp*; Jeune gente fresche et entiere *Qq*; Cuer de doulceur s. et r. *Qr* — 145–57 *Xe tries to maintain the eight-line stanzaïc format of the first part of the poem by adding three lines (145bis, 147bis, 152bis) to Stanza XIX's thirteen-line structure, making a total of sixteen lines, out of which are created two eight-line stanzas (Stanza XIX and a false XX), adding indentation at lines 151 and 158; Xe is also unique and curious in that, from Stanza XX to Stanza XXX, the thirteen-line stanzas are broken into two stanzas of six or seven lines, only presenting the full thirteen-line stanzas in the last exchange between the lover and the lady (Stanzas XXXI–XXXVI)* — 145–69 *Pf continues to present eight-line stanzas, only moving to thirteen-line stanzas at l. 170, thus creating 37 stanzas in total, rather than 36. It is also one of two manuscripts, with Pj, that presents an additional, thirty-eighth stanza, at the end (lines 379–88)* — 145bis Ou est tout delit et plaisir *Xe* — 146 [...]eur e. d.*Qp*; De doulceur e. d. plaisant c. *Xe* — 147 Q. fait e. *Pa, Pe, Pk, Xa, Xd*; Q. sont e. vo b. plainiere *Pb, Qh*; f. vostre b. *Pl, Qn*; Q. fait e. v. b. sourir *Qa*; [...] faict e. v. *Qp*; Q. sont en b. planiere *Qq*; f. en vous en vous b. *Qx*; v. si beau f. *Xe* — 147bis Checun savez entretenir *Xe* — 148 m. d. plainiere *Pb, Qh*; m. d. priere *Pk*; [...] e. m. *Qp*; m. joye p. *Qx* — 149 Qui mamour avez t. e. *Pa, Pb, Pd, Pe, Pk, Pl, Po, Qa, Qb, Qd, Qh, Qn, Qq, Qx, Xa, Xd, Xe*; Car mamour avez t. e. *Pf, Pj*; *line missing Pp*; [...]amour avez t. e. *Qp* — 150 et *missing Pb*; [...]int v. v. *Qp*; v. ou m. *Qx* — 151 n. me v. *Pe*; Las vous ne v. s. *Po* — 152bis Par vous il me faudra mourir *Xe* — 153 Faictes en donc a v. b. *Pb, Qh, Qq*; a v. bandon *Po*; a v. plaisir *Qb*; f. en v. *Qx* — 154-55 *lines inverted Pl, Xe, so rhyme is incorrect* — 154 Car je suis v. f. *Pa, Pb, Pd, Pe, Pf, Pj, Pk, Pl, Po, Qa, Qb, Qd, Qh, Qn, Qp, Qq, Xa, Xd*; Car il es v. f. *Qx*; Et si suis v. f. *Xe* — 155-57 *lines missing Pe* — 155 Jesperere vueillez o. n. *Pa*; Jay espoir vueillez vous o. n. *Pb, Qh*; J. vueillez o. *Pd, Pk, Po, Pp, Qd, Qn, Qp, Qx, Xa, Xd*; Jexploiterary v. o. *Pf, Pj*; Jay espoir vuilles o. n. *Qq*; Espoir auray vueilles o. n. *Qr*; Je attendray vueillez o. n. *Xe* — 156 Que vous naurez ja l. r. *Pb, Qh, Qq*; p. de r. *Qp, Xa* — 157 o. ou d. *Qp, Xd*

Stanza XX

158-70 and 184-96 *lines inverted Qx* — 158-83 *(Stanzas XX–XXI) lines missing Po* — 158 q. me s. *Xe* — 159 Espereray j. e. *Pa, Pk, Qp, Xa*; Je vous s. j. *Pb, Qh*; s. et j. *Qd* — 160 je *missing*, t. pour bien h. *Pa, Pf, Pj, Pk, Qd, Qh, Qn, Qp, Qx, Xa*; je *missing*, t. pour m. *Pb, Pd, Xd, Xe*; E. me t. pour m. *Pe, Qb, Qp*; E. men t. pour m. *Pl, Qq*; je *missing*, t. pour mon honnorelz *Qa* — 161 j. vous f., trop *missing Pa, Pd, Pe, Pk, Pl, Qa, Qb, Qd, Qn, Qp, Xa, Xd, Xe*; s. j. vous suis ennuyeux *Pb, Qh, Qq*; j. vous f. tout le mieux *Pf, Pj*; j. vous f. le mieux *Qx* — 162 d. c. pour piteux *Pk*; c. pas j. *Qx* — 163-64 *lines inverted Pb, Qb, Qh, Qq* — 163 d. e. exploie *Pf, Pj*; Qui de douleur est esploure *Pp*; Qui de doleur est esprouve *Qr* — 164 E. tellement e. *Qb* — 165 q. v. plest *Qx* — 166-68 *lines missing Qh* — 166 m. commande q. *Qa*; A c. q. j. m. [...] *Qx* — 167 Sans vous requerir r. *Pa, Pb, Pd, Pk, Pl, Qd, Qp, Qn, Qq, Xa, Xd, Xe*; Du mal qui me charge si fort *Pb, Qh*; v. requerir r. *Pe, Pf, Pj, Qa, Qx*; D. v. requerir [...] *Qx* — 168 n. v. desplaist *Qx* — 169 S. vous ayme e., ma *missing Pa, Pk, Qp, Xa, Xd*; e. s. mon malaise *Pb, Qh*; ma *missing Pd, Pe, Pf, Pj, Pl, Pp, Qa, Qb, Qd, Qn, Qx, Xe*; e. s. mal aise *Qq* — 170 Sans vous requerir resconfort *Pb, Qh*; *line missing Qq*; A ce n. v. *Qx*

Stanza XXI

171-83 *lines missing Qx* — 171 c. et voy bien a. *Qr* — 172 q. damours r. *Pa, Pd, Pk, Qb, Qp, Qr, Xa, Xe* — 173 p. de d. *Pa, Pd, Pe, Pf, Pj, Pk, Pl, Qa, Qb, Qd, Qh,*

Qn, Qp, Qq, Xa, Xd, Xe; S. mort mort n. p. de d. *Pb*; n. pas g. *Pp, Qr* — 174 Mais
jay plus chier de v. *Pa, Pk, Qp, Xa*; N. jay plus chier v. *Pb, Pd, Pl, Qb, Qd, Qh,
Qn, Qq*; vivre *missing Pe, Qa, Xd*; mieulx *missing Pf, Pj*; Nostant jayme plus v. e.
Xe — 175 Encores p. q. *Pa, Pd, Pf, Pj, Pk, Qd, Qp, Qq, Xa, Xe; line missing Pb, Qh*;
Vivre encore plus que s. *Pe, Qa*; Encores p. q. j. n. vueil *Pl, Qn*; Encore p. q. j. n.
s̶e̶u̶l̶ sueil *Qb*; p. asses q. *Qr*; Vivre encor p. q. j. me s. *Xd* — 176 Ne q. d. *Qa* — 177
E. en e. *Pb, Qh*; E. eussez v. *Qr* — 179 Ja n. m. *Pa, Qp, Xa, Xd*; Jamais n. m. *Pk*; Ja
n. m. voyes v. *Xe* — 180 q. doulceur m. *Pk*; q. la mort m. *Qr* — 180bis Ja ne seray
de mal delivre, *Pb, Qh*; n. m. agreable *Qd, Xe* — 182 m. soit p. *Pd, Pl, Qd, Qn*; m.
nest p. *Qa*; mest *missing Qh* — 183 *line missing Pb, Qh, Qq; the additional line
180bis in Pb and Qh maintains the thirteen-line stanza, but the rhyme scheme is
broken*; j. a v. *Pd*; je *missing Pk, Qp, Xa*; v. bien en v. *Pl, Qn*; v. jen v. *Qd*

Stanza XXII

Rubric: La dame *Pa, Pb, Pd, Pf, Pj, Po, Pp, Qa, Qb, Qp, Xe*; Lamie *Pk*; Responce
Pe, Qd, Xd — 184 Q. dame e. *Pd, Pe, Po, Qa, Qb, Qd, Qh, Qn, Qq, Xd, Xe*; Q.
dame a h. *Pl*; Q. dames en amour s. *Qr*; Q. dame e. h. s. tient *Qx* — 185 r. a c. *Pk*
— 186 Et q. l. *Pb, Pf, Pj, Qa, Qb, Qh, Qx*; Quant on l. r. *Xe* — 187 q. en desdaing
l. *Po*; e. qua d. *Qa* — 188 s. s. tient *Pa, Pk, Xa*; s. s. contient *Pd, Pl, Qd, Qn*;
Pour cause s. s. soutient *Pe*; P. se femme s. contient *Pf, Pj, Qp*; Pour ce se elle s.
contient *Po, Xe*; Pour ce quelle s. c. *Pp*; *line missing, but appears at l. 196bis in
Qa*; Pour ce celle s. c. *Qr*; *fragment damaged in upper left corner,* [...] selle se
maintient *Qx*; P. se ferme elle se tient *Xd* — 189 Sans q. b. p. lamolie *Pa, Pb, Pd,
Pf, Pj, Pk, Pl, Po, Pp, Qb, Qd, Qh, Qn, Qp, Qq, Xa, Xe*; Sans q. bel p. lamolie *Pe,
Qa, Xd*; [...] b. p. lamolie *Qx* — 190 S. naurez j. *Qa*; [...]es j. m. *Qx*; n. la m. *Xd*
— 191 vous *missing Pa, Pb, Pd, Pk, Pl, Po, Qa, Qb, Qd, Qh, Qn, Qp, Qq, Qr, Xa,
Xd, Xe*; s. dure ou s. *Pa, Pd, Pk, Qa, Qb, Qp, Xa, Xd*; s. dure ne s. *Pb, Qh*; Qui
soit dure ou s. *Pe*; Se je suis trop rude ou s. *Pf, Pj*; s. du tout s. *Pl, Po, Qd, Qn,
Xe*; s. dure et s. *Qq*; s. trop plus s. *Qr*; [...] dure ne sauvache *Qx* — 192 C. assez
apres d. *Pf, Pj, Qd*; C. assez a peu de l. *Qr*; [...] a. a. peu de l. *Qx*; a. beaucoup
d. *Xe* — 193 d. a u. *Pb, Qh, Qq*; [...] d. b. *Qx* — 194 Q. q. me t. *Pb, Pe, Pk, Pl, Pp,
Qd, Qh, Qn, Qq, Xe*; Q. q. me t. ou f. *Po*; *line missing Qa*; [...] me tient ou sotte
ou s. *Qx* — 195 Je nauray jamaiz l. c. *Pe, Qa*; Q. ja n. je l. *Pl, Qn*; n. j. tel c. *Qr*;
Itel nauray ja l. c. *Xe* — 196 D. moy f. *Pa, Pb, Pk, Pp, Qb, Qd, Qh, Qp, Qq, Qr,
Qx, Xa*; 196bis Pour cause selle se contient *Qa*

Stanza XXIII

197-209 *and* 210-22 *(Stanzas XXIII-XXIV) lines inverted Pa, Pd, Pk, Pl, Po, Qd,
Qn, Qp, Qr, Xa* — 197 v. v. mamerez *Pb, Pf, Pj, Qb, Qh, Qq* — 198 Ou s. n. *Pa,
Pe, Pk, Po, Pp, Qa, Qp, Xa, Xd, Xe*; v. en l. *Pl, Qd, Qn* — 199 p. p. constraindre
Pd; y *missing Pf*; v. y vueil p. *Pp*; Ne j. n. *Qa*; pas *missing Qa, Qx*; Ame n. v., pas

missing Xe — 200 q. damour vous p. *Pd, Pe, Qa, Qd*; q. damours m. *Pp, Qr, Qx*;
Et q. damour m. *Xe* — 201 m. blasme n. *Pb, Qh, Qq*; J. de m. *Pk, Qp, Xa, Xd*; J.
de m. blasme n. *Qb, Xe*; J. pour m. *Qn* — 202 C. vous n. d. pas c. *Pb, Qh*; v. pas
c. *Pd, Pe, Pl, Po, Qa, Qb, Qd, Qn, Qq, Xe*; ja *missing Qx* — 203 p. clamer e. *Pb,
Qh*; p. gemir e. *Pe, Qa*; p. crier e. *Qq*; p. ame ou p. *Qx* — 204 Et *missing Pp*; v.
quy se c. *Qb*; s. s. contente *Qp* — 206 q. le reffuser v. *Pa, Pb, Pd, Pe, Pk, Pl, Po,
Qa, Qb, Qd, Qh, Qn, Qp, Qq, Xa, Xd*; q. le reffus si v. *Pf, Pj*; q. le refuser si me
g. *Qx*; q. le reffus fort v. *Xe* — 207 Car p. m. *Pl*; Je nen puis mais j. s. *Qq*; m. je
s. [...] *Qx*; m. lasse d. *Xe* — 208 eu *missing Pa, Pb, Pd, Pe, Pf, Pj, Pk, Pl, Po, Qa,
Qb, Qd, Qh, Qn, Qp, Qq, Qr, Qx, Xa, Xd, Xe*; j. dame e. *Pe*; s. javoie d. *Po*; j. d.
[...] *Qx* — 209 Je feisse r. p. *Pa, Pb, Pd, Pe, Pf, Pj, Pk, Pl, Po, Qa, Qb, Qd, Qh,
Qn, Qp, Qq, Qr, Xa, Xd, Xe*; Je feisse [...] *Qx*

Stanza XXIV

210–22 (Stanza XXIV) lines missing Xe; *210–378 (Stanzas XXV–XXXVI) lines
missing Qx* — *209bis line 209 repeated at the start of this stanza, giving it
fourteen lines Qa* — 211 Chose qui vostre m. p. *Pa, Pb, Pd, Pe, Pf, Pj, Pk, Pl,
Qa, Qb, Qd, Qh, Qn, Qp, Xa, Xd*; Chose qui vostre mal p. *Po*; m. vous p. *Pp, Qr*;
Chose que nostre mort vous p. *Qq* — 212 N. pourquoy v. *Pa, Pb, Pd, Pe, Pf, Pj,
Pk, Pl, Po, Qb, Qd, Qh, Qn, Qp, Qq, Xa, Xd*; Ne *missing*, c. si s. d. *Pp*; N. par moy
v. *Qa*; Ou d. q. *Qr* — 213 o. nul jour q. *Pa, Pd, Pe, Pf, Pj, Pk, Po, Qa, Qd, Qp, Qr,
Xa, Xd*; o. mais jour q. *Pb, Pl, Qh, Qn*; C. encor oncques q. *Pp*; o. a nul jour q.
Qb; C. oncquesmais jour q. *Qq* — 214 e. une p. *Qq* — 215 Chose parquoy je vous
desveille *Pa, Pb, Pk, Po, Qh, Qp, Xa, Xd*; Chose q. pour rien je desveille *Pd, Pe,
Pl, Qa, Qd, Qn*; Chose pourquoy de riens me dueille *Pf, Pj*; q. je n. *Pp, Qr*; Chose
pour quoy je le desveulle *Qb, Qq* — 216 r. q. tout bien vous vueille *Pa, Pd, Pk, Pl,
Po, Qb, Qd, Qn, Qp, Xa, Xd*; r. q. bien je vous vueille *Pb, Qh, Qq*; r. q. tout bien je
vous vueille *Pe, Qa*; q. beau v. *Pf, Pj, Qr* — 217 Vous mainte doulceur f. *Pa*; Car
vous mavez maint honneur fait *Pb, Qh, Qq*; Car vous mavez maint honneur f.
Pd, Pe, Pf, Pj, Pk, Pl, Po, Qa, Qb, Qd, Qn, Xa, Xd; Vous mavez mainte doulceur
f. *Qp* — 218 Et sc vous avez p. t. *Pa, Pd, Pe, Pf, Pj, Pl, Po, Qa, Qb, Qd, Qn, Qp,
Xd*; Et se vous aves p. trait *Pb, Qh, Qq* ; Et se vous avez traittie paine *Pk, Xa*; m.
p. faitte *Pp* — 219 q. s. tout bas et hault *Pa, Qp, Xd*; b. q. ce vault *Pb, Pe, Pk, Qh,
Qq, Xa*; b. que a ce f. *Pd, Pf, Pj, Pl, Po, Qa, Qd, Qn*; b. q. vault *Qb* — 220 d. joye
en tout bien p. *Pa, Pd, Qp, Xa, Xd*; d. e. honneur parfait *Pb, Qh, Qq*; d. en tous
biens p. *Pe, Pl, Po, Qd, Qn*; V. d. joye e. *Pp*; e. honneur p. *Qb* — 221 Telle que j.
la vous s. *Pa, Pd, Pe, Pj, Pk, Pl, Po, Qa, Qb, Qd, Qn, Qp, Xa, Xd*; Qui soit tout a
vostre souhait *Pb, Qh*; Telle que la vous s. *Pf*; A. comment j. *Pp*; *line missing Qq*;
c. le vous s. *Qr* — 222 v. grant doulceur v. *Pa, Pd, Pk, Pl, Qd, Qn, Qp, Xa*; Comme
v. doulceur l. v. *Pb, Qh*; v. doulceur l. *Pe, Pf, Pj, Po, Qa, Qb, Xd*; c. bien l. *Qr*

Stanza XXV

Rubric : Lamant *Pa, Pb, Pf, Pj, Po, Pp, Qb, Xe*; Lamoureux *Pd, Qa*; Complaincte *Pe, Qd, Xd;* Lamy *Qp, Xa* — 223 m. demande me c. *Pa, Pb, Pk, Qh, Qp, Qq, Xa*; m. r. ne passez *Pp, Qr* — 224 j. tous p. *Qa* — 225 Car n. p. *Pa, Pb, Pd, Pe, Pf, Pj, Pk, Pl, Qa, Qb, Qd, Qn, Qp, Xa, Xd, Xe*; n. ne d. *Pe*; n. m. demante *Pf, Pj*; Que n. p. *Qh, Qq* — 226–27 *lines inverted Pd, Pf, Pj, Pk, Pl, Po, Qa, Qb, Qd, Qh, Qn, Qp, Qq, Xa, Xd, Xe* — 226 Tant que mes espris sont lassez *Pa, Qp, Xd*; Tant qua m. suis t. *Pb, Pd, Pe, Pk, Pl, Po, Qa, Qb, Qd, Qh, Qn, Qq, Xa, Xe* — 227 Et ay eu des durs m. a. *Pa, Pk, Qp, Xa*; Jay eu des durs m. a. *Pb, Pe, Pl, Qa, Qb, Qd, Qh, Qn, Qq, Xd*; Jay endure des m. a. *Pd, Xe*; Jay eu des divers motz a. *Po* — 228 q. m. seque[…] *Qp* — 229 n. suis p. *Pb, Po, Qb, Qh*; n. suis p. n. en b. *Qa*; d. bon h. *Qr* — 230 Se damours nay aucun s. *Pa, Pb, Pd, Pe, Pf, Pj, Pk, Pl, Po, Qa, Qd, Qh, Qn, Qp, Qq, Xa, Xd, Xe*; S. damer nay aulcun s. *Qb*; Q. damer je nay nulz s. *Qr* — 231 Car oncques ne me trouve l. *Pa, Pd, Pf, Pj*; Car oncques ne me trouvay l. *Pb, Pe, Pk, Pl, Qa, Qb, Qd, Qh, Qn, Qp, Qq, Xa, Xd, Xe*; *line missing Po*; j. nen f. *Pp* — 232 De vous aymer en l. *Pa, Pb, Pd, Pe, Pf, Pj, Pk, Pl, Po, Qa, Qb, Qd, Qh, Qn, Qp, Qq, Xa, Xd, Xe* — 233 P. quainsi prins suis e. *Pa, Pf, Pj*; P. quainsi s. p. e. voz l. *Pb, Pd, Pe, Pf, Pj, Pl, Po, Qa, Qb, Qd, Qh, Qn, Qq, Xa, Xd*; P. quainsi fu p. *Pk*; P. quainsi s. p. e. […] *Qp*; P. quainsi prins suis e. voz l. *Xe* — 234 Si jen dy mille f. h. *Pa, Pb, Pd, Pe, Pk, Pl, Qa, Qd, Qn, Qp, Xa, Xd, Xe*; Si jen dy maintes f. h. *Pb, Qb, Qh*; Se jay dit mainteffoiz h. *Pf, Pj*; Den dire m. f. *Po*; Se en d. mainteffois h. *Qq*; Se une foiz men f. d. *Qr* — 235 Ce nest pas trop pour tel b. *Pa, Pd, Pe, Pf, Pj, Pk, Pl, Qa, Qb, Qd, Qn, Qq, Xa, Xd, Xe*; Se nest pas pour telle b. *Pb, Qh*; Cest bien pou pour telle b. *Po*; Ce nest pas trop pour tel b[…] *Qp*

Stanza XXVI

236 v. requiers a j. *Pb, Pd, Pe, Pf, Pj, Pl, Po, Qa, Qb, Qd, Qh, Qn, Qq, Xd, Xe*; Mais je vous prie a j. m. *Pp*; a j. […] *Qp* — 237 Belle et bonne q. t. *Pa, Pd, Pf, Pj, Pk, Pl, Po, Qb, Qd, Qn, Qp, Qq, Xa, Xd, Xe*; B. bonne q. t. *Pb*; Belle et bonne a t. *Pe, Qa*; t. l. […] *Qp* — 238 n. m. doubtez *Pe*; n. m. deboutiez *Pf, Pj, Po*; n. m. debou[…] *Qp* — 239 me *missing Pl*; j. m. […] *Qp* — 240 *line missing Pb, Qh*; S. assez de vous p. *Pl, Pp, Qd, Qn*; a. p. p[…] *Qp*; v. de si p. *Qq*; a. peu p. *Qr* — 241 v. l. escoutiez *Pf, Pj, Po*; v. l. esc[…] *Qp*; q. v. lescoutes *Qr* — 242 I. peut q. m. *Pf, Pj*; m. v. doubtiez *Pf, Pj, Po*; I. appert q. *Qa*; m. v. dou[…] *Qp* — 243 v. comment q. *Pb, Pd, Pe, Pf, Pj, Pl, Po, Pp, Qb, Qd, Qh, Qn, Qr, Xe*; Ains s. v. *Qa*; c. q. […] *Qp* — 244 q. est c. *Qp, Xa, Xd* — 245 Tout c. q. v. demanderiez *Pb, Qh, Qq*; v. me c. *Pe, Qa, Xa, Xe*; vous *missing Pf, Pj, Qr*; Tout c. q. *Pf, Pj, Po, Qb, Qr*; q. v. me commanderez *Pp*; v. luy commander[…] *Qp*; v. luy c. *Xd* — 246 Et s. d. v. venoit *Pa, Pb, Pd, Pe, Pf, Pj, Pk, Pl, Po, Qb, Qd, Qh, Qn, Qq, Xa, Xd, Xe*; Et s. a d. v. venoie *Qa*; Et s. d. v. ven[…] *Qp* — 247 Qui autant doulent e. s. *Pa, Pd, Pe, Pf, Pj, Pk, Pl, Po, Qa, Qb, Qd, Qn, Qq, Xa, Xd*; Qui autant courrouce e. s. *Pb, Qh*;

Qui autant dolent e. seroi[...] *Qp*; Autant dolant mon cueur s. *Xe* — 248 Belle c.
v. *Pa, Pd, Pk, Pl, Qd, Qn, Xa*; Comme vous mesmes en s. *Pb, Qh*; Belle que vous
me fines s. *Pe*; Ou plus que v. ne s. *Pf, Pj*; Belle dame c. v. *Po*; Belle c. v. len s. *Qa*;
Belle que c. v. en s. *Qb*; Belle c. v. en s. *Qp, Xd*; Comme vous meismes v. s. *Qq*; t.
belle com s. *Qr*; B. que vous mesmes s. *Xe*

Stanza XXVII

Rubric: Demande que lamant fait *Xe* — 249 e. q. advient *Po*; e. q. adven[...] *Qp*
— 250 v. ~~cueur~~ cuer t. *Pe*; c. t. devient *Po*; c. t. d[...] *Qp* — 251 A. que le mien fut
o. *Pa, Pd, Pe, Pf, Pj, Pl, Po, Qa, Qb, Qd, Qh, Qn, Qp, Qq, Xa, Xd, Xe*; c. le mien
f. *Pb*; A. com le mien f. *Pk* — 252 f. il c. *Pa, Pk, Pl, Qp, Qr, Xa, Xd*; p. f. convient
Po; par *missing Qq* — 253 Quautant d. mal il s. *Pa, Qp*; Quautant d. doleur s. *Pb,
Pe, Pf, Pj, Qh, Qq, Xd*; Que autant d. maulx s. *Pd, Pl, Qn*; Que autant d. mal s.
Pk, Qd, Xa, Xe; Que autant d. maulx sousteint *Po*; Q. des d. *Pp*; Q. tant d. d. s.
Qa, Qb; Autant d. douleur s. *Qr* — 254 *line missing Pb, Qh*; m. et a. *Pe*; Que m.
o. *Qb* — 255 Seriez vous contente a. *Pa, Pb, Pd, Pe, Pk, Pl, Po, Qa, Qb, Qd, Qh,
Qn, Qp, Qq, Xa, Xd*; Seriz vous bien contente doncques *Pf, Pj*; Il vous feroit bien
mal a. *Qr*; Seriez vous contente que a. *Xe* — 256 Quun ung a. f. *Pe*; ung *missing
Pf, Pj*; a. fust d. *Pk*; Ung a. f. *Xe* — 257 Quen f. vous au s. *Pa, Pf, Pj, Pk, Pl, Pp,
Qd, Xa*; Ne q. f. vous au s. *Pb, Qh*; f. vous au s. *Pd, Qa, Qb, Qn, Qq*; f. vous lors
au s. *Pe*; Mais q. f. vous au s. *Po*; Q. pourries faire au s. *Qr*; Ne quen f. vous au s.
Qp, Xd; f. vous donc au s. *Xe* — 258 V. ny s. *Pa, Pd, Pf, Pj, Pp, Qd, Qn, Qq, Xa*;
V. ny s. avoir c. *Pb*; V. ny s. donner c. *Pe*; V. ny s. trouver c. *Pk*; V. ny s. aucum
c. *Po, Qh*; n. seriez n. *Qa*; V. ny s. trouver n. c. *Qb*; Trouver vous ny sauriez c.
Qp; V. ny pourries trouver c. *Qr*; Trouver vous ny auriez c. *Xd*; V. ny s. meptre
c. *Xe* — 259 c. vous d. *Pa, Pb, Pe, Pf, Pj, Pk, Qa, Qb, Qh, Qp, Qq, Xa, Xd*; e. en c.
Pl, Qn; Pour ce vous pry a motz c. *Qr* — 260 m. teniez p. *Pf, Pj*; Quainsi vous n.
m. tenies p. *Po*; En c. p. *Pp*; n. mesloignez p. *Xe* — 261 Combien que ce nest pas
p. *Pa, Pb, Pd, Pe, Pf, Pj, Pk, Pl, Qa, Qb, Qh, Qn, Qp, Qq, Xa, Xd, Xe*; Combien
que ce nest mye p. *Po*; Combien que ce nest p. *Qd*

Stanza XXVIII

Rubric: La dame *Pa, Pb, Pd, Pf, Pj, Po, Pp, Qa, Qb, Qp, Xa*; Responce *Pe, Qd,
Xd*; Lamie *Pk*; Responce par la dame *Xe* — 262 v. est v. *Pb, Qh, Qq*; Je voy bien
par v. c. *Pp, Qr* — 263 E. a. grant douleur *Pk, Xa*; Que vous endurez paine m.
Pp, Qr; Endurer a. d. *Qa*; [...]ndure a. d. *Qp* — 264 Et forment vostre cueur s.
d. *Pa, Pk, Xa, Xd*; *line missing Pb, Qh, Qq*; En v. c. *Pd*; Car v. c. *Pe, Pf, Pj, Qa*;
Quant pour moy vostre cuer s. d. *Pp, Qr*; [...] fourment vostre cueur s. d. *Qp*;
Dont v. c. *Xe* — 265 o. n. point par crainte *Pf*; n. point p. *Pj*; o. doit amer sans
c. *Pp, Qr*; p. p. contraire *Qa*; [...]is o. n. *Qp* — 266 A. amour s. *Pa, Pl, Qn*; A.
seroit lamour f. *Pb, Qh, Qq*; [...]ltrement amour s. *Qp* — 267 [...] n. q. *Qp* — 268

[…]sse c. c. *Qp* — 269 s. le v. *Pb, Pf, Pj, Qh, Qq*; s. v. voulsissez *Pd*; m. souffist s. v. *Pe*; […]e p. s. *Qp*; s. v. voulisses *Qr*; m. p. bien mes quon voulysse *Xe* — 270 p. vous p. *Pb*; p. n. parlissez *Pd, Qr*; Q. de plus ne men p. *Pe*; n. me p. *Pl*; ce *missing*, n. me p. *Qa*; p. vous ne p. *Qh*; p. n. parlassez *Qn*; […] d. c. *Qp*; p. n. me parlysse *Xe* — 271 […]ue l. c. *Qp* — 272 Et quaultre d. advisissiez *Pa, Pb, Pd, Pk, Qh, Qq, Xa*; a. d. advisissies *Pe, Pl, Qa, Qd, Xd*; a. d. amissies *Po*; Et quaultre d. amissies *Qb*; a. d. avisissez *Qn*; […]uautre d. advisissiez *Qp*; Mais quaultre d. choisisses *Qr*; E. voustre cueur aultre choysse *Xe* — 273 *line missing Pb*; d. m. voulsisies *Po*; Qui feist ce que demandissiez *Pp*; A qui voz plaintes monstressiez *Qa*; d. m. joissies *Qb*; La ou passer temps vous peussiez *Qh*; […] m. q. *Qp*; Qui fist ce que commandisses *Qr*; m. luy voulisse *Xe* — 274 j. pas d. *Pa, Pd, Pe, Pf, Pj, Pk, Pl, Po, Qb, Qd, Qn, Qp, Qq, Qr, Xa, Xd, Xe*; d. je n. s. pas d. *Pb, Qh*; C. dame n. *Qa*; […] d. n. *Qp*

Stanza XXIX

Lines 275–87 and 288–300 (Stanzas XXIX-XXX) inverted Pp — 275 d. bien q. *Pa, Pb, Pd, Pe, Pf, Pj, Po, Qa, Qb, Qd, Qh, Qp, Qq, Xa, Xd, Xe*; d. bien q. adviengne *Pe*; moult *missing Pl, Qn*; q. me c. *Pl*; […]e d. b. *Qp* — 276 p. long v. entretiengne *Pa, Qp, Xd*; Que p. l. *Pe, Qh, Qq*; […] p. l. *Qp* — 276bis *line 280 duplicated here, giving this stanza 14 lines Xa* — 277 p. vous l. s. *Pe*; v. et v. *Qa*; […] c. p. *Qp* — 278–80 *lines missing Pl, Qn* — 278 […]ncques m. q. *Qp*; q. men s. *Pp* — 279 q. son propos t. *Pa, Pd, Pk, Po, Qa, Qd, Qp, Qq, Xa*; v. homs q. son propos t. *Pb*; s. corps t. *Pe*; Nen v. n. *Pf, Pj, Xe*; se *missing Pp*; q. son pourpos t. *Qb, Xd, Xe*; v. oncques q. son propos t. *Qh*; […]y n. q. *Qp* — 280 Ainsi comme tenu lavez *Pa, Pb, Pd, Pf, Pj, Pk, Po, Qa, Qb, Qd, Qh, Xa, Xd*; c. t. […] *Pe*; Aussi comme tenu lavez *Pl, Qn*; […]si comme tenu lavez *Qp*; Si bien c. tenu laves *Qq*; Ainsi que vous tenu lavez *Xe* — 281 s. v. retenez *Pl, Qb, Qn*; s. v. revenez *Qa*; […] s. s. *Qp* — 282 Tant que vous dictes de griefz m. *Pa, Pb, Pd, Pf, Pj, Pk, Po, Qa, Qb, Qd, Qh, Qq, Xa, Xd, Xe*; Tant que vous dictes de griefz […] *Pe*; Tant que vous dictes de maulx *Pl, Qn*; […] que vous dictes de griefz m. *Qp*; p. les autre les m. *Qr* — 283 Plusieurs ont de pensers n. *Pa, Pb, Pd, Pe, Pf, Pj, Pk, Pl, Po, Qa, Qb, Qh, Qn, Qq, Xa, Xd, Xe*; […]ieurs ont de pensers n. *Qp* — 284 j. dont ilz ont m. *Pa, Pd, Pk, Qp, Qq, Xa*; j. dont ilz font m. *Pb, Pe, Pl, Qa, Qb, Qh, Qn, Xd*; j. dont y font m. *Pf, Pj*; j. dont il font m. *Po*; j. qui font bien m. *Xe* — 285 M. se vrais sont v. d. tresbeaulx *Pa, Pb, Pd, Pe, Pf, Pj, Pk, Pl, Po, Qa, Qb, Qd, Qh, Qn, Qp, Qq, Xa, Xd, Xe*; d. plaisans e. *Pp* — 286 Vous estes decevant e. f. *Pa, Pb, Pd, Pe, Pf, Pj, Pk, Pl, Po, Qa, Qb, Qd, Qh, Qn, Qp, Qq, Xa, Xd*; e. joyeulx ou f. *Pp*; Vous estes decepveur ou f. *Xe*

Stanza XXX

288 Me v. v. mectre e. d. *Pb, Pd, Pe, Pf, Pj, Pl, Po, Qa, Qb, Qd, Qh, Qn, Qq, Xd, Xe*; v. moy m. *Pk, Xa*; Chascun doit doubter les d. *Pp, Qr* — 289 f. p. mensongiers

Pa, Po, Qn, Qp; f. parleurs l. *Pe, Qa, Xe*; D. maints envieux l. *Pp, Qr*; D. telz f. *Qb*; D. ses parleurs l. *Qq*; c. f. parleurs mensongiers *Xd* — 290 D. par eulx est tout mal r. *Pa, Pk, Qp, Xa*; m. nen r. *Pb*; que *missing Pf, Pj, Pl, Qn*; m. ne r. *Po*; Par lesquelz maint mal est r. *Pp, Qr* — 291 I. blasment les gens v. *Pp, Qr* — 292 d. souvent p. *Pa, Pb, Pd, Pe, Pf, Pj, Pk, Pl, Po, Qa, Qd, Qh, Qn, Qp, Qq, Xa, Xd, Xe*; d. des maulx p. *Pp*; d. souvent p. dung t. *Qb* — 293 f. parle n. *Pe*; f. parler n. *Qa* — 294–300 *lines missing Xe* — 294 Et pour ce ung amoureux parfait *Pp*; Pour ce ung amoureux parfaict *Qr* — 295 Doit tousjours fuyr telz meschants *Pp, Qr* — 296 e. s. tresdesplaisans *Pe, Xd*; Il vous en seroit d. *Pf, Pj*; s. bien d. *Pk*; Aussi e. s. *Po*; Ne dire nulz motz d. *Pp, Qr*; s. bien d. *Qh*; Car v. e. *Qp* — 297 d. mes a. *Pa, Pd, Pe, Pf, Pj, Pk, Pl, Po, Qa, Qb, Qd, Qh, Qn, Qq, Xa, Xd*; v. estiez d. *Pb*; Et pou parler pour les perilz *Pp*; Et peu parler pour tous perilz *Qr* — 298 Je me doubte de m. *Pp, Qr*; s. tant fort m. *Qh* — 299 Le monde est present mal disant *Pa, Qp, Xd*; *line missing Pk, Xa*; f. vois d. *Pl*; f. vrais d. *Po, Qb*; Car q. l. *Pp, Qr* — 299bis Et lun va lautre desprisant *Pa, Qp, Xd* — 300 Ainsi que mortel ennemis *Pa, Qp, Xd*; Lors e. s. du pis *Pf, Pj*; Ce seroit malement du p. *Pp, Qr*; c. le p. *Qa*; E. diroient ilz p. *Qb, Qq*

Stanza XXXI

Rubric: Lamant *Pa, Pb, Pf, Pj, Po, Pp, Qb*; Lamoureux *Pd*; Complaincte *Pe, Qd, Xd*; Lamy *Pk, Qp, Xa*; Lamant en se complaignent *Xe* — 302 Pour serviteur m. r. *Pa, Pd, Pe, Pf, Pj, Pk, Pl, Po, Qa, Qd, Qn, Qp, Xa, Xd, Xe*; E. pour servant m. *Pb, Qh, Qq*; Je vous pry que m. r. *Pp, Qr*; Ou pour servant m. r. *Qb* — 303 Par grace et par g. a. *Pa, Pd, Pe, Pf, Pj, Pk, Po, Qa, Qb, Qd, Qp, Qq, Qr, Xa, Xd*; Vous serez dame de pitie *Pb, Qh*; par grace et a. *Pl, Qn*; Vostre servant par a. *Pp*; Par grace et par a. *Xe* — 304 Et *missing*, s. vous l. *Po* — 305 Quelque beau train que vous tenez *Pa, Qp, Xd*; Je vous dy que vous m. *Pb, Pd, Pe, Pl, Pp, Qa, Qb, Qd, Qn, Qq, Xe*; Votre honneur sans vous m. *Pf, Pj*; *line missing Pk, Xa*; J. diray q. *Po*; Je vous dy q. v. mesprouves *Qh*; Trop malement vous m. *Qr*; s. a. lentrepenez *Xe* — 306 Vous e. d. *Pa, Pk, Qp, Xa, Xd*; E. estes du tout s. *Pb, Qh, Qq*; E. estes d. *Pe, Pl, Po, Qa, Qb, Qd, Qn, Xe*; En tant questez si s. p. *Pf*; E. tant questez si s. p. *Pj*; Comme une d. s. *Pp, Qr* — 307 s. pour v. *Pf, Pj, Po*; Et par vous suis si m. t. *Pp*; S. par vous suys si m. *Qr*; Et j. s. pour v. *Qa, Qb*; s. de v. *Xe* — 308 Se m. n. *Qb* — 309 p. drap d. *Pa, Pb, Pd, Pf, Pj, Pk, Po, Pp, Qa, Qb, Qd, Qh, Qp, Xa, Xd, Xe*; *line missing Pe*; p. drap d. d. couleur forte *Pl, Qn*; d. n. forte *Pp*; Drap porteray d. n. *Qr* — 310 C. doulx m. qui de j. h. *Pa, Pd, Pk, Pl, Qd, Qn, Xa*; C. doulx moys qui de j. h. *Pb, Pe, Qa, Qb, Qh*; en ce moys que j. h. *Pf, Pj*; Et diray que de j. h. *Po*; Comme en qui d. j. nabonde *Qp, Xd*; C. doulx ~~jour~~ mois qui de j. h. *Qq*; En m. o. *Qr*; Se don nay qui de j. h. *Xe* — 311 j. soyt m. *Qr* — 312 Et *missing*, q. s. deporte *Po*; E. com c. q. s. deporte *Pp*; E. comment c. *Qa*

Stanza XXXII

314 E. sestre puis de vous a. *Pa, Pb, Pd, Pe, Pf, Pj, Pk, Pl, Qa, Qd, Qh, Qn, Qp, Qq, Xa, Xd*; Sestre puys de vous a. *Po*; E. puis estre d. *Qb*; Si puis estre de vous a. *Xe* — 315 Et vostre doulce amour sappointe *Pb, Qa, Qh*; Et vostre doulceur amour sa pointe *Pe*; q. m. desapointe *Pf, Pj*; a. me d. *Pl, Qn*; S. c. quautrement desapoincte *Po*; Et que chose sappointe *Pp*; q. nul m. *Qb*; Et nostre doulce amour sappoincte *Qq*; Et que nostre amour sapointe *Qr*; S. que q. *Xa*; ce *missing Xe* — 316 J. puis bien d. *Pa, Pb, Pd, Pe, Pf, Pj, Pk, Pl, Po, Qa, Qb, Qd, Qh, Qn, Qp, Qq, Qr, Xa, Xd, Xe* — 317 j. la tresbelle et c. *Pa, Pd, Pe, Pk, Pl, Po, Qa, Qb, Qd, Qn, Qp, Xa, Xd*; j. la plus belle et c. *Pb, Qh, Xe*; Jaime la plus belle et c. *Qq* — 318 q. mort n. desappointe *Pa, Pd, Qp*; m. n. desappointe *Pb*; q. mort n. desacointe *Pk, Xa*; q. mort me desappointe *Pl, Qn, Xe*; q. mort men desapoincte *Po, Qd, Xe*; m. men d. *Pp*; m. me d. *Qr* — 319 n. me v. *Pa, Qp, Xa, Xd*; n. me v. departir *Pb, Qh, Qq*; Nul n. me verra r. *Qr*; m. voires r. *Xe* — 320 c. vueillez c. *Pa, Pd, Pe, Pk, Pl, Pp, Qd, Qn, Qp, Qr, Xa, Xd, Xe*; E. se vous voulez c. *Pb, Qh, Qq* — 321 s. a u. *Pa, Pk, Qp, Xa*; s. en u. *Pb, Pd, Pe, Pf, Pj, Pl, Po, Pp, Qa, Qb, Qd, Qn, Qq, Qr, Xd, Xe*; d. amours cueurs s. en u. *Qh* — 322 Q. sera a nous deux c. *Pa, Pf, Pj, Pk, Qd, Qp, Xa, Xd*; Q. sera a tous deux c. *Pb, Pd, Pe, Pl, Po, Qa, Qb, Qh, Qn, Qq, Qr, Xe* — 323 y *missing Pa, Qp, Xa*; *line missing Pf, Pj*; nul *missing Xe* — 324 L. amoit l. *Qa* — 325 *line missing Pb, Qh, Qq*; f. a s. *Pl, Qn* — 326 A tant que la m. n. *Pa, Qp, Xd*; Jusque que m. si n. *Pk, Xa*; m. n. de porte *Pe*

Stanza XXXIII

327 et *missing Pa, Pb, Pk, Pl, Pp, Qb, Qd, Qh, Qn, Qp, Qq, Xa, Xe*; s. e. dererechief *Pd*; s. tout d. *Pe, Qa, Qr, Xd* — 328 Dictes moy a u. seul m. b. *Pa, Pb, Pd, Pe, Pf, Pj, Pk, Pl, Qa, Qb, Qd, Qh, Qn, Qp, Qq, Qr, Xa, Xd*; m.dissies a u. *Po*; Dittez moy en u. seul m. *Xe* — 329 Des biens que jay vers vous r. *Pa, Pd, Pk, Pl, Qd, Qn, Qp, Xa, Xd, Xe*; Ce dont j. v. *Pb, Qh, Qq*; Se vostre grace ay conquis *Pe*; c. dont j. *Pf, Pj, Qr*; Des biens q. je vous ay r. *Po*; Se ce dont j. v. *Qa*; Ce dont j. v. a. tant r. *Qb* — 330 Croissez ma peine et mon m. *Pa, Pd, Pf, Pj, Pk, Po, Qp, Xa, Xd, Xe*; Croisse ma paine et mon m. *Pb, Pl, Qd, Qh, Qn, Qq*; Si seray hors de ce m. *Pe*; Croistes m. p. *Qa*; Croissies ma payne et mon m. *Qb*; Vivray je ades en ce m. *Qr* — 331-32 *lines missing Pe* — 331 O. que j. viengne toust a c. *Pa, Pb, Pd, Pf, Pj, Pk, Qa, Qb, Qd, Qh, Qn, Qp, Xa, Xd*; v. tout a c. *Pl, Xa*; Et me banisses derechief *Po*; *line missing, but line 332 copied twice Qq*; O. au moins q., tost *missing Xe* — 332 j. vers vous tant q. *Pa, Pk, Pl, Qn, Qp, Xa, Xd*; Des biens quay de vous tant q. *Pb*; Des biens q. j. vers vous tant q. *Pd, Pf, Pj, Qb, Qd, Xe*; De vostre amour q. tant j. *Po*; Davoir ce dont j. l., si *missing Pp*; Des biens q. je vous ay tant q. *Qa*; Des biens quay devers vous tant q. *Qh*; Des biens quay vers vous tant acquis *Qq* — 333 a. d. nay quis *Pa, Pl, Qn, Qp, Xd*; a. d. je ne quis *Pb, Qh, Qq*; a. d. ne quis *Pe, Pf, Pj, Qa, Qr*; n. me p. *Po*; O. autre autre d. ne requis *Pp*; a. d. ne requis *Qb*; O.

tant d. je nen quis *Xe* — 334 Estre ne me peut r. *Pa, Pb, Pe, Pf, Pj, Pk, Pl, Po, Qa, Qb, Qd, Qh, Qn, Qp, Qq, Qr, Xa, Xd*; Estre ne peut r. *Pd*; Estre n. m. *Qp*; Estre ne me peut reprouche *Xe* — 335 b. amy t. *Pa, Pd, Pe, Pf, Pj, Pk, Pl, Po, Qa, Qb, Qd, Qn, Qp, Xa, Xd, Xe*; Bien scay que a. avez t. *Pb, Qh, Qq*; b. autrui t. *Pp*; b. a. trouver *Qa*; Puet estre quauries t. *Qr* — 337 v. m. approuve *Pb, Qh, Qq*; v. m. esprouver *Qa*; v. mavez e. *Qp* — 338 Vous trouveres cler et p. *Pe*; I. seroit b. p. v. trouver *Qa* — 339 e. ung t. *Pd, Pl, Qn*; Quon nen trouveroit nul autel *Pp*; l. n'est n. e. *Qa*; l. nen a n. *Qr*

Stanza XXXIV

Rubric : Lamie *Pa, Pk, Qp, Xa*; La dame *Pd, Pf, Pj, Po, Pp, Qa, Qb, Xe*; Responce *Pe, Qd, Xd* — 340 cueur *missing Pe*; M. c. tramble tressault et sue *Qb* — 341 Je suis p. t. *Pf* — 342 plus *missing Pa, Pb, Pd, Pf, Pj, Pk, Pl, Po, Pp, Qa, Qb, Qd, Qh, Qn, Qp, Xa, Xe*; En moy na mes n. d. *Pa, Pk, Qp, Xa*; Ne j. ny s. *Pb, Qb, Qh*; Ne j. ny voy n. *Pd, Pf, Pj, Pl, Qd, Qn, Xe*; Ne j. n. *Pe, Qr, Xd*; Quant j. ny s. *Po*; s. mais n. *Pp*; Et j. ny s. *Qq* — 343 Mon cueur se sent d. f. *Pd, Pl, Qn*; C. j. sens damours la venue *Pe*; J. men s. *Pk*; Car *missing*, s. bien d. *Po*; s. damer f. *Qh, Qq* — 344 V. bel p. m. vertue *Pe*; V. bel p. *Qa* — 345 t. p. pourpense *Pb, Qh, Qq*; m. p. et p. *Pd, Po*; p. quant p. *Pf, Pj, Qa, Qb*; p. my p. et p. *Pl, Qn*; Qui moult m. p. tant p. *Qr*; Qui plus desire e. p. *Xe* — 346 […]ieu d. ce qui est s. o. *Xe* — 347 E. que l. c. atant s. passe *Pa, Pk, Qp, Xa*; E. que l. c. bien s. passe *Pb, Pd, Pe, Pf, Pj*; E. que l. c. en bien s. passe *Pl, Po, Pp, Qa, Qb, Qd, Qh, Qn, Qq, Qr, Xd, Xe* — 348 vous *missing Pf, Pj*; v. refuse l. *Qa* — 349–50 *lines inverted Pb, Qh, Qq* — 349 M. c. se rend et se rendra *Pa, Pb, Pd, Pe, Pf, Pj, Pk, Pl, Po, Qa, Qb, Qd, Qh, Qn, Qp, Qq, Xa, Xd, Xe*; Et m. c. se rent et rendra *Pp, Qr* — 350 J. en n. *Pb, Pd, Pl, Qh, Qn*; J. en n. temps n. *Po*; a *missing*, j. je n. c. *Pp* — 351 r. pour a. *Qa*; Q. jamaiz p. a. lamasse *Qr* — 352 s. comment i. *Pe, Qa*; s. com i. *Pk*; s. quil men advendra *Xe*

Stanza XXXV

353 p. maimer par h. *Pa, Pb, Pd, Pk, Pl, Po, Qa, Qb, Qd, Qh, Qn, Qp, Qq, Qr, Xa, Xd*; p. maimer pour h. *Pe*; v. p. amer par amours *Pf, Pj, Xe* — 354 p. p. ne m. *Pa, Pd, Pf, Pj, Pk, Pl, Po, Qa, Qd, Qn, Qp, Xa, Xd, Xe*; p. ne p. m. *Pb, Qb, Qh, Qr, Qq*; p. p. ou m. *Pe* — 355 Ne me vueillez jamais changer *Pa, Pd, Pk, Qp, Xa, Xd*; Vous ne me vueillez c. *Pb, Qh, Qq*; Vous ne me vueilliez point c. *Pe, Qa*; Vous ne me veulliez ja c. *Pf, Pj, Pl, Qb, Qd, Qn, Xe*; Vous ne me voulsissies c. *Po* — 356–57 *lines inverted Pd, Pl, Po, Qb, Qd, Qh, Qn, Xe* — 356 Je laisseray t. r. *Pa, Pb, Pe, Pf, Pj, Pk, Qa, Qh, Qp, Qq, Qr, Xa, Xd*; Et laisseray t. r. *Pd, Pl, Qb, Qd, Qn, Xe*; Et laisseroie t. r. *Po* — 357 Pour vous aymer comme mon cueur *Pa, Qp, Xd*; v. o. tout mon cueur *Pb, Qh, Qq*; Je v. o. *Pd, Pl, Qb, Qd, Qn*; Je v. octroiroye m. *Po*; o. toute m. *Qa*; v. abandonne m. *Xe* — 358 f. jamais d. *Pa, Pb, Pd, Pk, Pl, Po, Qa, Qb, Qd, Qh, Qn, Qp, Qq, Xa, Xd*; S. jamais en faire d. *Pe, Pf, Pj, Qr, Xe* — 359 v.

v. plus e. *Pa, Pd, Pf, Pk, Pl, Po, Qd, Qn, Qp, Xa, Xd*; Si n. v. *Pf, Pj*; v. v. point e.
Qa — 360 Car c. q. *Pb, Qb, Qh, Qq*; q. j. escripvez *Qa*; Et *missing Xe* — 361 g.
me s. *Pa, Pb, Pe, Pf, Pk, Qp, Xa, Xd*; Vous ne vous verrez ja p. *Pp*; g. me faictes p.
Qa — 362 n. devroit e. *Pb, Qh*; Doncques d. *Pf, Pj*; ne *missing Pf, Pj, Pl, Qb*; Des
biens dont chascun nest pas l. *Pp*; D. d. devroit e. *Qq* — 363–64 *lines inverted*
Pb, Qh — 363 Mais s. s. *Pb, Pd, Pe, Pf, Pj, Po, Pp, Qa, Qb, Qd, Qh, Qn, Qq, Qr, Xe*
— 364 t. b. [...] *Pe*; Et de blasme tout delivre *Pp*; s. ton b. *Qr* — 365 p. dont j. *Pa,*
Pb, Pd, Pe, Pf, Pj, Pk, Pl, Po, Pp, Qb, Qd, Qh, Qn, Qp, Qq, Xa, Xd, Xe; j. vo[...] *Qp*

Stanza XXXVI

367 A. que men avez p. *Pf, Pj* — 368 Si fois je vous de bien bon c. *Pa, Pd, Pe,*
Pk, Pl, Po, Qa, Qn, Xa, Xd; Si fais je vous d. t. *Pb, Qd, Qh, Qq, Qr, Xe*; S. feray je
vous de bon c. *Pf, Pj*; v. requier d. *Pp*; Sy foys je veul de t. c. *Qb*; Si fays je vous
de bien bon c[...] *Qp* — 369 Qua m. l. *Pb, Qh, Qq*; l. v. ~~seres~~ soyez *Pe*; En m. l.
Po — 370 q. pour riens n. *Pf, Pj* — 371 le *missing Pb, Pf, Pj, Qd, Qh, Xe*; n. vous
v. *Pe*; Car je vous ay donne mon ceur *Po*; v. pour n. *Qb*; l. vouldray a n. *Qp, Xa,*
Xd; a n. feu[...] *Qp* — 372 M. trop plus que f. ne s. *Pa, Pk, Qp, Xa*; Mais *missing*
Pe; c. vostre s. *Pl*; c. vostre e. *Pp, Qn*; f. e. s[...] *Qp*; Ainsi c. f. ne s. *Xd* — 373–74
lines inverted Pb, Qh — 373 Nous entraymons tous deux ensemble *(unique line*
with incorrect rhyme) Pb, Qh; m. v. ay[...] *Qp* — 374 E. ja p. rien q. nous o. *Pa,*
Pb, Pd, Pf, Pj, Pk, Pl, Po, Qd, Qh, Qp, Xa, Xe; E. ja p. rien q. nous voyons *Pe,*
Qa, Xd; Ne ja p. rien q. *Pf, Pj*; E. que p. riens q. nous o. *Qb*; E. ja p. riens q. nous
ayon *Qn*; q. n. oy[...] *Qp*; *line missing Qq*; Se vostre cuer au mien sassemble *Qr*
— 375 Que *missing*, n. se d. *Pa, Pb, Pd, Pe, Pk, Po, Qa, Qb, Qd, Qh, Qq, Xa, Xd*;
La n. a. n. se dessamble *Pf, Pj*; Que *missing*, a. n. se dessemble *Pl, Qn, Xe*; N. a.
n. desassembl[...] *Qp* — 376–77 *lines inverted Pl, Qn, Xe*; *lines missing Po* — 376
Et s. n. *Pa, Pb, Pd, Pe, Pk, Pp, Qb, Qd, Qh, Qp, Qr, Xa, Xd, Xe*; E. souvent n.
entretenons *Pl, Qa, Qn* — 377 *line missing Qq*; Dun mesme vouloir nous s. *Xe* —
378 Si aurons temps joyeulx e. *Pa, Pk, Qp, Xa*; A. aurons bon temps e. *Pb, Pd, Pe,*
Pf, Pj, Pl, Po, Qa, Qb, Qd, Qh, Qn, Qq, Xd, Xe; Si aurons temps joyeulx en[...] *Qp*

Explicit

Explicit la belle dame ou a mercy *Pb, Qh*; Le vostre moitie plus que sien Car en
tout son met il na rien *Pe*; Explicit le livre de la belle dame a mercy *Pf*; Explicit
la dame qui eust mercy de son amant *Pj*; Explicit *Pk, Pl, Pp*; Et ho *Po*; Explicit la
complainte d'amours *Qa*; Explicit *Qb*; Explicit la belle dame ou a mercy *Qh*; Cy
finit la belle dame ou mercy *Qn*; Cy fine le x. livre *Qp*; Explicit la belle dame ^{ou}
a mercy *Qq*; Explicit deo dicacur laus et hympnus *Qr*; Le vostre moitie plus que
sien, Car en tout son cueur il n'a rien *added by Du Chesne in square brackets,*
with marginal note Aiousté du Ms. *Xd*; Explicit deo gracias *Xe*

Addendum

379–88 Pf and Pj present an additional ten lines before the explicit; Pl and Qn do also, but it is a different text. Pf breaks the lines into two stanzas; Pj presents a single stanza.

Text from Pf and Pj:

[L'Amant]	[The Lover]
Je vous mercye humblement	I thank you humbly
Comme tout plain de reconfort,	As one completely filled with comfort,
Car j'estoie bien prés de mort	For I was very near to death
Se je n'eusse en alegement.	If I had not had relief.
Nous vivrons tresjoyeusement,	We will live most joyously,
Sans faire l'un a l'autre tort.	Without wronging each other.
Et tant que j'auray sentement,	And for as long as I am of sound mind,
Ne vueil aillieurs faire deport.	I have no desire to depart.
Vous estez ma vie et le port	You are my life and the harbour
Dont vient tout mon esbatement.	From which all of my happiness comes.

Text from Pl and Qn:

[L'Amant]	[The Lover]
Puis que veoir ne vous puis, Belle,	Since I cannot see you, Fair One,
Par devers vous mon cuer s'en va,	To your side goes my heart,
Qui de par moy vous comptera	Which, through me, will give you
De mon estat pouvre nouvelle.	News of my poor condition.
Or vueillez donc, ma damoiselle,	Now, please, my damsel,
Moy mander ce qu'il vous plaira,	Command me as you wish,
Car vous estes la seule celle	For you are the only one
Pourquoy mon cuer joyeux sera,	For whom my heart will be happy.
Ne pour autre ne vous changera	And it will never abandon you for another,
En confortant vostre querelle.	Thus calming your argument.

Le Dialogue d'amoureux et de sa dame

Title: D'un amoureux parlant a sa dame par amour *Pa, Pc (modern hand), Qp, Xa*; Dialogue dun amoureux et de sa dame *Xd*; Epistre d'un amant a sa dame (*for Stanzas XIX–XXI*), Rescrit de la dame au dit amant (*for Stanzas XXII–XXIV*) *Xn*

Stanza I

1–180 (*Stanzas I–XVIII*) *lines missing Po, Xn* — 2 m. s. plai[…] *Qp* — 5 d. l. desplaisance *Pa, Qp, Xa, Xd* — 6 p. s. sent[…] *Qp*; m.fait p. *Xd* — 9 l. p. esjouir *Pa, Qp, Xa, Xd*

Stanza II

11 q. vous d. *Pa, Xa, Xd*; f. q. vous deu[…] *Qp* — 12 Ny p. d. *Pa* — 14 l. puist d. *Pa* — 15 v. v. dou[…] *Qp* — 17 h. g. aulta[…] *Qp* — 18 p. luy m. *Pa*; p. soy m. *Qp, Xd*; moy *missing Xa* — 19 m. tour ne s. *Pa*

Stanza III

28 v. server m. *Xd*; m. ou q. *Pa, Qp, Xa, Xd*

Stanza IV

Rubric: La dame *Pa, Qp, Xa, Xd* — 33 n. vous v. *Pa, Qp, Xa, Xd* — 35 f. n. f. *Xa*; f. et n. *Xd* — 36 […e] n. u. *Qp*; Ce n. pas un. *Xd* — 37 Honnourer cherir et doubter *Pa, Xa, Xd*; *line missing Pc*; […]norer cherir et doubter *Qp* — 38 […] q. u. *Qp* — 39 […] c. d. *Qp* — 40 […]il p. q. *Qp*

Stanza V

41 […]uand a m. *Qp* — 42 […]ont v. v. *Qp* — 43 […]e c. i. *Qp* — 44 […]e m. a. *Qp* — 45 […]e n. v. *Qp* — 46 Pourquoy m. d. *Pa, Xa, Xd*; […]ourquoy m. d. *Qp* — 47 […]e j. n. *Qp* — 48 […]ourquoy v. m. *Qp* — 49 […] p. v. *Qp* — 50 […] c. a. *Qp*

Stanza VI

55 s. mie d. *Pa, Qp, Xa* — 56 v. je p. *Pa, Xa, Xd*; v. ja p. *Qp* — 57 s. ja p. *Pa, Qp, Xa, Xd* — 58 et *missing Pa, Qp, Xa, Xd*; p. — 59 Daultres q. v. *Qp, Xd*

Stanza VII

Rubric: Lamoureux *Pa, Qp, Xa, Xd* — 61 q. ne suis pas a. *Pa, Qp, Xa, Xd* — 62 B. et v. *Pa, Qp, Xa, Xd* — 69 m. folleur na m. *Pa, Qp, Xa, Xd* — 70 M. envoyez u. *Qp*

Stanza VIII

72 P. me c. *Pa, Qp, Xa, Xd* — 73 v. requiers p. de m. *Pa, Qp, Xa, Xd* — 77 c. que tout entier vous l. *Pa, Qp, Xa, Xd*

Stanza IX

86 m. d. vostre office *Pa, Qp, Xa, Xd* — 90 E. comme h. *Pa*; E. comme h. tout r. *Qp, Xd*

Stanza X

Rubric: La dame *Pa, Qp, Xa, Xd* — 93 b. tout l. *Qp, Xd* — 94 De faire ce que je vouldroie *Pa, Qp, Xa, Xd; line missing Pc* — 99 n. vous p. *Xd*

Stanza XI

103 en *missing Pa* — 106 E. aussi c. trop g. f. *Qp, Xd* — 107 O. vostre m. *Pa, Qp, Xa, Xd* — 108 f. cy p. *Pa, Qp, Xa, Xd*

Stanza XII

116 Ou que je ne suis d. p. *Pa, Qp, Xa, Xd* — 117 N. m. requeres plus avant *Pa, Qp, Xa, Xd*

Stanza XIII

Rubric: Lamoureux *Pa, Qp, Xa, Xd* — 124 d. vous n. *Qp, Xa, Xd* — 125 p. vous n. *Xa, Xd* — 130 j. m. de valoir *Pa, Qp, Xa, Xd*

Stanza XIV

131 Q. de m. *Pa, Qp, Xa, Xd*; p. v. che[...] *Qp* — 132 c. com c. *Pa, Qp, Xa, Xd* — 133 c. a chois[...]*Qp* — 136 c. a m. *Pa, Xa, Xd*; a ma m[..]*Qp* — 138–39 *lines missing Qp* — 139 Je vous promectz v. a. *Pa, Xd*; Je vous prometz v. aurez t. *Xa* — 140 a. d. d[...] *Qp*

Stanza XV

141 a. f. al[...] *Qp* — 143 n. vucil p. *Pa, Qp, Xa, Xd* — 144 q. le c. *Pa, Qp, Xa, Xd* — 145 Namours quant il me c. *Pa, Qp, Xa, Xd* — 147 maiz *missing*, A t. s. department *Pa, Qp, Xa, Xd*   150 b. cueur r. *Pa, Qp, Xa, Xd*

Stanza XVI

Rubric: La dame *Pa, Qp, Xa, Xd* — 151 s. tresbien est m. *Pa, Qp, Xa, Xd* — 152 v. vous d. *Pa, Qp, Xa, Xd* — 153 E. que plus il nen soit p. *Pa*; s. plus p. *Qp*; E. que il nen soit plus p. *Xa, Xd* — 159 J. v. respons quoy que men die *Pa*; J. v. responds bien quen amye *Qp, Xd*; Je vous respons bien quen maniere *Xa*

Stanza XVII

164–65 *lines inverted Pa, Qp, Xa, Xd* — 164 Par a. n. par m. t. *Pa, Qp, Xa, Xd* — 165 Q. je p. *Pa, Qp, Xa, Xd* — 167 [...] s. o. *Qp* — 168 J. a faire a q. *Pa, Xa*; [...] ay a. a *Qp*

Stanza XVIII

172 […]ui n. s. *Qp* — 173 […] s. v. *Qp* — 174 […] j. v. *Qp* — 175 […] s. b. *Qp* — 176 […]ue v. m. *Qp* — 177 Et vostre amie reclamer *Pa, Qp, Xa, Xd; line missing Pc* — 180 […]e l. e. *Qp*

Stanza XIX

Rubric: Lamoureux *Pa, Qp, Xa, Xd*; Epistre d'un amant a sa dame *Xn* — 181 […] las m. d., et *missing Qp*; H. madame e. *Xn* — 185 P. me d. *Pa*; Et ma donne de la t. *Po*; P. me d. joye e. *Qp, Xa*; P. me d. pleurs e. *Xd*; Vivant pour vous en grant t. *Xn* — 186 S. durement q. *Xn* — 188 f. quen d. *Pa, Po, Qp, Xa, Xd* — 189 n. mie e. *Pa, Po, Qp, Xa, Xd*; n. point e. *Xn* — 191 a. n. reposer *Qp*; N. en riens mon e. *Xn* — 193 V. mon cas un peu poser *Xn*

Stanza XX

194 Car s. n. *Pa, Po, Qp, Xa, Xd*; Las s. n. v. p. me g. *Xn* — 195 E. ma douleur f. *Pa, Po, Qp, Xa, Xd*; Sante ne pourray acquerir *Xn* — 196 Par v. b. *Pa, Qp, Xa, Xd*; Par humble response a. *Po*; En souffrant peine douloureuse *Xn* — 197 j. que s. *Pa, Po, Qp, Xa, Xd*; En chemin suis la mort querir *Xn* — 198 Il m. c. b. finir *Pa, Po, Qp, Xa, Xd*; Non cessant par tout l'enquerir *Xn* — 199-200 *lines inverted Pa, Po, Qp, Xa, Xd* — 199 Par une douleur savoureuse *Pa, Qp, Xa, Xd*; Par une douleur rigoureuse *Po*; Pour une douleur envieuse *Xn* — 200 Se vous nestes de moy piteuse *Pa, Po, Qp, Xa, Xd*; S. de moy vous nestes p. *Xn* — 201 d. j. mesmerveille *Po*; Qui fort me poinct j. g. *Xn* — 202 q. j. repose ou je v. *Po*; me *missing*, o. je v. *Xn* — 204-05 *lines missing Pa, Qp, Xa, Xd* — 204 Jen ay .xx. puces en loreille *Po*; Qui dict p. s. *Xn* — 205 Qui d. q. *Po* — 206 P. me d. *Po, Xn*

Stanza XXI

207 n. s. sil adviendra *Xn* — 209 e. a m. *Xn* — 210 q. me f. *Pa, Po, Qp, Xa, Xd*; J. pense b. q. me f. *Xn* — 211 A mon advis et conviendra *Xn* — 212 C. doresenavant m. *Pa, Po, Qp, Xa, Xd, Xn* — 213 A vous seule je me complains *Pa, Po, Qp, Xa, Xd, Xn* — 214 D. mon grief mal qui ne vient moindre *Xn* — 215 Qui me faict souspirer et plaindre *Xn* — 216 s. nen f. *Pa, Po, Qp, Xa, Xd*

Stanza XXII

Rubric: La dame *Pa, Po, Qp, Xa, Xd*; Rescrit de la dame au dit amant *Xn* — 220 q. voz c. *Pa*; Sil e. q. vostre c. s. *Po*; Sil est ainsi que fort s. d. *Xn* — 221 Vostre cueur et largement cueille *Xn* — 222 De d. q. *Xn* — 223 i. pourtant force que v. *Xn* — 224 e. q. racueille *Pa, Po, Qp, Xa, Xd* — 225 v. p. regretz *Pa, Po, Qp, Xa, Xd, Xn* — 226 p. n. faiz *Pa, Po, Qp, Xa, Xd, Xn*; Pour m. n. *Xn* — 227 v. mavez d. *Pa, Po, Qp, Xa, Xd*; q. a. on entendit *Xn* — 228 e. vos l. *Pa*; e. vostre l. *Po*; Par vostre faict et vostre dict *Xn* — 229 Que vostre cueur est de nuict f. *Xn* — 230 Et qui tressaut et contredit *Xn* — 231 Tous voz raisons vous mavez dict *Xn* — 232 Mais vous nestes point fort m. *Xn*

Stanza XXIII

233 e. moy s. *Pa, Qp, Xa, Xd*; Si languissez e. m. *Xn* — 234 m. servies e. *Po*; m. s. doresnavant *Xn* — 235 Mais entendez a vostre affaire *Xn* — 237 v. monstre n. *Po*; v. monstre n. *Xa*; Ne vous monstra chere en devant *Xn* — 238 Ne chose fis qui vous peust p. *Xn* — s. j. rude a bien faire *Xn* — 240 Peu cherissant m. a. *Xn* — 241 Bien me garder fort e. *Xn* — 242 c. et qui v. *Po*; Pense c. c. *Xn* — 244 q. ne suis humble et p. *Pa, Qp*; j. suys humble et p. *Po*; j. ne suis humble et p. *Xa*; q. ne suis humble et p. *Xd*; q. suis damantz p. *Xn* — 245 Dautres que vous trouver faudra *Xn*

Stanza XXIV

247 est *missing Po* — 249 n. h. saveur *Xn* — 250 N. par a. n. par c. *Pa, Po, Qp, Xa, Xd, Xn* — 251 T. sen q. *Pa, Po, Xa, Xd*; Sen tienne q. v. *Qp*; Se tienne q. v. *Xn* — 252 En moy nest p. v. *Xn* — 258 Du bon chemin tres loing s. *Xn* — *The envoi that follows line 258 and ends the text in Xn appears below. Its third line has the same reading as line 169 in Stanza XVII. The fourth line in this envoi is similar to line 170 in that same stanza.*

Amant a moy sans plus muser
Bref soyez content sil vous plaist
Prenez en gre le reffuser
Je nen puis mais sil vous desplaist.

Stanza XXV

Rubric: Lamant *Pa, Po*; Lamoureux *Qp, Xa, Xd* — 259–414 *lines missing Xn* — 261 c. pour a. *Pa, Po, Qp, Xa, Xd* — 265 j. s. conte[...] *Qp* — 267 m. par v. *Pa, Po, Qp, Xa, Xd* — 268 p. nulle a. *Pa, Po, Qp, Xa, Xd* — 270 je *missing*, n. p. reconforte *Pa, Po, Qp, Xa, Xd*

Stanza XXVI

273 q. f. nest content *Pa, Qp, Xa, Xd* — 275 t. a p. *Pa, Po, Qp, Xa, Xd* — 277 n. b. h[...] *Qp* — 280 v. cueur a. *Pa, Qp, Xa, Xd* — 282 E. regardes b. *Pa*; Je vois que la mort ja matainct *Po* — 283 d. l. empraint *Pa, Qp, Xa, Xd*; Je suys desja palle et detainct *Po* — 284 Dune douleur qui mon ceur larde *Po*

Stanza XXVII

287 m. livrent a. *Pa, Qp, Xd* — 289 Si fort que ne men puis saillir *Pa, Po, Qp, Xa, Xd*; *line missing Pc* — 294 d. a nul mentente *Pa, Po, Qp, Xa, Xd* — 295 m.

r. si bien *Pa, Qp, Xa, Xd*; E. puis epoir m. dit acten *Po* — 297 q. g. ten contente *Pa, Po, Qp, Xa, Xd*

Stanza XXVIII

Rubric: La dame *Pa, Po, Qp, Xa, Xd* — 298 S. b. secretement aymez *Pa, Po, Qp, Xa, Xd* — 299 Et b. loiaument vous servez *Pa, Xa, Xd*; Ou se loyaulment vous serves *Po*; [...]t b. loyaulment vous servez *Qp* — 300 [...] n. a. *Qp* — 301 Ou s. b. *Pa, Qp, Xa, Xd*; Ou se en gre v. recepves *Po* — 302 q. v. aymez *Pa, Qp, Xa, Xd*; Tout le mal que compte maves *Po* — 303 p. ou d. *Pa, Qp, Xa, Xd*; n. men p. *Po* — 305 f. a v. *Po*; [...]e q. f. *Qp* — 306 j. ne s. *Pa, Po, Qp, Xa, Xd* — 307 h. ce nest a t. *Po* — 309 s. lealle t. *Xa*

Stanza XXIX

312 n. ser v. *Pa* — 313 [...]oit d. m. *Qp* — 314 [...]e j. p. *Qp* — 315 [...]e q. u. *Qp* — 316 Q. me d. *Qp, Xd* — 319 o. ne fiz n. n. feray *Pa, Qp, Xa, Xd*; Jamaiz je ne masserviray *Po* — 320 Je nay cure de telle atache *Po*

Stanza XXX

324–36 *stanza missing Pa, Po, Qp, Xa, Xd*

Stanza XXXI

Rubric: Lamant *Pa, Po, Qp*; Lamoureux *Xa, Xd* — 337 Cest c. d. *Pa, Qp, Xa*; Esse d. q. *Po* — 338 E. par l. *Qp, Xa, Xd* — 339 d. ou d. *Po* — 342 M. feissent p. *Pa, Qp, Xa, Xd*; M. fassent p. *Po* — 343 J. cuide q. *Pa, Qp, Xa, Xd*; ce *missing Qp, Xd* — 344 q. scet l. *Pa, Po, Qp, Xa, Xd* — 345 et *missing Pa, Po, Qp, Xa, Xd* — 346 *line missing Pa, Qp, Xa, Xd, but in all except Xa, there is an additional line (350bis) that has the correct rhyme to make it fit as line 346:* De ce forfeit et grant diffame; Que jay tousjours servy sans blasme *Po* — 347 f. d. dicelle *Po* — 349 j. len r. *Po*

Stanza XXXII

350 q. t. jendure *Po* — 351 U. doulceur q. *Xa* — 353 L. p. terrible et obscure *Po* — 354 Q. longuement e. *Po* — 355 l. ia a d. *Pa, Qp, Xa, Xd*; Et semble quamours lait jure *Po* — 356 Puisque mon ceur est endure *Po* — 357 De d. e. de t. *Po* — 358 Pour v. m. *Po* — 359 Je pers m. b. et m. c. *Po* — 361 M. tresoultrageuse d. *Po* — 362 n. plus rien q. *Pa, Qp, Xa, Xd*

Stanza XXXIII

364 v. avez a. *Xa* — 366 Quant rien il n. v. *Pa, Po, Qp, Xa, Xd* — 367 Mais a servy s. n. *Pa, Po, Qp, Xa, Xd* — 368 d. c. et d. *Pa, Po, Qp, Xa, Xd* — 369 q. sa t.

Po — 370 g. nen s. *Pa, Po, Qp, Xa* — 371 v. le c. *Po* — 373 e. ja tout p. *Po* — 375 Pour v. pour lamour de m. d. *Pa, Qp, Xa, Xd*; Pour vostre amour ma chere d. *Po*

Stanza XXXIV

Rubric: La dame *Pa, Po, Qp, Xa, Xd* — 376 Dia p. d. *Pa, Qp, Xa, Xd*; Mais p. d. *Po* — 377 e. du p. *Pa, Po, Qp, Xa, Xd* — 380 f. en p. *Pa, Po, Qp, Xa, Xd* — 383 Et d. s. *Xa* — 387 d. b. largement *Pa, Qp, Xa, Xd*; D. d. et du tourment *Po* — 388 n. devez b. *Pa, Po, Qp, Xa, Xd*

Stanza XXXV

389 f. et d. *Po* — 390 e. est mon entente *Po* — 391 d. vostre r. *Pa, Qp, Xa, Xd* — 392 n. a. lentente *Pa, Qp, Xa, Xd*; q. n. si attempte *Po* — 393 n. par m. *Pa, Po, Qp, Xa, Xd* — 394 *line missing Pa, Qp, Xa, Xd* — 395 Si a. m. *Pa, Qp, Xa, Xd* — 396 *scribe mistakenly put a capital E here as if it marked the beginning of a new stanza Pa* — 397 c. mie p. *Pa, Po, Qp, Xa, Xd* — 399 Vous vous debates pour neant *Po*; v. aye n. *Xa* — 400 Car vostre mal nest pas si grant *Po* — 401 Qui faille que la mort endure *Po*; Que p. l. *Pa, Qp, Xa, Xd*

Stanza XXXVI

402 Oncques j. n. *Po* — 404 e. d. et ataine *Pa, Qp, Xd*; Pour tel d. soubdaine *Po*; e. d. et atainte *Xa* — 405 s. f. aiguir *Pa, Qp, Xa*; s. f. arguir *Xd* — 406 f. b. esjouir *Pa, Xa, Xd*; n. le f. b. esjouyr *Po, Qp* — 407 A a. s. *Pa, Qp, Xa, Xd* — 410 a m. rien ne feroie *Pa, Qp, Xa, Xd*; j. nen s. *Po* — 411 Si a. v. *Pa, Qp, Xa*; Guerir vous aves a. a. *Po* — 412 Q. vous peut bien r. *Pa, Po, Qp, Xa, Xd*; r. e. [...] *Qp* — 413 j. n. sauroie *Pa, Po, Qp, Xa, Xd* — *No explicit Pa, Qp, Xa, Xd*; Et ho *Po*

Table 1A.
Missing, Inverted, and Additional Lines in
La Belle Dame qui eust mercy using the Base Manuscript, Paris, BnF f. fr. MS 1131 (*Pc*)

Missing	Inverted	Additional
—	↕	+

Line(s)	Pc	Pa	Pb	Pd	Pe	Pf	Pj	Pk	Pl	Po	Pp	Qa	Qb	Qd	Qh	Qn	Qp	Qq	Qr	Qx	Xa	Xd	Xe
1																							
1–112																		—		—			
9–12		—																			—		
9–16																	—						
121–36																				—			
129–36 /		↕	↕	↕	↕	↕	↕	↕	↕	↕		↕	↕	↕	↕	↕	↕	↕			↕	↕	↕
137–44																							
134–35					—																		
145bis																							+
147bis																							+
149											—												
152bis																							+
154–55										↕													↕
155–57					—																		

Line(s)	Pc	Pa	Pb	Pd	Pe	Pf	Pj	Pk	Pl	Po	Pp	Qa	Qb	Qd	Qh	Qn	Qp	Qq	Qr	Qx	Xa	Xd	Xe
158–70 / 184–96																				↕			
158–83										|													
163–64			↕										↕		↕			↕					
166–68													|										
170																		|					
171–83																				|			
175			|												|								
180bis			+												+								
183			|									|			|			|					
188												|											
194												+											
196bis																							
197–209 / 210–22		↕		↕				↕	↕	↕				↕		↕	↕		↕		↕		
209bis												+											
210–22																							
210–378																				|			|
221																		|					
226–27				↕		↕	↕	↕	↕	↕		↕	↕	↕	↕	↕	↕	↕			↕	↕	↕

Table 1A

Line(s)	Pc	Pa	Pb	Pd	Pe	Pf	Pj	Pk	Pl	Po	Pp	Qa	Qb	Qd	Qh	Qn	Qp	Qq	Qr	Qx	Xa	Xd	Xe
231																							
240																							
254																							
264																							
273																							
275–87 / 288–300											↕												
276bis		+																			+		
278–80																							
294–300																							
299																							
299bis		+															+					+	
305																							
309																							
323																							
325																							
331																							
332																							

Line(s)	Pc	Pa	Pb	Pd	Pe	Pf	Pj	Pk	Pl	Po	Pp	Qa	Qb	Qd	Qh	Qn	Qp	Qq	Qr	Qx	Xa	Xd	Xe
332bis																		+					
349–50			↕												↕			↕					
356–57				↕					↕	↕			↕	↕	↕	↕							↕
363–64			↕												↕								
373–74			↕												↕								
374										—								—					
376–77									↕							↕							↕
377																		—					
Total lines missing	0	4	7	0	8	1	1	2	3	29	1	2	3	0	6	3	8	9	0	310	6	0	20

Table 1B.

Rhyme Schemes and Gender

Missing, Inverted, and Additional Lines in
Le Dialogue d'amoureux et de sa dame using the Base Manuscript,
Paris, BnF f. fr. MS 1131 (*Pc*)

	Missing		Inverted		Additional	
	—		↔		+	

Manuscript-Incunabula / Line Number(s)	Pc	Pa	Po	Qp	Xa	Xd	Xn
1–180			—				—
37	—						
94	—						
138–39				—			
164–65		↔		↔	↔	↔	
177	—						
199–200		↔	↔	↔	↔	↔	
204		—		—	—	—	
205		—		—	—	—	
204–05			↔				
259–414							—
289	—						
324–36		—	—	—	—	—	
346[1]		—		—	—	—	
350bis		+		+		+	
394		—		—	—	—	
Envoi[2]							+
Total no. of missing lines	4	15	193	17	17	15	336

[1] Line 346 is missing in *Pa, Qp,* and *Xd*, but appears at the end of the stanza as line 350bis.
[2] *Xn* presents only lines 81–140, or six stanzas (XIX–XIV), followed by a four-line envoi, which uses line 169 as its third line.

TABLE 2

Rhyme Schemes and Gender

The rhyme schemes used in *La Belle Dame qui eust mercy* and *Le Dialogue d'amoureux et de sa dame*, including a breakdown by gender, are detailed in the grid and the outlines below.

La Belle Dame qui eust mercy	Rhyme Gender in Poem 1 (lines 1–144) and Poem 2 (lines 145-378)		
	Poem 1 = Total of 144 rhymes	Poem 2 = Total of 234 rhymes	Poems 1 & 2 = Total of 378 rhymes
Masculine Rhymes	57% (82 rhymes)	62% (145 rhymes)	60% (227 rhymes)
Feminine Rhymes	43% (62 rhymes)	38% (89 rhymes)	40% (151 rhymes)

Le Dialogue d'amoureux et de sa dame	Rhyme Gender in Poem 1 (lines 1-180) and Poem 2 (lines 181-414)		
	Poem 1 = Total of 180 rhymes	Poem 2 = Total of 234 rhymes	Poems 1 & 2 = Total of 414 rhymes
Masculine Rhymes	74.5% (134 rhymes)	56% (131 rhymes)	64% (265 rhymes)
Feminine Rhymes	25.5% (46 rhymes)	44% (103 rhymes)	36% (149 rhymes)

La Belle Dame qui eust mercy

Poem 1: Stanzas I—XVIII

There are eight possible *abc* rhyme schemes in a *huitain*: abc / a'b'c'/ a'b'c / a'bc'/ ab'c'/ abc'/ ab'c /a'bc (where the apostrophe indicates a feminine rhyme). All of these are used at least once in the eighteen stanzas in Poem 1. The most common rhyme schemes are #1 (found in five stanzas, all of which contain only masculine rhymes) and #5 (found in five stanzas, all of which contain a feminine "b" rhyme). Two rhyme schemes are used twice each, and the

TABLE 2   85

remainder are used once. Masculine rhymes account for 57% of the rhymes used in Poem 1.

Scheme #1: a b a b b c b c

I	a = os	b = er	c = é
IV	a = és	b = ien	c = uis
VII	a = er	b = ours	c = aint
VIII	a = ir	b = ant	c = et
XVIII	a = a	b = ay	c = y

Scheme #2: a b' a b' b' c' b' c'

II	a = ent	b' = endre	c' = iengne
IX	a = ent	b' = ire	c' = oye

Scheme #3: a' b a' b b c' b c'

III	a' = ie, ye	b = is	c' = ame, asme

Scheme #4: a' b' a' b' b' c' b' c'

V	a' = ose	b' = ouche, oulce	c' = esse
VI	a' = ee	b' = ise	c' = aulte

Scheme #5: a b' a b' b' c b' c

X	a = oint	b' = aine	c = int
XI	a = ir	b' = ance	c = er
XIV	a = ist	b' = elle	c = é
XV	a = oy	b' = omple, onte	c = ieulx, ieux
XVI	a = eu	b' = ure	c = ier

Scheme #6: a b a b b c' b c'

XII	a = er	b = aiz, ayz	c' = ictes, ites

Scheme #7: a' b' a' b' b' c b' c

XIII	a' = euse	b' = aire	c = oys

Scheme #8: a' b a' b b c b c

XVII	a' = eille	b = ir	c = oir

Poem 2: Stanzas XIX—XXXVI

Ten of the sixteen possible *abcd* rhyme schemes are used in the eighteen *treizains* in Poem 2.[1] No particular scheme stands out: three have all masculine rhymes (#1) and three have feminine 'a' and 'd' rhymes (#4). Four schemes are used twice each, four are used only once. Masculine rhymes make up slightly less than two-thirds of the rhymes in this section (62%).

Scheme #1: a a b a a b b c c d c c d

XXVI a = ains	b = és	c = oit	d = és
XXX a = iers	b = aict, ait	c = ans	d = ys, is
XXXIII a = ief	b = uis	c = é	d = el

Scheme #2: a' a' b a' a' b b c c d c c d

XXIX a' = iegne	b = és	c = aulx, eaulx	d = al

Scheme #3: a' a' b' a' a' b' b' c' c' d c' c' d

XXIV a' = ace, ache	b' = eulle, ueulle	c' = aicte, aycte	d = ault
XXXIV a' = ue	b' = ence, ense	c' = ace, asse	d = a

Scheme #4: a' a' b a' a' b b c c d' c c d'

XIX a' = iere	b = ir	c = on	d' = icte, ite
XXVIII a' = ainte	b = eult, eust	c = iés	d' = ine, igne
XXXII a' = ointe	b = ir	c = ung, un	d' = arte

Scheme #5: a a b' a a b' b' c c d c c d

XXV a = és	b' = eure	c = as, acs	d = é
XXVII a = ist	b' = onques	c = us	d = eil

Scheme #6: a a b' a a b' b' c' c' d c' c' d

XXII a = ient	b' = ie	c' = age	d = ous

Scheme #7: a a b' a a b' b' c' c' d' c' c' d'

XXI a = eul, ueul	b' = ee	c' = able	d' = ivre
XXIII a = és	b' = aindre	c' = ente, empte	d' = iefve

[1] abcd / a'b'c'd'/ a'bcd / a'b'cd / a'b'c'd / a'bc'd / a'b'c'd'/ a'bcd'/ a'b'cd'/ ab'cd / ab'c'd / ab'c'd'/ ab'cd'/ abc'd'/ abc'd/ abcd'.

TABLE 2 87

Scheme #8: a a b a a b b c' c' d' c' c' d'

XXXI a = és   b = ié   c' = orte   d' = onde

Scheme #9: a a b a a b b c' c' d c' c' d

XX   a = ieulx, yeulx b = é   c' = aise, ayse d = ort

Scheme #10: a a b a a b b c c d' c c d'

XXXV   a = our   b = ier   c = é   d' = arge
XXXVI a = és   b = eur, ueur   c = on   d' = emble

Le Dialogue d'amoureux et de sa dame

Poem 1: Stanzas I—XVIII

Of the sixteen possible *abcd* rhyme schemes, eight are used in Poem 1 of *Le Dialogue*, one of which (#7) appears in four stanzas, two appear in three stanzas each, three appear twice, and two appear once. Masculine rhymes account for amost three-quarters (74.5%) of the rhymes in Poem 1.

Scheme #1: a b a b b c c d c d

II   a = eulx, eux   b = er   c = ant   d = oit
VI   a = eur   b = er   c = y   d = iés, és
XIII   a = y   b = és   c = on   d = oir

Scheme #2: a' b a' b b c c d c d

V   a' = ie, ye   b = é   c = ir   d = ant
XII   a' = euses   b – ié, é   c = ent   d = u
XVII   a' = ouche   b= ent   c = er   d = aist

Scheme #3: a' b' a' b' b' c c d c d

I   a' = aine   b' = ance   c = ir, yr   d = oir

Scheme #4: a' b a' b b c c d' c d'

III   a' = ee   b = ent   c = ay   d' = oye
IV   a' = ire   b = a   c = er   d' = ance

Scheme #5: a b' a b' b' c c d c d

| XIV | a = y | b' = elle | c = ort | d = eul |
| XVIII | a = oy | b' = euse | c = er | d = ans |

Scheme #6: a b' a b' b' c c d' c d'

| X | a = oir | b' = oye, oie | c = é | d' = ance |

Scheme #7: a b a b b c' c' d c' d

VII	a = és	b = er	c' = esse	d = art
IX	a = a	b = our	c' = ice	d = é
XI	a = ous	b = oir	c' = ie, ye	d = és
XVI	a = é	b = ant	c' = ie	d = ir

Scheme #8: a b a b b c c d' c d'

| VIII | a = yeulx, ieulx | b = ent | c = aiz | d' = elle |
| XV | a = er | b = a | c = ent | d' = asse |

Poem 2: Stanzas XIX — XXXVI

Poem 2 of *Le Dialogue* uses eleven *abcd* rhyme schemes, two of which are used in three stanzas each, three are used twice each, and the remainder once each. Masculine rhymes account for 56% of the total rhymes.

Scheme #1: a a b a a b b c c d c c d

| XXXIV | a = ys, iz | b = on | c = ent | d = ous |

Scheme #2: a' a' b a' a' b b c c d c c d

| XXX | a' = iere | b = oit | c = er, ier | d = ours |

Scheme #3: a' a' b a' a' b b c' c' d c' c' d

| XIX | a' = esse | b = uis, uys | c' = ance | d = er |
| XXXII | a' = ure | b = é | c' = esse | d = ort |

Scheme #4: a' a' b a' a' b b c c d' c c d'

| XXII | a' = eulle | b = aiz, etz | c = ist, it | d' = ade |

Table 2   89

Scheme #5: a' a' b' a' a' b' b' c c d' c c d'

XXXV   a' = empte, ente   b' = ee   c = empt, ent, ant   d' = ure

Scheme #6: a a b' a a b' b' c' c' d c' c' d

XX a = ir	b' = euse	c' = eille	d = ault
XXIII a = ant	b' = aire	c' = euse	d = a
XXVIII a = és	b' = aire	c' = ee	d = ort

Scheme #7: a a b' a a b' b' c' c' d' c' c' d'

XXIV a = eur	b' = ire	c' = esse	d' = arge
XXXVI a = ir, yr	b' = aine	c' = oye	d' = ye, ie

Scheme #8: a a b' a a b' b' c c d' c c d'

XXVI a = ent	b' = eure	c = aint	d' = arde
XXIX a = a	b' = ose	c = ay	d' = ache
XXXIII a = ait	b' = ee	c = er	d' = asme, ame

Scheme #9: a a b a a b b c' c' d' c' c' d'

XXXI   a = er   b = on   c' = elle   d' = ayme, ame

Scheme #10: a a b a a b b c' c' d c' c' d

XXI   a = a   b = aims, ains   c' = aindre   d = ant

Scheme #11: a a b a a b b c c d' c c d'

XXV a = oir	b = ent	c = é	d' = ivre
XXVII a = ir	b = ault	c = ien, iens	d' = ente, empte

TABLE 3

Rhyme Gender, Quality, and Frequency

The gender, quality, and frequency of rhyme words found in *La Belle Dame qui eust mercy* and *Le Dialogue d'amoureux et de sa dame* are detailed below.

NB: For the purposes of these tables, 'rhyme words' include all possible rhymes developed within a given stanza, from assonant to leonine pluperfect, meaning that a single word at the rhyme may be counted more than once. In Stanza IX, for example, there is a feminine leonine simple rhyme between three words, *folie* : *mirencolie* : *amye*. In addition, there is a feminine leonine pluperfect rhyme between two of those words, *folie* : *mirencolie*. Thus, this example produces five rhyme words.

Table 3   91

La Belle Dame qui eust mercy

Rhyme Gender & Quality	Rhyme Words in Poem 1 (lines 1–144) and Poem 2 (lines 145–378)		
	Poem 1 = total of 187 rhyme words	Poem 2 = total of 327 rhyme words	Poems 1 & 2 = total of 514 rhyme words
Masculine Rhymes			
Assonant	34 words / 18.2%	71 words / 21.7%	105 words / 20.4%
Consonant	32 words / 17.1%	40 words / 12.2%	72 words / 14%
Leonine Simple	23 words / 12.3%	66 words / 20.1%	89 words / 17.3%
Leonine Perfect	10 words / 5.4%	20 words / 6%	30 words / 5.8%
Leonine Pluperfect	2 words / 1%	2 words / 0.6%	4 words / 0.75%
Equivocal	8 words / 4.3%	14 words / 4.3%	22 words / 4.25%
Subtotal - Masculine Rhyme Words	109 words / 58.3% of all of the rhyme words in Poem I	213 words / 64.9% of all of the rhyme words in Poem II	322 words / 62.5% of all of the rhyme words in La Belle Dame qui eust mercy
Feminine Rhymes			
Leonine Simple	52 words / 27.8%	79 words / 24.3%	131 words / 25.6%
Leonine Perfect	20 words / 10.8%	23 words / 7.1%	43 words / 8.4%
Leonine Pluperfect	2 words / 1%	10 words / 3.1%	12 words / 2.35%
Equivocal	4 words / 2.1%	2 words / 0.6%	6 words / 1.15%
Subtotal - Feminine Rhyme Words	78 words / 41.7% of all of the rhyme words in Poem 1	114 words / 35.1% of all of the rhyme words in Poem 2	192 words / 37.5% of all of the rhyme words in La Belle Dame qui eust mercy

Le Dialogue d'amoureux et de sa dame

Rhyme Gender & Quality	Rhyme Words in Poem 1 (lines 1-180) and Poem 2 (lines 181-414)		
	Poem 1 = Total of 217 rhyme words	Poem 2 = Total of 302 rhyme words	Poems 1 & 2 = Total of 519 rhyme words
Masculine Rhymes			
Assonant	107 words / 49.3%	118 words / 39%	225 words / 43.35%
Consonant	12 words / 5.5%	35 words / 11.6%	47 words / 9.06%
Leonine Simple	24 words / 11%	22 words / 7.28%	46 words / 8.9%
Leonine Perfect	14 words / 6.4%	6 words / 2%	20 words / 3.85%
Leonine Pluperfect	0 words / 0%	0 words / 0%	0 words / 0%
Equivocal	6 words / 2.8%	2 words / 0.67%	8 words / 1.5%
Subtotal - Masculine Rhyme Words	163 words / 75% of all of the rhyme words in Poem 1	183 words / 60.6% of all of the rhyme words in Poem 2	346 words / 66.7% of all of the rhyme words in Le Dialogue d'amoureux et de sa dame
Feminine Rhymes			
Leonine Simple	42 words / 19.3%	93 words / 30.8%	135 words / 26%
Leonine Perfect	2 words / 1%	18 words / 6%	20 words / 3.85%
Leonine Pluperfect	8 words / 3.7%	8 words / 2.65%	16 words / 3.1%
Equivocal	2 words / 1%	0 words / 0%	2 words / 0.39%
Subtotal - Feminine Rhyme Words	54 words / 25% of all of the rhyme words in Poem 1	119 words / 39.4% of all of the rhyme words in Poem 2	173 words / 33.3% of all of the rhyme words in Le Dialogue d'amoureux et de sa dame

GLOSSARY

Abbreviations

adj.	adjective
adv.	adverb
adv. phr.	adverbial phrase
conj.	conjunction
fem.	feminine
fut.	future
impers.	impersonal
inf.	infinitive
intr. v.	intransitive verb
loc.	locution
masc.	masculine
n.	noun
p.	past
p. p.	past participle
pl.	plural
pers.	person
prep.	preposition
pres.	present
sg.	singular
subj.	subjunctive
tr. v.	transitive verb

Glossary

Acointance, fem. sg. n. B87: *acquaintance, company, involvement*
Acointe, masc. sg. p. p. Accointer, tr. v. B314: *to be favoured, known, preferred*
Actraire, inf. Attraire, tr. v. B100: *to beguile, attract, seduce*
Adonques, conj. B255: *then*
Advance, 3rd pers. sg. pres. Avancer, tr. v. B84: *to favour, prefer, promote*
Advenant, masc. sg. adj. D50: *welcome, becoming, appropriate*
Advenist, 3rd pers. sg. pres. Avenir, impers. v. B249: *to happen, come to pass*
Adviser, inf. Aviser, tr. v. B124: *to consider, decipher, understand, perceive*
Ains que, conj. B18: *first, beforehand*
Aist, ainsy m'___ Dieu, adv. phr. B13: *So help me God*

Alegerés, 2nd pers. pl. fut. Alléger, tr. v. B11: *to soothe, assuage, ease, comfort*
Amer, inf. Aimer, tr. v. B172: *to love*
Amolie, 3rd pers. sg. pres. subj. Amollir, tr. v. B189: *to weaken, soften*
Amoureux, masc. sg. adj. B251: *loving, filled with love*
Apensee, fem. sg. adj. B43: *sophisticated, intelligent, prudent*
Appartient, 3rd pers. sg. Appartenir, impers. v. B185: *to be appropriate*
Appeller, inf. tr. v. B2: *to call, label*
Apris, masc. sg. adj. B20: *well-bred, educated, mannerly*

Bien, masc. sg. n. D2, B16: *happiness, reward, boon, gift, well-being*
Blasonnés, 2nd pers. pl. pres. Blasonner, B27: *to flatter, praise, honour*
Bon, a vostre ___, adv. phr. B153: *as you please, at your will*
Briefz, masc. pl. adj. B3: *brief, short, few*
Brisay, 1st pers. sg. p. Briser, tr. v. B232: *to end, cease*

Cause, sans ___, adv. phr. B298: *for no reason, groundlessly*
Celee, fem. sg. adj. B42: *hidden, secret*
Celler, inf. Celer, tr. v. B4: *to hide, keep hidden*
Changier, inf. Changer, tr. v. B355: *to abandon, betray, be inconstant toward*
Chief, a ___, adv. phr. B331: *fully, completely*
Chiere, fem. sg. n. B99: *countenance, aspect, look*
Clamours, fem. pl. n. D333: *complaint, demand, request*
Cointe, fem. sg. adj. B317: *beautiful, gracious*
Combien, ___ que, conj. B182: *however much, even though*
Conforter, inf. tr. v. B91: *to comfort, aid, console*
Consceil, masc. sg. n. B258: *counsel, idea, thought*
Contraint, 3rd pers. sg. pres. Contraindre, tr. v. B54: *to compel, constrain, oblige*
Contredire, inf. v. tr. D33: *to argue, counter, dispute*
Convenist, 3rd pers. sg. p. Convenir, impers. v. B252: *to force, be necessary, so happen*
Courage, avoir le ___ de, loc. B195: *to be disposed, have the heart/thought, be inclined [to do something]*
Crains, 1st pers. sg. pres. Craindre, tr. v. D132: *to fear, revere, adore*
Cremeur, fem. sg. n. D250: *fear, awe, respect*
Croistre, inf. tr. v. D212: *to strip, remove, eliminate*
Cuydasse, 1st pers. sg. imp. subj. Cuider, tr. v. B350: *to believe, think*

Dangier, masc. sg. n. D80: *resistance, refusal*
Deboutés, 2nd pers. pl. pres. Débouter, tr. v. B238: *to reject, spurn*
Dechoit, 3rd pers. sg. pres. Déchoir, tr. v. D329: *to fall low, diminish, be reduced*
Demaine, masc. sg. n. B77: *domain, authority*

Demeure, 3rd pers. sg. pres. Demeurer, intr. v. B225: *to remain, be left*

Departir, sans _____, adv. phr. D7: *steadfastly, relentlessly*

Derechief, adv. B327: *once again, once more*

Desacointe, 3rd pers. sg. pres. subj. Desaccointer, tr. v. B315: *to separate, break up*

Desassemble, 3rd pers. sg. pres. Désassembler, tr. v. B375: *to rend asunder, break apart*

Desceuvre, 1st pers. sg. pres. Découvrir, tr. v. D294: *to reveal, expose*

Desdaigneuse, fem. sg. adj. D243: *disdainful, scornful, haughty*

Despite, fem. sg. adj. B157: *disdainful, spiteful*

Despointe, 3rd pers. sg. pres. subj. Dépointer, tr. v. B318: *to dispossess, eliminate something from someone*

Deult, 3rd pers. sg. pres. Se Douloir, refl. v. B264: *to suffer, grieve*

Doint, 3rd pers. sg. pres. subj. Donner, tr. v. B220: *to give, grant*

Dolent, masc. sg. adj. B163: *doleful, sad, sorrowful*

Doubter, inf. Douter, tr. v. D15: *to revere, adore*

Doubtés, 2nd pers. pl. pres. Douter, tr. v. B242: *to fear, be on guard against, be wary of*

Douloir, inf. tr. v. D10: *to suffer, feel pain*

Ennuyeulx, faire l'_____, loc. B161: *to annoy, bother, be annoying, be bothersome*

Enquerir, inf. Enquérir, tr. v. D47: *to seek, seek to know, demand, request*

Enté, masc. sg. adj. B6: *adorned, embellished, replete*

Entendre, inf. tr. v. B30: *to understand, comprehend*

Entente, fem. sg. n. B208: *intention, will*

Entiere, fem. sg. adj. D327: *whole, unspoiled, pure, sincere*

Entreprinse, fem. sg. n. B42: *intent, endeavour, undertaking*

Entrepris, faire ___ , tr. v. B21: *to intend, endeavour, undertake to do, aim*

Entrevoyon, 1st pers. pl. pres. Entrevoir, tr. v. B376: *to see each other*

Esbahie, fem. sg. adj. D41: *bewildered, baffled, perplexed*

Eschiet, 3rd pers. sg. pres. Échoir, tr. v. D115: *to happen, befall*

Eschivé, masc. sg. p. p., Esquiver, tr. v. B364: *to avoid*

Escondire, inf. tr. v. B69: *to rebuff, reject, dismiss*

Escondisseur, masc. sg. n. D53: *someone who refuses, resists, rejects*

Eslire, inf. Élire, tr. v. D252: *to choose, select*

Esplouré, masc. sg. adj. B163: *tearful*

Espris, masc. sg. p. p. Éprendre, B23: *taken captive, seized, ensnared*

Esprouvé, masc. sg. p. p. Éprouver, tr. v. B337: *to put to the test, judge, evaluate*

Estrangier, inf. Étranger, tr. v. B359: *to keep at a distance, keep at bay*

Estrivé, masc. sg. p. p. Estriver, tr. v. B360: *to resist, refuse*

Fainte, fem. sg. adj. B266: *false, deceitful*

Faveur, fem. sg. n. D249: *affection, predilection, preference, inclination*

Ferue, fem. sg. p. p. Férir, tr. v. B343: *to strike* (feru *modifies masculine noun* cueur; *feminine form used incorrectly because needed for the rhyme*)

Feur, a nul ___ , loc. B371: *not for anything, not at any price*

Fiance, fem. sg. n. B85: *vow, pledge, promise*

Force, par ___ , adv. phr. B252: *by force or constraint*

Forment, adv. B264: *grievously, mightily*

Fors, prep. B8: *except, if only, but*

Fors que, conj. B290: *except that, nothing but*

Foyson, fem. sg. n. D339: *multitude, abundance, large quantity*

Franc, masc. sg. adj. B154: *free, willing, sincere*

Franche, fem. sg. adj. D389: *free, independent, unfettered*

Franchyse, fem. sg. n. D273: *nobility, privilege, freedom*

Garder, inf. tr. v. B88: *to preserve, maintain, keep*

Garison, fem. sg. n. D193: *remedy, cure, protection*

Gracieulx, masc. sg. adj. B336: *gracious, benevolent, amiable, sweet*

Gré, en ___ , adv. phr. B7: *favourably, willingly*

Griefve, 3rd pers. sg. pres. Grever B206: *to pain, hurt, wound*

Hardement, masc. sg. n. D22: *boldness, courage, force, determination*

Haulte, fem. sg. adj. B46: *bold, presumptuous, pretentious, overconfident*

Honneur, masc. sg. n. B12: *honour, virtue*

Humblement, adv. B9: *humbly, kindly, graciously*

Ja, ne ___ , adv. B14: *never*

Juree, fem. sg. p. p. Jurer, tr. v. B177: *to swear, solemnly declare*

Lacs, masc. sg./pl. n. B233; Laiz, D77: *snare, trap, net*

Laisserés, 2nd pers. plg. fut. Laisser, tr. v. B198: *to forsake, cease, stop*

Largement, adv. B27: *greatly, generously*

Largesse, fem. sg. n. D253: *generosity, abundance*

Las, masc. sg. adj. B231: *tired, weary*

Legier, de ___ , masc. sg. adj. B128: *slight, trifling, trivial*

Los, masc. sg. n. B1: *praise, honour*

Losengiers, masc. pl. n. B289: *slanderers, gossips, rumourmongers*

Maint, masc. sg. adj. B127: *many, a good number*

Mendre, fem. sg. adj. B12: *less, diminished*

Mercy, masc. sg. n. B183: *mercy, compassion accorded out of grace, pity*

Merveille, fem. sg. n. B129: *amazement, surprise, astonishment*
Mesaise, fem. sg. n. B169: *anguish, distress, discomfort*
Meschief, masc. sg. n. B330: *distress, chagrin*
Mesdisans, masc. pl. n. D178: *gossipmongers, gossips, liars*
Mesprendre, inf. Méprendre, tr. v. B13: *to do harm, do wrong*
Mie, ne ___ , adv. B6: *not [negation]*
Mire, masc. sg. n. D158: *healer, doctor*
Monte, 3rd pers. sg. pres. Monter, tr. v. B114: *to amount to*
Moult, adv. B160: *very, extremely*
Muser, inf. tr. v. D332: *to waste one's time, linger, dawdle*

Neantmains, adv. B174: *nonetheless*
Nette, fem. sg. adj. D327: *pure, innocent, faultless, unsoiled*
Nice, fem. sg. adj. B32: *naïve, simple, innocent, unworldly;* masc. sg. n. D89: *dolt, simpleton, idiot*
Noblesse, fem. sg. n. D254: *privilege, nobility*
Nuysans, masc. sg. adj. B295: *harmful, injurious*

Octroyeray, 1st pers. sg. fut. Octroyer, tr. v. B357: *to grant, offer, gift*
Onques mais, adv. B105: *never before*
Ordonné, masc. sg. p. p. Ordonner, tr. v. B110: *to ordain, order, set to rights*
Orguelleuse, fem. sg. adj. B157: *arrogant, proud, vain*
Orray, 1st pers. sg. fut. Ouïr, tr. v. B36: *to hear, listen to*
Oultrageuse, fem. sg. adj. B46: *excessive, outrageous, shocking*
Ouÿr, inf. tr. v. B9: *to listen to, hear*

Paine, fem. sg. n. B74: *effort, pain, distress*
Painer, se ___ , inf. Se Peiner, refl. v. B76: *to suffer pain or distress*
Parler, masc. sg. n. B5: *speech, language, manner of speaking*
Part, a ___ , adv. phr. B88: *on one's own, all alone*
Party, masc. sg. p. p. Partir, D57: *divided, split, shared*
Penitance, fem. sg. n. D5: *punishment, penance*
Plaigniés, 2nd pers. pl. pres. Plaindre, tr. v. B95: *to complain*
Pourchace, 3rd pers. sg. pres. Pourchasser, tr. v. B211: *to bring about, cause*
Pourvoye, 3rd pers. sg. pres. subj. Pourvoir, tr. v. B70: *to consider, contemplate*
Poy, masc. sg. n. B28: *little, small amount;* adv. B43: *little, barely*

Poyse, 3rd pers. sg. pres. Péser, tr. v. B48: *to trouble, weigh upon*
Prendray, 1st pers. sg. fut. Prendre, tr. v. B309: *to dress in, don*
Privé, masc. sg. adj. B361: *deprived;* B363: *discreet, prudent, reserved*

Querir, inf. Quérir, tr. v. B133: *to seek*

Quicte, masc. sg. adj. B154: *free of obligations or restrictions*

Quis, masc. sg. p. p. Quérir, tr. v. B332: *to request, seek, desire*; B333: *to seek, try to find*

Rebelle, fem. sg. adj. D80: *contrary, hostile, resistant*

Reconfort, masc. sg. n. B167: *comfort, aid, succour*

Reconfort, 3rd pers. sg. pres. Réconforter, tr. v. B308: *to comfort, aid, succour*

Rectraict, masc. sg. p. p. Retraire, tr. v. B290: *to emanate from, come forth*

Recueul, 3rd pers. sg. pres. Recueillir, tr. v. B172: *to reap, gather, amass*

Reffraint, 3rd pers. sg. pres. Refraindre, tr. v. B56: *to alleviate, temper, moderate, calm*

Regarder, inf. tr. v. B7: *to see*; B86: *to search, look (for)*

Regretz, masc. pl. n. D225: *complaints, despair, heartache*

Renom, masc. sg. n. B1: *reputation, high repute, renown, fame*

Reprendre, inf. tr. v. B15: *to reproach, blame, criticize, condemn*

Reprouvé, masc. sg. p. p. Réprouver, tr. v. B334: *to blame, reproach, criticize, condemn*

Requerir, inf. Requérir, tr. v. D46: *to woo, implore, beseech*

Retenir, inf. tr. v. B57: *to retain, keep, recognize*

Retraire, inf. tr. v. B101: *to back down, retreat*

Rigour, masc. sg. n. B356: *obstinacy, opposition*

Rudesse, masc. sg. adj. D69: *coarseness, roughness, lack of refinement*

Rusé, masc. sg. adj. D88: *tricked, duped, deceived*

Sachés, 2nd pers. pl. pres. subj. Savoir, tr. v. B18: *to know, understand, comprehend*

Saige, fem. sg. adj. B2: *wise, reasonable, prudent*

Santé, fem. sg. n. D269: *relief, health, well-being*

Sauvage, fem. sg. adj. B191: *cruel, harsh, fierce*

Sayson, fem. sg. n. D342: *time of life, season*

Secret, masc. sg. adj. B62: *discreet, private, secret*

Semblant, masc. sg. n. D19 : *deceit, deception, falsehood*; D45: *sign, gesture*; D216: *inclination*

Sequeure, 3rd pers. sg. pres. Secourir, tr. v. B228: *to bring aid, succour, comfort*

Servant, masc. sg. n. B58: *servant*

Seul, 1st pers. sg. pres. Souloir, intr. v. B175: *to be accustomed to, used to*

Solas, masc. sg. n. B230: *solace, pleasure, consolation*

Souffrant, pres. p. Souffrir, tr. v. B169: *to suffer, endure pain*

Souvenir, masc. sg. n. D291: *thought, memory*

Tache, fem. sg. n. D320: *stain, mark, blemish*

Talent, masc. sg. n. D164: *intent, desire, will*

Targe, fem. sg. n. D258: *shield, armour, armament, protection*

Tiegne, 3rd pers. sg. pres. subj. Tenir, tr. v. B276: *to keep, hold*; B279 *to hold to, remain steadfast to*

Toutesfoys, adv. B17: *nonetheless, in any case*

Trespassés, masc. sg. p. p. Trépasser, intr. v. B226: *to die*

Tresrude, fem. sg. adj. B5: *rough, crude, unpolished, ungracious*

Tressault, 3rd pers. sg. pres. Tressaillir, tr. v. B340: *to leap, jump, shiver*

Tressue, 3rd pers. sg. pres. Tressuer, tr. v. B340: *to perspire, sweat abundantly from shaking (under the effect of fear, anxiety, pain, passion, etc.), burn*

User, inf. tr. v. B50: *to spend, pass [time]*

Vaillant, masc. sg. adj. D62: *worthy, deserving*

Variable, masc. sg. adj. B179: *fickle, inconstant, disloyal*

Voir-disans, masc. pl. adj. B299: *those who speak truthfully or sincerely*

Vouloir, masc. sg. n. D24: *desire, will*

Ystra, 3rd pers. sg. fut. Issir, intr. v. B39: *to spring forth, come out of*

'

www.ingramcontent.com/pod-product-compliance
Lightning Source LLC
Chambersburg PA
CBHW072356030726
47505CB00014B/1861